Being Transgender

Being Transgender
What You Should Know

THOMAS E. BEVAN, PhD

FOREWORD BY DALLAS DENNY

 PRAEGER™

An Imprint of ABC-CLIO, LLC

Santa Barbara, California • Denver, Colorado

Library of Congress Cataloging-in-Publication Data

Names: Bevan, Thomas E., author.
Title: Being transgender : what you should know / Thomas E. Bevan, PhD.
Description: Santa Barbara, California : Praeger, 2017. | Includes bibliographical references and index.
Identifiers: LCCN 2016030447 (print) | LCCN 2016034762 (ebook) | ISBN 9781440845246 (hardcopy : alk. paper) | ISBN 9781440845253 (ebook)
Subjects: LCSH: Transgender people—Psychology. | Transgenderism.
Classification: LCC HQ77.9 .B48 2016 (print) | LCC HQ77.9 (ebook)
 | DDC 306.76/8—dc23
LC record available at https://lccn.loc.gov/2016030447

ISBN: 978–1–4408–4524–6
EISBN: 978–1–4408–4525–3

21 20 19 18 17   2 3 4 5

This book is also available as an eBook.

Praeger
An Imprint of ABC-CLIO, LLC

ABC-CLIO, LLC
130 Cremona Drive, P.O. Box 1911
Santa Barbara, California 93116-1911
www.abc-clio.com

This book is printed on acid-free paper ∞

Manufactured in the United States of America

This book discusses treatments (including types of medication and mental health therapies), diagnostic tests for various symptoms and mental health disorders, and organizations. The author has made every effort to present accurate and up-to-date information. However, the information in this book is not intended to recommend or endorse particular treatments or organizations, or substitute for the care or medical advice of a qualified health professional, or used to alter any medical therapy without a medical doctor's advice. Specific situations may require specific therapeutic approaches not included in this book. For those reasons, we recommend that readers follow the advice of qualified health care professionals directly involved in their care. Readers who suspect they may have specific medical problems should consult a physician about any suggestions made in this book.

Contents

Foreword

Even twenty years ago it was difficult for transgender and gender-nonconforming people to find information. Today we are in the news and on television and enjoying an until now unheard-of popularity. And yet many of us are unemployed and unemployable, denied public services, harassed, misgendered, and all too often murdered. It is still, in the second decade of the twenty-first century, difficult for us to come to terms with ourselves and make informed decisions about our lives.

Fortunately, we have a wide variety of allies, laws to protect us in some locations, and an explosion of material we can read, view, or listen to to help us make sense of ourselves.

Along with YouTube transition videos, blogs and vlogs, and social media we still have an old standby—books. Books provide a level of detail unobtainable with other media and remain an essential component of our self education. Reading is still important. It will always be important.

Drawing upon her own experience and existing literature, Thomas Dana Bevan provides a narrative that can educate and inform trans people, allies, professionals, and the general public about who we are, why we are the way we are, and what we can do about it. It's all there—from terms and their definitions to discussion of the roles biology and culture play in the development of transgender identity and expression, to ways to make sense of it all and deal with ourselves, here is a narrative with a positive message. And you know what? In a world that discriminates against us, we need positive messages.

Dallas Denny, MA
Transgender Educator and Advocate
Recipient Virginia Prince and Trinity Awards

Preface

In spite of what some people say, being transgender does not mean that a person is broken or diseased or immoral or has made a conscious lifestyle choice. Being transgender is a natural behavior that is based on biology. It is part of the healthy diversity of nature that has allowed human beings to survive and be successful so far.

This book is about what science can tell us about being transgender, but even if you got turned off by your last science class in school, we will try to make the experience understandable and interesting. We will describe transgender experiences, including my own and others, to give the science context. Science provides facts about being transgender that are important to transgender people, parents, journalists, and the public.

Most important, this book seeks to provide reassurance to transgender people that they are not at fault for their transgender behavior which frequently violates the expectations of other people in the culture. Although life may be difficult for transgender people because of mistreatment, bullying, discrimination, and violence, transgender people need to know that they are basically complete, healthy, and blameless human beings.

As you read this book, you should understand that it presents a snapshot of the available transgender science at this time. You should expect changes in our understanding based on future science. Indeed, you should *demand* future science and increased understanding.

The paragraphs above were written in the summer of 2015. I write these last paragraphs a year later in a climate of hostility. Since last summer, both legal and cultural rejection has been fueled by the opportunity to make money and political hay by propagating lies about being transgender. As a result, I can no longer easily visit my family which requires driving across several states that now have laws rejecting my existence. In North Carolina, I cannot go to public restrooms at highway rest stops. In other states, I could be denied access to gas stations, restaurants, hotels, or other public accommodations if the management refuses to serve me on religious grounds. And there are many more discriminatory laws in the works, particularly in the states surrounding Georgia, where I live. Hopefully, by the time you read this, most of these laws will be struck down or rescinded after losing their power as wedge issues in the November 2016 election. It is still disappointing and stressful to me to know that some people do not welcome me in my own country.

I do have faith that all of this rejection will be overcome. All I can do is provide the scientific facts to help transgender people to deal with the *next* wave of rejection. I am reminded of the George Orwell quote:

> In a time of deceit—telling the truth is a revolutionary act.
> —George Orwell, *1984*

I only intend to help people understand being transgender. I have never wanted to be a revolutionary. But by telling the truth based on science and facts, based on Orwell's definition, I now have unintentionally become one.

Acknowledgments

I want to thank my children, Lesley and Cynthia, for their love and acceptance. Thanks also to Maggie and her family for their understanding. Special thanks to Patricia Bell for her excellent graphics and support. I want to thank Genny B. Jacks, Chelsea Rose Wendt, milesa phar and Carmel Greer for their encouragement. Thanks to Dallas Denny for her insightful forward. Finally, I want to express my love for my wife, Nancy, who continues to inspire me.

Acronyms and Glossary

Active coping mechanisms: Ways to reduce the psychological harm from stressful situations

Advancing age: One of three triggers for decisions about keeping transgender behavior a secret

Amygdala: Brain structure coordinating emotion

Androgen insensitivity syndrome (AIS): Syndrome in which body cells do not respond to testosterone

Asexual: Not attracted to either sex in sexual orientation

Autism spectrum: Group of neurodevelopmental differences

Bakla: Third gender category in the Philippines

Being transgender: behaving in transgender manner

Berdache: Misnomer term given to Native American third gender people

Binary gender system: System with two gender behavior categories

Biomarkers: Structural and functional differences between humans

Bisexual: Person attracted to people of both sexes

BNST: Basal nucleus of the stria terminalis

Boy/Man/He/Sir: Words associated with Western culture masculine gender behavior category

Bugis: Indonesian subculture with five gender behavior categories

Bullying: Minor assaults and batteries intended to coerce or dominate

CAH: Congenital adrenal hyperplasia; genetic condition in resulting high levels of testosterone produced by the adrenal glands

Chromosome: Division of DNA; humans have 46

Chukchi: Asian culture with three gender behavior categories

Cisgender: Gender system where gender behavior category is assigned solely based on birth sex

Congenital adrenal hyperplasia: Genetic phenomenon in which high levels of testosterone are secreted by the adrenal glands

Crossdresser: One who dresses in clothes of non-assigned gender behavior category

Crosspresentation: Dressing in clothes and comportment of non-assigned gender behavior category

Culture: Rules, values, and customs for behavior

Dead name: Name of transsexual prior to name change

Declarative knowledge: Knowledge acquired through reading and facts

DES: Diethylstilbestrol, a drug formerly given to prevent miscarriages; modifies DNA and DNA expression

DNA: Deoxyribonucleic acid; molecule that carries body and behavior blueprint information

Drag: Crossdressing for theatrical performance

DSD: Differences in sexual development, intersex

DSM: Diagnostic and Statistical Manual of Mental Disorders; list of diseases for insurance reimbursement

Emotional knowledge: Knowledge of learned emotional responses such as sexual arousal and fear

Epigenetics: Non-DNA influences on development that modify or change the expression of DNA

Evidence-based practice: Medical or psychological treatment based on scientific evidence

Existential crisis: One of four life realizations that tend to change behavior

Experiential knowledge: Knowledge gained through experiences

Fa'afafine: Samoan third gender behavior category

Fakaleiti: Third gender category of Tonga

Feminine: Western culture gender system behavior category

Feminization surgery: Surgery to improve female appearance

Femminiello: Third gender behavior category of Naples, Italy

Flexible gender system: System that allows movement between GBC

Fraternal twins: Nonidentical in terms of DNA at conception

FTM: Female-to-male transsexual (and sometimes transgender)

Gay: Male attracted to another male; also sometimes includes females attracted to other females

Gender: Gender behavior category determined by culture

Gender behavior category (GBC): Behaviors determined by culture

Gender behavior predisposition: Biological predisposition with regard to gender behavior categories

Gender dysphoria: Unhappiness with assigned gender behavior category; pathological term when person is distressed or unable to function because of being transgender

Gender fluid: Person who moves between or combines gender behavior categories

Gender identity: Verbalization of congruent gender behavior category

Gender identity disorder (GID): Pathological term when person is distressed or unable to function because of being transgender

Gender presentation: Expression of gender behavior category

Genderqueer: Those not having a congruent gender behavior category

Gender system: System and rules for gender behavior categories

Gene: Part of the DNA molecule that provides information on body and behavior traits

Genetic markers: Places on the DNA molecule that are associated with particular traits (e.g., being transgender)

Genital plastic surgery: Procedures in transsexual transition that change genital organs

Girl/Woman/She/Ma'am: Words associated with Western culture feminine behavior category

GnRH: Gonadotropin releasing hormone that controls production of sex hormones

Guevadoces: Children who appear female until childhood when their sex organs change to male due to a genetic block of forming an enzyme

Gynecomastia: Breast growth in older males because of hormonal changes

Handedness: Preference for use of left or right hand for particular tasks

He-she: Pejorative for a transgender person

Hijra: Third sex subculture in South Asia

HT: Hormone therapy in transsexual transition

ICD: International Classification of Diseases; list of categories for health insurance reimbursement

Identical twins: Twins having identical DNA at conception

INAH: Interstitial nucleus of anterior hypothalamus

Inflexible gender system: System that does not allow movement between gender behavior categories

Inheritable: Trait that can be passed through DNA inheritance

Intersex: Differences in sexual development

Kathoey: MTF second type of woman from Thailand

Kinship theory of gender evolution: Theory that human survival depends on the fitness of the group regardless of individual sex

Lesbian: Female attracted to another female

LGBTQQIA: Acronym for lesbian, gay, bisexual, transgender, genderqueer, questioning, intersex and asexual

Lhamana: Zuni third gender behavior category

Mahu: Tahitian/Hawaiian third gender behavior category

Marriage flight: Getting married in an attempt to deal with being transgender

Masculine: Western culture gender system behavior category

Masculinization surgery: Surgery to increase male appearance

Microassaults: Minor verbal and nonverbal threats of violence or bullying

Microbatteries: Minor physical violence acts

Military flight: Joining the military in an attempt to deal with being transgender

Misgendering: Using incorrect gender pronouns

Modeling: Learning by observation of the actions of others

Mosaic: Person having more than one DNA type

Motor knowledge and memories: Knowledge gained through observation of modeling behavior and skill learning

MRI: Magnetic resonance imaging; provides images of brain anatomy and activation

MTF: Male-to-female transsexual (or transgender person)

Muxe: Third gender behavior category in Southern Mexico

Nadleeh: Navajo third gender behavior category

Natural experiment: Unplanned experiment that occurs without control of a scientist

Naturalistic decision-making: Simple process for making decisions under time pressure

Nonbinary gender system: Gender system having other than two gender behavior categories

Pathology: Study of diseases and disorders

PCOS: Polycystic ovary syndrome that occurs in some females resulting in high levels of testosterone

Population frequency: Percentage of occurrence; equivalent to prevalence in pathological terms

Positive interpretation of events: Active coping mechanism to reduce long term stress

Prenatal Testosterone Theory of Transgenderism (PTTT): Theory that extreme levels of prenatal testosterone cause being transgender

Puberty blocking: Prevention of puberty using non-sex hormones

Purging: Throwing out items needed for congruent gender presentation

Putamen: One of the brain structures for sensation and movement

Queer: Those who are neither cisgender nor heterosexual

Questioning: Person unsure of their gender behavior category and/or sexual orientation

Realization of being transgender: Understanding of incongruent GBC assignment

Realization of Death: One of the four existential crises that tend to change behavior

Realization of Isolation: One of the four existential crises that tend to change behavior

Realization of Meaninglessness: One of the four existential crises that tend to change behavior

Realization of Personal Freedom: One of the four existential crises that tend to change behavior

Relaxation response: Learned response to relax in the face of stress

Reparative therapy: Therapy aimed at elimination of being transgender or changing sexual orientation

Samurai: Warriors who used active coping strategies

Secrecy: Using denial and deception to protect the information that you are transgender

Sex: Sex organs; biological organs enabling reproduction

Sexual arousal: Physiological preparation for sexual behavior

Sexual orientation: Romantic attraction to people of a particular sex

Sexual perversion: Sexual behavior considered to be pathological and motivated by sexual arousal

Shim: Pejorative for transgender person

Social transition: Full-time test period behaving in congruent gender behavior category

SRY gene: Gene that triggers male sex organ formation

Testosterone: Sex hormone produced by male sex organs but also by the adrenal glands in both sexes

Tetragametic chimera: Person with two types of DNA due to cell merger shortly after conception

Top surgery: Mastectomy involving breast removal and male reconstruction

Traditional sex-based evolutionary theory of gender: Theory that sex characteristics determine gender tasks and behaviors

Trait: Physical or behavioral characteristic determined by genes

Tranny: Pejorative for transsexual or transgender person

Transgender (TG): Being transgender; Incongruency between assigned gender behavior category and congruency with another gender behavior category

Transman: FTM transsexual (or transgender person)

Transposons: Genes that hop from one chromosome location to another

Transsexual (TS): Transgender person who seeks sexual organ body modification through transition procedures

Transsexual transition: Procedures to change sex organs

Transvestism: Term for being transgender that attributes sexual arousal as the cause of the behavior

Transwoman: MTF transsexual or transgender person

Twin study: Studies in which twins are compared for genetic traits

Two-factor theory: Theory that genetics and epigenetics are causal factors in being transgender; genetic mechanisms are primary factors but can be blocked by epigenetic mechanisms

Two-Spirit: Native American gender-flexible people

Waria: Indonesian third gender behavior category

Whakawahine: Maori third gender category in New Zealand

Winkte: Lakota third gender behavior category

WPATH: World Professional Association for Transgender Health; sets guidelines for transgender treatment

Xanith: Omani third gender behavior category

Zhe, Ze, Yo, Xe, Ve, etc.: Nontraditional gender-neutral pronoun systems

Zen warriors: Warriors who used active coping strategies

CHAPTER 1

Being Transgender: What You Need to Know

The purpose of this book is to tell you what you need to know about being transgender. Whether you are transgender, think you are transgender, or just want to know more about transgender people, this book will provide the needed information. The information comes from two sources: (1) analysis of over 3,000 scientific articles and (2) transgender experience, both from me and from what other transgender people have said. My experience includes being a transgender person in the closet for 50 years, starting at age 5. I then started gradually coming out, and after 9 years, I have completed transsexual transition. I cannot say that my experience was representative of all transgender people, so I will include quotes indicating the experience of others.

The intent of this book is to make science and experience complementary. By providing relevant experience, the science should be more interesting. The science should also show that the experiences are not isolated to me or to a few transgender people but apply to many transgender people.

Most of the information we see on the Internet or on the news about being transgender is not based on scientific facts but rather on unsubstantiated opinion. We see many supposedly authoritative talking heads with opinions, but there are very few scientific experts on the subject, and they do not often get heard. As a result, people may come to believe that opinion is the only thing available to resolve transgender issues. For this reason people are surprised to learn that there actually is a body of science that tells us important things about being transgender. Being transgender can be hard to understand but science provides definitions, evidence, and facts that can be clear. That does not mean that all questions can be answered by science because there are gaps in our knowledge. Recognizing these gaps helps us to better define the questions and how to answer them in the future.

Many of these questions need to be resolved so that mental health professionals and medical doctors can follow **evidence-based practice** when dealing with transgender people. Evidence-based practice simply means that treatment is based on scientific evidence. In the past and even today, this is not so. As we will see, the use of scientific evidence in counseling and medicine does not mean that there is anything wrong with being a transgender person. Transgender people mostly seek counseling for things other than being transgender. All people need counseling sometimes, but transgender people have some additional burdens because being transgender is a violation of our culture. Transgender people sometimes need help with the rejection that comes from this violation. Evidence-based practice does not mean that being transgender can be changed or "cured."

I got a call from Diane Sawyer's producer a couple of days before her interview with Bruce, soon to be Caitlyn Jenner, saying that she had just discovered that there was actual science about being transgender and if I could help her understand it. She had run across my previous books. We talked for several hours, but it was too late to impact Diane Sawyer's interview with Caitlyn. I wrote her a seven-page critique of the interview from a scientific point of view, so maybe the next time around an interview with Caitlyn will be more meaningful. Many people, including the producer, are surprised to learn that there are actual scientific studies concerned with being transgender.

Transgender experiences are included in this book because they explain why a particular piece of science is important to being transgender. Some people are turned off by science or do not know why they need to learn about it. The hope is that combining transgender experiences with relevant science will motivate you to get through any resistance you may have to learning science. We also will include stories about being transgender because psychological studies have shown that people retain more information if it is included in a story. We intend not to talk down to the reader about science but to make it as easy as possible to learn and retain it.

In this book, I have done my best to eliminate all traces of pathology about being transgender. Pathological words and statements suggest that there is something wrong with being transgender and that transgender people have a disorder or disease. In some cases, I have substituted non-pathological, neutral terminology in place of the pathological terminology. For example, instead of talking about the "prevalence" of being transgender, which has pathological connotations in the study of the extent of medical diseases, we will talk about "population frequencies" of being transgender. This term provides a neutral noun that is the mathematical equivalent. I have also substituted "being transgender" for the term "transgenderism" because many transgender people object to the "ism" part. To them it sounds patho-logical and is also used to indicate different ideologies and schools of thought. Being transgender is neither of these two things. Clinicians may find terminology changes as unfamiliar but the "medical model" of being transgender has long since been discarded. The medical model is a tradition in medicine in which the idea is that the medical professional first has to iden-tify a disorder or disease in order to find a "cure." Since mental health research and medicine have conceded that there is no cure for being trans-gender, the medical model is no longer useful for understanding being trans-gender. Many clinicians have gotten away from using terms of pathology, but old habits diehard.

I recently went to a training course for mental health and medical profes-sionals that included a lecture on transgender treatment. At the outset, the speaker said that he was no longer going to use the pathological term "gen-der identity disorder." The organization that sponsored the training course had gone on the record against using the term. But old habits die hard. He had included the term in every PowerPoint slide and used the term in his speaking several times per slide. I had to go out of the room to avoid laughing out loud at his predicament. In his defense, it took me a few years to shake some pathological terms, and I still use them to communicate when it is unavoidable. The term "transgender" actually started out as a pathologi-cal term, but it would be difficult to eliminate it because the transgender community has changed it's meaning, co-opted and depathologized it.

In this chapter, we will discuss the primary questions that people have about being transgender and point to other chapters where more detailed answers can be found. The primary questions people have about being trans-gender are:

1. What is being transgender?
2. What is the difference between being transgender and being transsexual?
3. If I am a transgender person, am I diseased?
4. Am I transgender because of my biology?
5. When and how does being transgender usually begin?
6. Is being transgender common? How many transgender people are there?
7. How does someone get to be transgender?
8. Why do people reject transgender people?
9. Is it this way in other cultures?
10. Should you be blamed for being transgender?
11. If a person is transgender, does that mean they are gay or lesbian?

12. Are people transgender because they get sexually aroused from crossdressing?
13. Should you keep the secret of being transgender?
14. Does being transgender mean that you will have to change your sex?
15. What are effective ways to deal with cultural rejection for being transgender?
16. What does being transgender feel like?
17. Will things get better for transgender people?
18. How can transgender people deal with pseudoscience and lies about being transgender?

1. WHAT IS BEING TRANSGENDER?

Being transgender is behaving as a girl when people say you are a boy or behaving as a boy when people say you are a girl. Acting as a girl or a boy is called gender. A grown-up girl is called a woman, and a grown-up boy is called a man. People sometimes say that you are a boy if you have male body parts or a girl if you have female body parts, but, as we will see, that is not true for transgender people.

When nearly all people are born, a doctor declares their **sex**, whether male or female, by looking at the visible sex organs between the legs. These sex organs and others are the some of the organs that are used in human reproduction. In our culture, a baby is immediately assigned to one of two **gender behavior categories**, masculine or feminine, based on sex. Culture consists of rules for behavior within a group of people as decided by the group and is continued by teaching their children. The gender behavior categories of our culture contain the behaviors and rules for behaviors in that category. People expect males to behave in the masculine category and females to behave in the feminine category, as set by our Western culture.

Transgender people behave in a gender category that is different from the one people expect, because cultural rules are not based on biology. Transgender people do this because their biology does not agree with their cultural gender assignment. Some people are surprised or are afraid when they see transgender people because their behavior is not what they expect according to culture. They sometimes do not understand why transgender people behave that way. As we will see, there is scientific evidence that indicates that we are born with a biological **gender behavior predisposition** that we get from our parents.

Being transgender usually involves **crossdressing** or **crosspresenting**, which means that a person dresses, grooms, and comports themselves consistent with their congruent or preferred gender category which is not the one that they were assigned to at birth. **Crossdressers** are people who present themselves in this way. Not all people who crossdress are being transgender. For example, some crossdress to be entertaining, some crossdress for economic reasons, and some crossdress as a form of political protest. Entertainers who crossdress on the stage may or may not crossdress off the stage. If they crossdress and crosspresent all the time, then they are transgender.

I am transgender. When I was a child, I always knew that I was a girl and now I know that I am woman even though I started out with male body parts. And I have always wanted to behave as a girl or woman, although sometimes culture and duty got in the way. Some transgender people who know they are boys or men start out with female body parts.

As I grew up, I somehow always knew that I was not doing anything wrong, but I often got confused because of all the scary pathological words that were associated with being transgender. Transgender itself is a strange word. In order to understand the words, where they came from and what they mean, we will explain them in Chapter 2: Definitions.

2. WHAT IS THE DIFFERENCE BETWEEN BEING TRANSGENDER AND BEING TRANSSEXUAL?

Transsexuals are a subset of transgender people. Transsexuals want to behave in their preferred gender all the time, and they tend to change their body parts to be more like what people and culture expect. All transsexuals are transgender people, but not all transgender people are transsexuals. Transsexuals go through a medical process called **transsexual transition** to change their bodies. This process may involve hormones, surgery and other medical treatments.

About nine years ago, I decided that I was transsexual and began to change my body. Some transgender people know that they are transsexuals from childhood, but some realize it only later in life. If you are transgender, it does not mean that you will automatically become transsexual.

We will talk more about what being transgender and transsexual means in Chapter 2. In Chapters 6 and 7, we will talk more about what happens to transgender and transsexual people in the course of their lifetimes.

3. IF I AM A TRANSGENDER PERSON, AM I DISEASED?

Being transgender is perfectly natural and not a disorder or disease. The idea that being transgender means that you are broken or diseased comes from the words used by the mental health and medical communities. The words come from a time when they tried to understand being transgender as a medical problem that needed to be cured, like a disease. They no longer attempt to "cure" transgender people, but they do provide help to transgender people to deal with the social problems that occur because they are transgender. Most transgender people do not seek mental health help. They are perfectly happy to be transgender and work out their social problems on their own. Some transgender people do have problems that they find they cannot deal with on their own, usually problems with family members. Before people undergo transsexual transition to change their bodies, medical guidelines indicate that they should go to a mental health provider in order to be sure that they do not have some real mental disease that could be a problem. Medical doctors do not usually allow certain treatments for transsexual people like taking hormone drugs or getting certain surgeries without clearance or letters from mental help providers. There are written international guidelines for mental health and medical providers about treating transgender people.

When I first knew that I was a transgender person, I went to the library and tried to find information on being transgender. There was not much information, and the words they used were scary. They made me feel as if I had a disease or was a bad person because I was transgender. Being transgender was lumped with some really bad mental problems in the books. These were mental problems that resulted in people hurting other people or being hurt themselves. I could never see why what I wore or my gender behavior could actually hurt anyone in any way, so I never believed that being transgender was like these scary problems.

In Chapter 2, we will discuss some of the words that have indicated in the past that transgender people are diseased, and in Chapter 6, we will deal with transsexual transition. Chapter 3 provides information on why I believe that being transgender results from a biological predisposition, making it perfectly natural.

4. AM I TRANSGENDER BECAUSE OF MY BIOLOGY?

Being transgender occurs because your biology conflicts with what people and culture expect from you in terms of gender behavior. All people seem to have a gender behavior predisposition that is formed by biology. People have all sorts of predispositions like being more left-handed than right-handed or being good at music or art or baseball. Gender predisposition has to do with which gender behavior category seems more natural or comfortable.

For most people, their gender behavior predisposition does not conflict with their assigned gender category, but for transgender people, it does.

When I was a child, behaving like girls felt more natural than behaving like boys did. It was similar to me being more comfortable swinging a baseball bat or golf club from where left-handers do. (We will see that transsexuals tend to use their left hands more for certain tasks.) I usually liked to play with girls more than I liked to play with boys. Girls liked to play at the things that I had seen my parents do to take care of people. Boys only wanted to play rough games and talk about sex as though it was a dirty thing. Because I was big for my age until I got to high school, I was pretty good at rough games, but they became boring after a while. I did not know much about sex (and my fellow students did not know either), but their comments seemed to be hurtful to girls. My parents always taught me to be a gentleman, but many of the things that gentlemen were supposed to do, like having consideration for others, seemed more like what girls did than what boys did.

In Chapter 3, we will provide the scientific evidence that being transgender involves the development of a biological gender predisposition.

5. WHEN AND HOW DOES BEING TRANSGENDER USUALLY BEGIN?

People realize that they are transgender starting at about the age of 4–5. Most transgender people realize it by about the age of 7, but some do not realize it until they are grown-up adults. This comes as a surprise to many people because they think that children do not know about gender at such an early age. But most children understand the basics of gender at about age 2–3 by watching grown-ups and listening to what they say. Transgender children may not know what words to use to explain that they are transgender, but they know which gender category is natural for them.

I remember that at the age of 2, my first granddaughter would only wear pink because that was what she had learned girls were supposed to wear. I will never forget her running down the street dressed in a pink tutu with pink shoes and a pink barrette in her hair. By then, I knew that there was no biological reason for girls to wear pink, only that they were supposed to do that according to culture.

Transgender behavior usually starts in childhood. Transgender children begin by trying on clothing of their preferred gender from family members or in nursery school "dress up" stations or in play at home. At first, only single pieces of clothing may be enough, but this gradually increases in teenage and adult years to dressing completely. For males who believe that they should be in the feminine gender category, this includes wearing makeup, perfume, and heels. Females who believe they should be in the masculine gender can sometimes go undetected since culture says it is okay for girls to wear boys' clothes and behave like "tom-boys," at least in early childhood and teenage years.

At the age of about 4 ¾, I told my mother that I was a girl and not a boy. I know it was Christmas time because I had a beautiful pink balloon that said "Merry Christmas" on it. I still have a picture of it that I put on the cover for my first book. Because it was Christmas, I know the date with some precision.

Because being transgender begins so early in life, it is one of the pieces of evidence that support the idea that biology contributes to being transgender. We will talk more about this in Chapter 3.

6. IS BEING TRANSGENDER COMMON? HOW MANY TRANSGENDER PEOPLE ARE THERE?

The earliest estimates of the frequency of being transgender were based on records from clinics in Europe. These estimates were absurdly low. Most transgender people never go to a clinic or to a mental health professional because they never need their services. Current estimates are that at least 1–2% of people are transgender. This amounts to at least 20 million transgender people in the United States, which is equivalent to the populations of several U.S. states. Being transgender is not rare at all, making it more likely that being transgender involves biology.

When I was in psychology graduate school, I saw the numbers from the European clinics and felt lonely even though I knew that a group of clinical patients was usually not typical of the population from my study of psychology. Later I found out that if you count the number of people going to transgender support groups or those who say they are transgender when asked in a survey, there are clearly many more transgender people than those early estimates. We will discuss the available information on the frequency of being transgender in Chapter 3.

7. HOW DOES SOMEONE GET TO BE TRANSGENDER?

There are three things that need to happen to make someone transgender. The first thing is that they have a biological predisposition or preference for one gender behavior category over another. It is likely that all people have a predisposition or preference for one gender category or the other. Transgender people get this way due to the genes that they get from their parents. Genes contain the information needed to form the human body and create behavior. Chapter 3 is concerned with how this biological predisposition is formed.

The second thing that needs to happen is that the person needs to be born into a culture that has limited gender behavior categories, gender category is assigned by sex alone and one does not allow people to move between categories. This has to do with the rules that culture sets up. In our culture, there are only two gender behavior categories, and people are not expected to move between them. This makes our culture **binary** (meaning two), **cisgender** (gender must match birth sex), and **inflexible** (moving between categories is banned). This is not the case in other cultures and subcultures, as we shall see in Chapter 4.

The third thing that needs to happen is that the person needs to learn about gender behavior categories. As we described earlier, most children know the fundamentals about gender at the age of 2–3. Most transgender people realize that they are transgender shortly after they learn about gender at ages 4–6.

As I was growing up, I tried to find out all the information that I could on being transgender because I wanted to find out how I got this way. The first clue came from a psychology teacher who happened to mention that transgender people were found all over the world. I reasoned that if being transsexual was not unique to a particular location, then it was more likely to be a feature of human biology. In Chapter 3, we will provide information showing that being transgender occurs in many places in Western culture. In Chapter 4, we will provide information on non-Western cultures that have different gender systems than we do.

8. WHY DO PEOPLE REJECT TRANSGENDER PEOPLE?

Many people learn to reject transgender people from their family and community. Culture is passed on through families and communities. Transgender people are rejected because they violate Western cultural rules by expressing themselves. Transgender people are different because they behave in an unexpected gender behavior category. People who reject transgender people do so because they see transgender people as being different. Humans have strong emotional reactions to people who are different, which may include fear, sexual arousal, and hatred.

Some people may associate being transgender with having a mental disorder because they have seen it in the media. Some people associate being transgender with street crime. Many transgender people are rejected by their parents, their churches, and their communities. They become homeless and have no choice but to sell themselves or push drugs on the street. Police are trained to believe that transgender people are likely to be engaged in street crime and their experience often confirms this. Some police have been trained to believe that being transgender is a mental disorder.

My first scary rejection episode occurred one night when I was traveling and staying in a hotel. As I often did, I went to a transgender support group meeting, and I went to it crossdressed. I was on my way back to my hotel room when a young girl and her mother passed me in the hall. They followed me to my room and later complained to the hotel. A few minutes later, after I had changed clothes and taken off my makeup, a young security guard came to my door and told me that I had scared some people in the hotel. I said I was sorry and that I did not mean to scare anyone. He asked if I had any drugs or if I was a prostitute. I told him, no. He asked if he could come in my room and whether he could search it. Since I had nothing to hide, I told him that he could. He proceeded to go through all my things and lay them out on the bed. He was looking for hypodermic needles, drugs, and devices to prevent sexually transmitted diseases. Finding none, he was about to leave and told me that I needed to see a psychologist. I told him that I would. (I did not do this for at least a decade later.) I got up the courage to ask him where he had learned about transgender people pushing drugs, working in prostitution, and needing mental health help. He told me that he had learned it in his police courses in the nearby community college. He was a part-time hotel rent-a-cop who was studying at night to join a real police force.

I believe that people reject transgender folks primarily out of ignorance or being misinformed as the rent-a-cop did. In fairness to police, since their primary job is to deal with criminals, their only experience with transgender people may be with those transgender people who are also criminals. As we shall see, transgender people are on the street because they have been thrown out of their homes or have left voluntarily because of rejection and abuse. Law enforcement on the street is a pretty stressful business for police, and they are sure to remember what they are taught or what they experience in the street.

In our culture, community leaders and organizations tell many people that there is something wrong with transgender people because they are different. Rather than inform people about being transgender, the media often uses stories about transgender people to get attention, improve ratings, and make money.

We will talk more about why culture teaches rejection in Chapter 4 and how to deal with some forms of rejection in Chapter 7.

9. IS IT THIS WAY IN OTHER CULTURES?

There have been other cultures that have different gender systems from our Western culture, and some of these cultures still exist. Many of them are now only found in pockets around the world as subcultures of Western culture. Many cultures had/have more than two gender behavior categories that are based not only on sex but also on childhood behavior. At least 100 Native American tribes had 3 gender behavior categories and about half of those had 4 categories. The other important thing about these diverse cultures is that many allowed movement between categories. One day a person could be dressed in feminine clothing and make pottery; the next day this same person could put on masculine clothing and become a warrior. There is even an existing subculture with five gender behavior categories. In our Western culture, we only have two gender behavior categories and movement between them is forbidden. It should be made clear that people in these other cultures who moved between gender behavior categories were not transgender. They were not transgender because they did not violate any cultural rules. They were following the rules of their culture.

When I was a young child, I loved music, dance, and art. Because I was assigned to be a boy, by the time I got to high school, I had been discouraged from all these things by my teachers and family. As a child, I was a good boy soprano and was in demand as a church and school soloist. But the moment my voice changed in puberty, the calls for my singing stopped. As for art, I remember vividly that, after looking at my drawing of a gnarled tree, my seventh grade art teacher told me that boys had no talent. That was the end of art for me. Instead, I was encouraged to be a football player and go into the military because that was required of a boy or man. I never got a chance to dance but I love music and I hopefully still have some time left. If I had grown up in other cultures, I may have been allowed to express my interests in these things.

We will provide more information on these gender diverse cultures in Chapter 4.

10. SHOULD YOU BE BLAMED FOR BEING TRANSGENDER?

Being transgender involves biology and culture. A transgender person is not responsible for either of these things. The first is a biological predisposition or preference for a gender that you were not assigned because of your sex. The second is the cultural rejection of those who engage in being transgender. You get your biology from your parents and you have no choice over the culture that you were born into.

One of the reasons I wrote this book is to educate people about being transgender so that they can change our culture. There is nothing anyone can do about biological predisposition, but culture does evolve and can be changed. We can be more tolerant and accepting of those who choose to be part of a particular gender or no gender at all.

We will explore the diversity of cultures in Chapter 4 and how to change culture in Chapter 9.

11. IF A PERSON IS TRANSGENDER, DOES THAT MEAN THEY ARE GAY OR LESBIAN?

Transgender people come in all forms of **sexual orientation**. There are gay, lesbian, bisexual, and asexual transgender people, just as in the larger population. Being transgender refers to a preference for gender behavior category; sexual orientation is determined by the sex of the person you come to love. We know that the biology of sexual orientation is different from being transgender. Sexual orientation is more connected with romantic love than it is with gender.

The sexual orientation of people can evolve and change. What seems right at one time in life can seem not right at other times. The same thing happens with transgender people, especially transsexual people after they change their bodies in transition. For example, about a quarter of male transsexuals who are initially sexually oriented toward females change their sexual orientation. They become sexually oriented to males. But most male transsexuals are still attracted to females after transition, which technically makes them lesbians. Some reject sexual orientation and become asexual. As we have seen with Caitlyn Jenner, she has not completed transsexual transition and is still unsure of what her sexual orientation will be at this point.

One of the things that fascinates me is the fact that many married couples stay together despite the fact that one may be transgender or a transsexual. One of my best friends is a member of a couple who have transitioned in opposite directions since getting married. She was a male and he was a female when they married. Despite problems with laws and culture, some couples manage to stay together despite one of them being transgender or transsexual. Love is a strong force keeping people together which is independent of gender and sex.

Often young transgender people are confused about whether they are transgender as well as about their sexual orientation. We will deal with the problem of "sorting it all out" in Chapter 5.

12. ARE PEOPLE TRANSGENDER BECAUSE THEY GET SEXUALLY AROUSED FROM CROSSDRESSING?

It is true that at the beginning of being transgender, people may get sexually aroused when they crossdress, but this does not continue for very long. Studies have shown that people engage in transgender behavior to feel more at ease, relaxed, and authentic, but not sexually excited.

At the beginning, people who crossdress probably experience sexual arousal for at least two primary reasons: (1) prior learning of sexual arousal to particular stimuli or (2) novelty. Sexual arousal to stimuli is learned during the time when people are going through puberty and early adulthood. At this age, people are spontaneously aroused or can easily arouse themselves. The stimuli that they are seeing or thinking about at the time also become arousing because the association is learned. We know that what can be learned in this way can also be unlearned or extinguished. Continued exposure to opposite gender clothing without arousal results in unlearning or extinction. Crossdressers may have learned to be aroused by clothing of their preferred gender behavior category but this is rapidly unlearned through exposure without sexual arousal.

We know that sexual arousal can be triggered by novelty or new stimuli. Crossdressers who have not previously dressed in clothing associated with their preferred gender behavior category will feel new fabrics and clothing designs that may trigger arousal, but repeated exposure will no longer be arousing.

My initial experiences with crossdressing as a transgender person were arousing, but I found that the arousal quickly went away both during and between crossdressing sessions. During a session, the arousal from feminine clothes and makeup had faded by the time I got to my support group. Between crossdressing sessions, I found that the clothing that had been arousing before was arousing for shorter time periods. Why did I make such observations? Well I am a scientist, so I take note of such things. Today, I do not get aroused at all by crossdressing.

We will talk more about sexual arousal and its relation to being transgender, sexual orientation, and love in Chapter 5.

13. SHOULD YOU KEEP THE SECRET OF BEING TRANSGENDER?

Keeping the secret of being transgender is a heavy burden that has both mental and medical consequences. Transgender people need to be aware of these negative effects if they want to keep their secret. Keeping a secret like being transgender can result in lying, high mental workload, isolation, loss of authenticity, depression, and attempted suicide. We will explore all of these effects in Chapter 6.

For me, there were degrees of "coming out" or revealing my transgender behavior that reduced the burden. Over a period of about 25 years, I started to go to support group meetings, saw psychologists, came out to my family and friends, and eventually worked in my preferred gender behavior category. On the other hand, coming out also has its price in terms of emotional conflicts with people, particularly family members. They may feel betrayed because they were lied to and later question their own feelings about transgender people, or they may come to question their own sexual orientation.

No one told me that keeping my secret about being transgender would be a heavy burden when I was a child, but gradually it became a burden I could no longer bear. I was constantly worried that I had not kept my lies straight. It was exhausting. I lost or never made friends because I feared that they would get close enough to learn my secret. I now find that I do not have an adequate support network of friends which studies show is vital for a longer life.

We will talk more about transgender secrecy in Chapters 6 and 7.

14. DOES BEING TRANSGENDER MEAN THAT YOU WILL HAVE TO CHANGE YOUR SEX?

Most transgender people do not change their sex organs. Some transgender people change their sex organs to make them more acceptable in their preferred gender category. Transsexuals and even some non-transsexual transgender people do this to some degree. Nearly all transsexual people take sex hormones, and some have surgery to change their breasts and appearance. Some non-transsexual transgender people take hormones on a do-it-yourself basis, which is very dangerous.

Only about 25% of transsexuals ever have surgery to change their genital organs. I prefer to call such surgeries, **transsexual genital plastic surgeries** (**GPS**), rather than sex change operations or other terms. I will explain in more detail in Chapter 10.

I liken transsexual transition to exploring a forest, not climbing a mountain. The success of transsexual transition is not measured on whether a person completes transsexual GPS but whether the transsexual feels comfortable being full time in their preferred gender category. Changing your body in transition involves a series of sequential decisions, not a race to the top.

There are many pathways you can follow as a transgender person, and we will explore these pathways in Chapter 6.

15. WHAT ARE EFFECTIVE WAYS TO DEAL WITH CULTURAL REJECTION FOR BEING TRANSGENDER?

There is a wide range of ways in which people in our culture reject transgender people. At one end of this range are microaggressions or minor insults. These range from deliberately using the wrong gender pronoun, to treating transgender people like they are not there, to making negative comments to others so that they can be heard by the transgender person. Next are direct comments aimed at insulting transgender people. These can involve sarcasm or calling transgender people names like "freak" and "tranny." Using pathological terms falls into this category because they imply that a transgender person is sick or diseased. Next in the range are minor microassaults and microbatteries. Microassaults are small verbal threats, while microbatteries are minor physical attacks such as bullying and bumping into people. Finally, there are major attacks, sometimes using weapons, which can result in permanent injury or death.

Transgender people experience rejection from every segment of society. Medical people refuse to treat transgender folks. Laws in many states discriminate against transgender people with regard to housing, jobs, public accommodations, identification documents, and now restrooms.

There are also whole sections of the country that do not accept transgender people. The Georgia governor has recently vetoed a law that would discriminate against transgender people, but there are no state laws protecting us. There are, however, laws for the City of Atlanta. All of the Southern states have either passed discriminatory laws or are thinking about it, including Georgia. About half of the U.S. states have joined in a lawsuit to prevent transgender children from using the restroom that is congruent with their presentation in school.

I was a football official for 14 seasons and I learned about "rabbit ears." This funny term means being too sensitive about insulting comments from the teams or fans. The comments I received ranged from disputing calls to threatening to beat me up after a game. When I was a sideline official, these comments were sometimes made inches from my ears. To be a good official I had to learn how to deal with all this rejection without getting angry. Some officials did not learn, lost it, and dropped out from officiating.

Last summer, I was dressed in white capris and sandals with a beautiful peacock multicolored blouse on top. My transgender friend and I decided to walk through her small town on farmers' market day. There were tourists and people selling all sorts of vegetables and crafts. As we were walking, a rough man in a group of seated workmen having lunch saw me. He sarcastically complimented me, "Honey, nice shirt." Due to my rabbit ear training, reflexively, I said, "Thank you, I like my blouse a lot, too." It was only later that my friend noticed that I was hurrying through the market. I dealt with his microassault but it still unsettled me.

We will discuss some of the forms of rejection in Chapter 4 and ways to deal with some of these rejections in Chapter 7.

16. WHAT DOES BEING TRANSGENDER FEEL LIKE?

Many transgender people describe transgender crossdressing and cross-presenting variously as feeling relaxed, authentic, and content. I would describe it as a "floating" feeling. Many say that being transgender is a gift and that even if there were a "cure" for being transgender, they would not take it. To me, having a gender predisposition that is different from other birth males is a "gift" from nature. It must be important for the survival and evolution of human beings. Otherwise, we would lose this predisposition through evolution. Predispositions are part of the natural diversity of species that allows them to adapt. For some, this gift stimulates spiritual experiences and for most transgender people it provides experiences in two genders that most people never have. I have learned about putting on feminine clothes and makeup, just as I have learned about football defenses and military skiing and what a male body can do playing football.

For me, the more I express being transgender, the more I feel free and able to deal with whatever comes along. It brings out the best in me. I talk to people more and am more honest with them. I cannot see going back into secrecy. In Chapter 8, we will discuss the "gift" of being transgender.

17. WILL THINGS GET BETTER FOR TRANSGENDER PEOPLE?

Indications are that both for each transgender person and for transgender people, as a whole, things have gotten better, and this progress is likely to continue. There are more opportunities than ever before for each transgender person to get help when they need it. Transgender advocates are well aware of the problems transgender people face and they are taking action on most of them. Significantly, they now have science to back up their arguments.

Transgender advocates have the knowledge and skills to change both laws and culture. The United States has over 50 years of constant social advocacy, including opposition to the Vietnam War and the Civil Rights Movement. From these experiences, our advocates have learned how to change both laws and hearts. Transgender advocacy is currently in full gear opposing discriminatory state laws and winning people over. Changing culture is mainly a matter of education, coming out, meeting with non-transgender people, and overcoming the arguments of those who would seek to profit from rejection of transgender people. Jennifer Boylan, best-selling author and transgender advocate, quoted her mother as saying, "It is impossible to hate someone whose story you know."[1] Her mother said this about reducing hatred and fear for all types of people as well as transgender people.

When I was a child, if I had let people know that I was transgender, I probably would have been locked up in the local state hospital. In that era, I might have been surgically or chemically castrated, experienced electroshock, insulin shock, emetic conditioning, cattle prods, or operant conditioning "therapy." I might have remained there for many years. The country was then on a rampage to eliminate people with unwanted genes to prevent them from passing these genes on to their offspring. The alternative was to try to "cure" these people. Today, we have progressed to the point where one of America's best male athletes, Bruce Jenner, can be out as Caitlyn Jenner and be accepted by many people.

Things have improved for transgender people, but we have a long way to go to gain full acceptance. It will require not only changing the laws but also changing the culture. We will discuss what we need to do in the future to make this happen in Chapter 9.

18. HOW CAN TRANSGENDER PEOPLE DEAL WITH PSEUDOSCIENCE AND LIES ABOUT BEING TRANSGENDER?

Every morning I flip on my computer and wait for the Internet to deliver the morning information about being transgender. I get clippings from all the online or print news sources. I get notices from the major professional provider organizations. I am interested in articles about transgender science and try immediately to include any original scientific papers to add to my analysis. I also encounter a lot of particularly distasteful anti-transgender news articles. Because I was taught in the military to know your enemy, I read these as well. I am not interested in hating or harming anti-transgender people; I am interested in their arguments. I want to know their arguments so that they can be refuted by science when appropriate. Chapter 10 provides a series of frequently asked questions that I derived from my reading of anti-transgender arguments and some suggested answers based on science.

NOTE

1. Boylan, J., *I Am Caitlyn*, E Channel, Episode S2 E2, aired March 13, 2016.

CHAPTER 2

Definitions

"When I use a word," Humpty Dumpty said, in a rather scornful tone,
"it means what I choose it to mean, neither more nor less."
—Lewis Carroll, *Through the Looking Glass*[1]

INTRODUCTION

In this chapter, we will define some of the words you will need in order to understand being transgender. Lewis Carroll, among other things, was a mathematician, and although his characters seem a little wacky, they are all based on logic and mathematics. The point of the above quote is that Humpty Dumpty used his personal definitions of words but did not share his definitions with others. He was therefore unable to communicate with others.

The purpose of this chapter is to share my definitions so that I can communicate with you about the science and experience of being transgender. I am sure that they will not be the only definitions you will encounter because many transgender people and others have their own definitions. But the ones in this chapter are used consistently throughout this book.

Many of the defined words in this chapter are downright scary because they were invented to suggest that being transgender was a disease or disorder. Their inventors used Latin and Greek root words in order to give the terms a sense of medical pathology and authority as if they knew all about being transgender. Many of these words were given a secondary meaning to suggest why transgender people behave the way they do. The medical model requires a cause for a disease before a treatment can be determined. This "medical model" of treatment works nicely when you can find a bacterium and the mechanisms that it uses to cause a disease and there is an antibiotic that can cure the disease. It does not work well when the model is constructed for something that is not a disease and therefore cannot be "cured."

Many of the scary words have evolved over the years because transgender people, being crafty, changed their meaning and used them to mean what they wanted them to mean, somewhat like Humpty Dumpty. The words also evolved in public discourse to have even more new, vague meanings. If they are to be used in science, they need clear scientific definitions that refer to observable behavior, not to speculative inner workings of the brain. We will give them those clear scientific definitions in this chapter. To me, the scientific definitions are all that matter because it is the only way to communicate precisely.

Admittedly the discussion of definitions can be tedious and boring, so we will try to weave them into stories about the history of transgender people. There is actually some psychological science that says that people remember better if the information is embedded in a story. While you are reading this book, if you lose track of word definitions, you should be able to return here to get information, and there is also a quick reference guide at the beginning of this book.

In order to help you learn about these words, the words will be divided into five groups:

1. The Story of How We Got to Being Transgender
2. Words Related to Being Transgender
3. Current Pathological Words Related to Being Transgender
4. Sexual Orientation Words
5. Controversial Terms

THE STORY OF HOW WE GOT TO BEING TRANSGENDER

In this section, we will tell the story and define the following words:

- Transvestite
- Sexual arousal
- Transsexual
- Crossdressing
- Intersex
- Differences in sexual development
- Gender
- Sex
- Transsexual genital plastic surgery
- Gender behavior category
- Culture

- Gender presentation and crosspresentation
- Transgender

The story of how we got to being transgender begins with a medical doctor in pre-World War I Germany, named Magnus Hirschfeld. He was one of the early prominent sexologists who established the topic of sex as a legitimate area of study. He specialized in what we now know as transgender people (although he did not use the word "transgender"). The word he coined was **transvestism** from the Latin word *trans*, meaning across, and the word *vestis*, meaning garment. The Latin root words do not point to any particular cause for transvestism, but Hirschfeld immediately gave it the meaning that a transvestite dressed in the clothes of the opposite gender because they became sexually aroused by them. **Sexual arousal** refers to the physiological changes, most of them pleasurable, that the body makes in preparation for sexual behavior. Although the idea that sexual arousal causes being transgender is false, it is still used to attack transgender people by saying that there is something immoral or perverted about being transgender. In addition to coining the term "transvestism," he was involved with the first transsexual genital plastic surgery. **Genital plastic surgery (GPS)** is sometimes performed on transsexuals and involves anatomical modification of the genital organs. To show that history is not totally dead, they recently made a movie about it, called *The Danish Girl*.

The word **transsexual** was introduced by psychiatrist David Cauldwell from German to English in 1949 and popularized by Harry Benjamin, an endocrinologist who treated transsexuals. Transsexual people are a subset of transgender people who change their bodies to make them look more like people expect from their **gender presentation**. Gender presentation refers to dress and behavior that our culture associates with particular **gender behavior categories**. A gender behavior category is culturally constructed and includes behavior, norms, and rules. Cauldwell rejected transsexual genital plastic surgery as being a correct treatment, preferring psychotherapy instead. Contrary to Cauldwell, Benjamin believed that body transformation was the best way to treat transsexuals. Benjamin was famous for helping transsexual people by supporting their transsexual transition using sex hormone therapy and finding surgeons who would perform transsexual genital plastic surgery. He also developed a set of guidelines for treating transsexual people that was later revised to include all transgender people. The association that Benjamin formed is now known as the **World Professional Association for Transgender Health (WPATH)**. It is the preeminent organization that sets guidelines for treating transgender people.

Starting in the United States in the 1950s, transgender (they were not called that yet) people started calling what they did, **crossdressing**. "Transvestism" and "transsexualism" were then pathological terms that did not apply to these transgender people, because they felt that their primary reasons for crossdressing were relaxation and authenticity rather than for sexual arousal. Many of them also did not want to change their bodies as transsexuals did. A **crossdresser** is a person whose gender presentation is different from the gender behavior category assigned at birth. People crossdress for various reasons, including theatrical performance, political protest, or to obtain a job usually reserved for their incongruent gender. Today, transgender people form a subset of crossdressers. Even in the 1980s and 1990s, many still used the term "crossdressing" because the term "transgender" had not become popular. When I started to go to support groups in the late 1980s, the people there referred to themselves as crossdressers, but the word "transgender" was just coming into vogue.

Crossdressing was the first word, and so far the only word, to refer to transgender people that was not derived from a pathological term. Although people had been crossdressing since antiquity, the term seems to be a homegrown term that sprang up during the 1950s from what is now the transgender and drag communities. (More on drag will be discussed later.) Crossdressing people had been meeting in informal groups since at least the 1930s. Those who could afford it, met for weekends or vacations in isolated homes like "Casa Susanna" in the Catskills.[2]

Paralleling the popularization of the term "crossdressing" in the 1950s were two developments by John Money, a psychologist at Johns Hopkins University, that would change our understanding of crossdressing. The first was that Money gave **gender** the scientific meaning it has today, that of behavior within cultural gender categories. He distinguished it from the word **sex,** meaning the organs of reproduction. The second was that Money carried a "natural experiment," which inadvertently supported the involvement of biology in being transgender. The experiment eventually undercut his own theories. We will discuss this somewhat notorious experiment in Chapter 3. Money worked with children and people whose sex could not be determined at birth by inspection of their bodies. Such people are now called **intersex** people or those with **differences in sexual development**. For a while these people were described as having "disorders of sexual development," but intersex people reject that term. Being intersex is not a disease, and so disorder just does not fit. It is a naturally occurring phenomenon. These people usually get that way because the genetic plan for growing their body is different from others. An intersex author describes their predicament:

That was when I realized that life was a multiple-choice test with two answers:
Male and Female, And I was None Of The Above.
—I.W. Gregorio, *None of the Above*[3]

Money theorized that any child could be successfully brought up in either
gender if parents started child rearing in that gender early enough. Money
repurposed the term "gender" from language grammars that categorized
nouns. He did this because he needed a word other than "sex" to describe
the cultural categories of behavior of masculine and feminine. So from a scientific point of view, "sex" came to describe the organs of reproduction and
"gender" came to describe behavior. Today, in public discourse, they are frequently used interchangeably, much to the chagrin of many scientists who
are trying to keep them separate. A particular scientific concern is that if we
confuse them and do not keep them separate, then current studies may be
uninterpretable sometime in the future. This would interfere with the
progress of science when the original scientists are no longer available to say
whether they really classified their subjects by sex or by gender.

The independence of sex and gender is important for transgender people,
because it means that it is possible to have a male sex and a feminine gender
or a female sex and a masculine gender. Because many people get confused,
transgender people often use a saying to explain the differences between sex
and gender. Most transgender people subscribe to a slogan that "sex is
between your legs and gender is between your ears."

Unfortunately after Money repurposed the word, some people liked the
word "gender" so much that they began using it as a "polite" word for sex.
This was just the opposite of what Money had intended. Today, the words
"gender" and "sex" are mixed up in many places, including the media and
the Internet.

Due to this confusion, most people in our culture assume that sex and
gender are the same thing. They do not know the difference. This creates
considerable difficulty in communicating with transgender people, scientists,
and also policymakers. I once attended a meeting to discuss what to do about
homeless transgender people here in Atlanta. The meeting included city leaders, police, social workers, homeowners, lawyers, and transgender advocates.
During the first meeting, it took the transgender advocates at least two hours
to get the message across to other attendees that sex and gender were different. Even then I was not sure that they understood. These people were not
stupid and they were professionals in their fields; they just did not know any
better. Here they were on this important taskforce without having done their
homework on being transgender.

"Sex" should always refer to the body parts or organs of reproduction. Sexual categories are male and female. Humans reproduce by combining DNA and other chemical information through the joining of cells of parents. DNA is a molecule that occurs in almost all cells of the body and has the basic blueprint for development and behavior. In sexual behavior, cells are combined using the two primary sex organs that are the vagina for the female and penis for the male. Secondary sex organs get the female and male genitals and bodies ready for sex. These secondary organs include the breasts, brain, nervous system, and even skin. These latter organs change the body when sex is anticipated. Being ready for sex in this way is called "sexual arousal."

Virginia Prince was one of the most visible transgender advocates in the second half of the 20th century, having started several magazines and newsletters, a chain of affiliated support groups and published some of the first scientific research papers on being transgender:

> Sex and gender are not the same thing. We are born into a society that is highly polarized and highly stereotyped, not only into male and female, but into man and woman. Man and male, female and woman are considered synonymous pairs of words for the same thing. But it is not so. Sex and gender are not the same thing.
>
> —Virginia Prince, "Sex vs. Gender"[4]

In order to define the word "transgender," we need to continue the story with a few more terms that pertain to the gender categories that Money recognized. **Culture** is a man-made way of life that consists of rules, values, and customs. Because it is man-made, culture can evolve or be changed. Our Western culture defines only two gender behavior categories as **masculine** and **feminine**. The English words that go with masculine are **boy, man, he, Sir**. The words that go with feminine gender behavior category are **girl, woman, she, Ma'am**. Proper use of masculine or feminine words is a big issue for transgender people.

Behaviors in the feminine gender behavior category include wearing makeup or a dress or having long hair. For the masculine gender category this might include wearing short hair, wearing a suit and tie, and wearing no makeup. Some of these behaviors have evolved over the years. For example, the English general Oliver Cromwell had all his soldiers cut their hair short. Before this, most men had long hair. You probably know about English Cavaliers who opposed Cromwell and Three Musketeers in France, who both sported long hair. His soldiers became known as the Roundheads. Cropping their hair was not a sanitary matter; it was a cultural statement.

The term "transgender" could only have been coined after sex and gender were separated and the term "gender" gained acceptance. The word **transgender** is a word that originally came from a psychiatrist named John Oliven in 1965. He did not use the word as we use it today. Oliven used the word "transgender" instead of transsexual, because he wanted to replace sex with gender as a causative factor. This was an acknowledgment that sexual arousal was not the motivation for transsexual behavior in his judgment. Since then, transgender people have changed the meaning of the word to include both transsexuals and non-transsexual transgender people. For some, it has become an umbrella term for several types of behavior. Some people add other types of people but I do not. The behaviors that these other people perform are quite different from being transgender but you should know about them. We will define them in the next section.

For the purposes of this book, I will define **being transgender** as showing observable behavior that is incongruent with one's assigned gender behavior category and congruent with another category. This behavior includes crossdressing or **crosspresentation** in the preferred gender behavior category or verbal expression of gender or **gender identity**. Presentation includes clothing, behavior, deportment, language, and other things that are included in gender behavior categories. We will discuss gender identity in Chapter 2 in the section "Current Pathological Words Related to Being Transgender". In Western culture, people are assigned a gender behavior category at birth according to biological sex. Being transgender includes crossdressing and presentation according to the rules of a gender behavior category that was not the one assigned at birth.

WORDS RELATED TO BEING TRANSGENDER

We need to define several words to fully explain the details about being transgender. In this section, we will define the following words:

- Transsexual
- Transsexual transition
- Transman and transwoman
- MTF/FTM transsexuals
- Binary gender system
- Cisgender gender system
- Genderqueer
- Biological gender behavior predisposition

Transsexuals are a subset of transgender people. The difference is that transsexual people change their sex organs and body parts more than most other transgender people. They change their bodies in order to meet cultural expectations of the sex associated with their congruent or preferred gender. Transsexuals go through a process called **transsexual transition** in which they change their bodies using sex hormones, surgeries, and other procedures under the supervision of medical doctors and mental health professionals. (More about transsexual transition will be presented in Chapter 6.) But as we will see in that chapter, a few non-transsexual transgender people modify their bodies for the same reason.

Virginia Prince was a transgender leader in the 1970s and 1980s, and one of the highest awards among transgender people is named after her for her pioneering work to benefit the transgender community. Surprisingly, although she espoused being transgender and not being transsexual, she evidently took sex hormones for breast development. Even now, a small minority of non-transsexual transgender people seek to modify their bodies in this and other ways.

There are two types of transgender people. Those with a congruent masculine gender behavior category are called **transman** or in plural **transmen**. Those with a congruent feminine gender behavior category are called **transwoman** or in plural **transwomen**. These words can be applied to both transsexual and non-transsexual people. The way to remember their gender behavior category is by the last part of the word. A transwoman follows the feminine behavior category and the transman, the masculine category.

There are similar words that apply to the two types of transsexual people. They are known as **male-to-female (MTF)** or **female-to-male (FTM)**. MTF means that at birth, the person was ruled male but through the process of transsexual transition, the person is changing her sex organs to be more like female organs. MTF transsexuals follow the feminine behavior category. Likewise, FTM means that at birth the person was ruled female but through the process of transsexual transition, the person is changing his sex organs to be more like male organs. FTM transsexuals follow the masculine gender behavior category. Be aware that sometimes transgender people who are not transsexual are said to be MTF or FTM instead of transwomen and transmen, respectively.

Because we have only two gender behavior categories, our Western **gender system** is called **binary**, meaning two. At birth, according to our culture, those that the doctor decides are males are automatically assigned to the masculine category. Those that a doctor decides are females are automatically assigned to the feminine category. Because this automatic assignment to gender behavior categories is based on sex, our gender system is also called **cisgender**. If a person is called cisgender, it means that their sex and gender are in alignment according to cultural rules. Cisgender is the opposite of transgender. As we shall see in Chapter 4, not all cultures are binary and cisgender.

There is one more characteristic of the gender system of Western culture that distinguishes it from other gender systems. Unlike other gender systems, which we will describe in Chapter 4, people are not free to move between gender behavior categories. So the Western gender system is **inflexible**. In summary, the Western gender behavior system is binary, cisgender, and inflexible. If Western culture were more flexible, transgender people might experience less rejection.

The biological gender behavior predisposition of some people does not easily fit into any of the available gender behavioral categories. These people call themselves **genderqueer** or **gender fluid**. They may follow none or both of the available categories, mixing clothing and behaviors. Both genderqueer and gender fluidity seem to be increasing, especially in younger people. Some include genderqueer under the transgender umbrella but I do not, primarily because very little scientific research has been done on it. Many of the genderfluid people I have met seem to be inclined to move back and forth between genders as they wish.

Being transgender also involves a biological **gender behavior predisposition**. Humans have all sorts of predispositions. For example, there is predisposition to use one hand or the other to do particular tasks. Predispositions can be talent for music, art, or playing football. All humans have a biological gender behavior predisposition. The gender predisposition of some people does not fit well with their assigned gender behavior category but fits better with another category. These people are transgender. Gender behavior predisposition is not determined by sex. There do seem to be biomarkers, neuroanatomical structures, and neurophysiological functions that correlate with it, but these are not those that create sex organs. We will provide the evidence for a biological gender behavior predisposition that results in being transgender in the next chapter.

Milton Diamond, professor of anatomy and reproductive biology at the University of Hawaii, is famous for his study of the persistence of gender behavior predisposition in the face of opposite-gender child rearing. We will encounter him in the next chapter in a scientific drama with John Money. He has described the nature of gender behavior predisposition:

> Sex and gender, and all the things that we learn associated with them, are encoded in our nervous system. This is manifest by a person's predisposition to learn and do certain things and avoid doing other things ... And with this

predisposition, comes a somewhat innate feeling of belonging to a social group of either boys or girls. What I think happens is that as kids grow they are keenly aware of differences and similarities. I don't think there is a brain template that simply says male or female, boy or girl, but I do think we have a template that basically says "same or different" and built-in predispositions which encourage and discourage certain behaviors over others ...

—Milton Diamond, quoted in D. Kotula,
In the Realm of the Phallus Place[5]

Now we have defined all the words we need to fully explain the conditions necessary for being transgender. **Being transgender** is <u>showing behavior that is incongruent with your assigned gender behavior category and congruent with another category</u>. Being transgender involves several things:

1. A gender system that includes gender behavior categories (Western culture has two categories and so it is binary)
2. A gender system that assigns gender behavior category based on sex but not on gender behavior predisposition (a cisgender system)
3. An inflexible gender system that does not allow movement between gender behavior categories
4. A biological gender behavior predisposition that does not fit well with assigned gender behavior category but fits better with another category
5. Knowledge of gender behavior categories, usually acquired in childhood by age 2–3

As Janet Mock put it:

These women believed they were raising a boy child, and boys do not wear dresses, according to the rules of Western culture's gender binary system, which is rigidly fixed between two poles (boy and girl; male and female; man and woman; masculine and feminine) for all people depending on assigned sex (based on the appearance of one's genitals at birth). The system proclaims that sex is determined at birth; gender is based on your sex assigned at birth; no variation exists in sex or gender; you should not change your sex or gender; and you should act according to your assigned sex and its correlating gender-appropriate behaviors.

—Janet Mock, *Redefining Realness*[6]

CURRENT PATHOLOGICAL WORDS RELATED TO BEING TRANSGENDER

There are words and terms that reveal transgender history and issues with pathology. **Pathology** is a term referring to the study of diseases and disorders. The medical and mental health professionals who initially tried to help transgender people considered transgender behavior as pathological. This is still somewhat true today. Since being transgender is neither a disease nor a disorder, there is a strong movement to eliminate being transgender from pathological terms. In this section, we will define the following words, listed in order of historical appearance:

- Gender identity
- Gender identity disorder
- DSM and ICD
- Gender dysphoria

Like the term "transgender," the term **gender identity** started out as a psychiatric disease term, but it is now in common usage by transgender people and the public as well. Its current meaning is a shortcut way of expressing a person's congruent gender behavior category based on their gender behavior. Likewise a transgender person might say that they identify with being transgender or being a man or woman. Transgender people repurposed the term after hearing mental health professionals using it.

Verbal expression of gender identity or identification is useful in everyday talk, but actual observation of gender behavior is the best evidence for science. Statements of gender identity are weaker evidence than actual behavior observation or objective reports for determining that someone is transgender.

Knowledge of where gender identity came from is important, because it has been used in the past and is still being used in the term **gender identity disorder**, which is a disease state. The component word "identity" was derived from psychiatrists and psychoanalysts Sigmund Freud and later Erik Erikson. The term "identity" is also used in the behavioral sciences to designate affiliation with societal and geographical groups as in "I am a Lutheran or an Atlantan." Robert Stoller, a psychologist at the University of California, Los Angeles (UCLA), combined the word "identity" from their work with the word "gender" from Money to form the term "gender identity disorder." Psychiatrist Richard Green inserted the term into a listing of disease terms (DSM, see later) used for insurance billing and claims where it stayed until 2014.

Although the term was originally derived from psychiatry and the social sciences terms with pathological and other meanings, "gender identity" is now used by transgender and other people to describe their behavior and that they are part of the transgender community. They use the term as in "my gender identity is masculine" or "my gender identity is feminine."

There are two listings of medical billing categories that mental health professionals and medical professionals use to collect money for treatment from insurance companies for treatment of diseases and disorders. These two listings are the **Diagnostic and Statistical Manual of Mental Disorders (DSM)** and the **International Classification of Diseases (ICD)**. The billing for the DSM list is done by matching DSM categories to ICD categories, and the ICD category is the one used in the actual submittal. The matchup logic is approved by agreement of both the DSM and ICD authorities, a process called "harmonization." The importance of this DSM/ICD system is that there are categories referring to being transgender and transsexual as pathological disorders in both listings. The existence of these categories is used by some anti-transgender people to say that transgender people have a mental disease or illness and that they should not have the rights they deserve. Transgender people and allies are currently working to eliminate these terms from use as pathological diagnostic and medical billing terms, and they have met with some success.

Gender identity disorder (GID) was a term used for over 40 years in the DSM and for many years in the ICD as a diagnostic category for transgender people. Although the requirements for GID specified in the DSM that a person had to be "in distress or incapacitated" by their transgender behavior in order to be diagnosed in this way, the term was and is often used without considering this requirement or even examining the transgender person. Because of this pathologization, GID was replaced in 2014 in the DSM with the term **gender dysphoria** and given its own section of the listing. The term "gender dysphoria" is a mixture of English "gender" and Greek "dysphoria," meaning simply that one is unhappy about one's assigned gender. The term had been used in psychiatric circles for several decades but as a description rather than a formal pathological insurance billing category. When many transgender people heard about this term, they joked that they did not have gender dysphoria but rather "gender euphoria," meaning that they were happy with their preferred gender.

Gender dysphoria is still in the DSM that remains a listing of disorders and diseases. It says so in the title. The words have changed from gender identity disorder to gender dysphoria, but the term is still a disease term for being transgender. Nothing about the ICD has been changed except that gender dysphoria in the DSM points to gender identity disorder in the ICD. The DSM change, away from gender identity disorder, is therefore meaningless except as a gesture. There is hope that the next version of the ICD will eliminate gender identity disorder and insert a category that will cover transsexual medical treatments. Unlike the DSM, the ICD has some categories that do not refer to diseases. An example of such a category is normal pregnancy, which is not pathological but nevertheless requires medical attention. It has been suggested that the transsexual treatment category should be put in this group. So if this happens, how will transgender people get counseling and, if needed, psychotherapy? The answer is simple. There are many categories in the DSM and ICD under which transgender people could get this treatment.

I have been seeing psychologists for the past 14 years, and none of them has ever used pathological codes from the DSM or ICD for me that refer to being transgender or transsexual. They helped me with marriage and other problems that required counseling but not for being transgender. Counselors in the United States are also reticent about using pathological codes, because they inevitably are seen by nonprofessional medical people and can hurt the reputations of their clients.

SEXUAL ORIENTATION WORDS

In order to understand the differences between being transgender and various forms of sexual orientation, there are several words and one acronym you need to know. Being transgender is independent from sexual orientation. It is particularly important to distinguish these terms from those pertaining to being transgender. Transgender advocates are often aligned with advocates representing people in these sexual orientation groups. You will often hear about joint efforts to pass nondiscrimination laws and change culture in coordination with these groups. But being transgender is quite different from gay or bisexual sexual orientation.

In this section, we will define the following words and terms:

- Gay
- Lesbian
- Bisexual
- Asexual
- Genderqueer
- Queer
- Gender fluid
- Androgynous
- Questioning
- GLBTQQIA

Sexual orientation refers to the sex of the person to whom one is attracted for romantic love. Being transgender does not determine one's sexual orientation. Transgender people have a wide range of sexual orientations. Transsexual people sometimes even change their sexual orientation after transition. About 25% of MTF and 40% of FTM transsexuals change their sexual orientation during or after transition.

A **gay** person is traditionally a male attracted to a male, and a **lesbian** is a female attracted to a female. The term "gay" is increasingly being used to refer to both gays and lesbians. **Bisexual** means that a person is attracted to both males and females. Some people come to understand that their true sexual orientation is not the one that they are living in and change their sexual orientation but that is not being bisexual. **Asexual** means that someone is not attracted to either sex.

Genderqueer means that a person does not feel like they fit into one of the two gender behavior categories that we have in our culture, whereas **queer** refers to those who are neither cisgender nor heterosexual. Genderqueer people borrow from each gender behavior category in terms of gender presentation. **Gender fluid** means that a person may vacillate between genders or borrow behaviors from each gender behavior category.

During my transsexual transition, my sexual orientation did not change. That makes me a proud lesbian. I really enjoy going to Lesbians Who Tech meetings whose members are mostly lesbian millennials who, like me, are involved in computer science. There are a few genderqueer or gender fluid people attend as well and I enjoy talking with them.

Questioning means that a person is unsure about whether they are transgender and/or their sexual orientation. I have met many questioning people at support group meetings.

You probably have seen or will see the acronym LGBTQQIA. We have now defined all of the words involved in this term. Shown below are the words contained in it:

- Lesbian
- Gay
- Bisexual
- Transgender
- Queer (Genderqueer)
- Questioning
- Intersex
- Asexual

People can fall into multiple categories. As I pointed out earlier, I am technically transgender, a transsexual, and a lesbian. Some transgender and about

15–20% of transsexual people are also asexual. Many transgender people are in the questioning group until they resolve whether they are transgender or gay or both or neither.

Advocates for each of these groups sometime try to get together to advocate for things like nondiscrimination laws. Injustice to one group usually means injustice to all, so there is still a reason to cooperate with these groups as well as others.

CONTROVERSIAL TERMS

It is very important to avoid certain words because they are offensive and hurtful to transgender people. Words can and have been rehabilitated, so here is the current status of some controversial words:

- Transvestite
- Tranny
- A transgender
- She-male
- Shim
- He-she
- Gender identity disorder
- Transgenders
- Transgendered
- Gender pronouns
- Transgenderism
- Transsexualism

Probably the most offensive words for transgender people are transvestite, tranny, and she-male. We have already defined **transvestite** as a transgender person who is thought by some to be motivated by sexual arousal to present in their congruent gender behavior category. We will present the evidence that this explanation is not correct in Chapter 7. "Transvestite" is still used in the drag entertainment industry. Presumably it continues there because drag performers do all they can to create sexual arousal in their patrons using exaggerated sexually stimulating theatrical presentations.

Tranny is a shortened form of transgender which at one time was a term of endearment that expressed affection among transgender people. It was originated in the drag community but later became commonly used in the sex and pornography industry. For this reason, the word fell out of favor. Transgender people keep trying to reclaim this word but currently only transgender people should use the word. These words should never be used outside of the transgender community and even then some will consider it offensive. As transgender actress Calpernia Addams commented on the evolution of "tranny" from a term of endearment:

> ... tranny has evolved, from scattered in-community usage by drag and trans entertainers to accreting negative connotations from its frequent use as a dismissive semi-insult—it's gone from "Those trannies kicked ass last night when they raided at Stonewall" to "Ugh, look at that hot tranny mess."
>
> —Calpernia Addams[7]

(She is referring to the Stonewall gay and transgender uprising in which transgender people rebelled at being strip-searched in public. It was the beginning of the GLBT movement.) "Tranny," along with **she-male**, is still used in pornography and prostitution, industries which exploit transgender people and portray them in a bad light.

He-she and **shim** (meaning a combination of she and him) are most commonly used on the street, in law enforcement or as a slur. There is an effort to get policemen retrained to not use these hateful words. The argument is made in their training that it is in their own interest to refrain from using pejorative words for transgender people. Police use of such words causes transgender people to get angry, and therefore, they will be less likely to cooperate with law enforcement.

Gender identity disorder and **gender dysphoria** are words implying that being transgender is an illness or disease. By their own DSM definitions these terms do not apply unless a person is distressed or incapacitated by problems resulting from being transgender. However, these terms are often misused to refer to transgender people who are not distressed or incapacitated, including discussions about transgender people and in the media.

The word **transgender** is an adjective and proper usage of the word should be, for example, "transgender people" or "being transgender." However, this word is sometimes <u>misused</u> when used as a noun, as in "He is **a transgender**" or "**two transgenders** walked down the street." Transgender people take offense at these usages, and so they should be avoided. **Transgendered** should also not be used because it makes it sound as though transgender people are no longer human but have been somehow changed. Despite journalistic standards, this language is sometimes deliberately used by writers either out of ignorance or for sensationalism.

Finally, some transgender people are starting to take offense at the words **transgenderism** and **transsexualism**, presumably because the –ism part in medicine is used to refer to diseases or in social science to refer to philosophies.

There are still some times when they are appropriate scientific terms but as we discussed in Chapter 1, in this book we intend to use as few words as possible with pathological overtones. So instead of transgenderism, we will use "being transgender," which puts emphasis on behavior, not pathology.

MY HISTORY WITH THESE WORDS AND DEFINITIONS

Growing up, I first encountered the word "transsexual" as I read about Christine Jorgensen in the early 1950s. I was only 5 or 6 then, and my mother was an elementary school teacher. She had taught me how to read at least well enough to read the captions under the pictures of Jorgensen. Christine was the Caitlyn Jenner of her day, a celebrity "transsexual." Although I did not know much about human sex, I knew that she had once been a male, and it gave me hope for the future.

At some point in my childhood, like most other children, I started to be curious about sex. My parents had not talked about it to me, and that made me even more curious. The Internet was yet to be invented, so in that day the only references were the encyclopedias. As I was looking up words that seemed to be about sex, there was the word "transsexual." Perhaps I was naïve but I had never realized that transsexuals actually changed sex organs until then. I just figured that being a transsexual allowed one to be the gender that they were.

My curiosity also led to words about what they called **sexual perversion**. I read all about it and it was pretty scary. But my curiosity was peaked to know all about the secret things of sex that no one talked about. In the midst of trying to understand sexual perversion, there was the word "transvestite," which I discovered was related to the word "transsexual" somehow. I had been crossdressing in secret by now for at least a decade, and I suddenly realized that the description of "transvestite" sort of fit what I was doing. At that point I was still getting sexually aroused by crossdressing, so I got really scared when I incorrectly concluded that I was a sexual pervert. I am sure some transgender children even now come to the same conclusion and need reassurance. I did not feel guilty about it, but it worried me because being a transvestite was described as a mental disorder, and by then I knew that people with mental disorders went to the nearest state hospital. For me, it would have been the psychiatric hospital in Ancora, New Jersey. Although there was a lot of joking by adults about Ancora, my experience was that two of my playmates in the house across the street disappeared there and I never saw them again. The adults said that it was "schizophrenia," yet another word that I knew nothing about and was even scarier. I did not want to disappear for being a transvestite, so I vowed to stay deep in the closet.

When I was in college, I decided to take the abnormal psychology course as soon as I finished the introductory courses. The course was affectionately known as "Nuts and Sluts," referring to all the mental disorders as well as nymphomania or uncontrolled sexual desire in women. (We never studied uncontrolled sexual desire in men, probably because it was the norm in our all-male college.) At first there was a lot of material on organic disorders like schizophrenia and manic depression but then the course turned to behavior disorders. They included all the disorders at the time, including homosexuality, transvestism, bisexuality, and asexuality. Homosexuality was described in the textbook as a disorder, but it seemed like the instructor did not believe it. From his defense of homosexuality, it seemed like he might be homosexual himself. Not that I minded.

With the disorders, there were also phobias which could be treated by exposing the patient gradually to more intense stimuli of the type that caused the fear. During this exposure, the patient engaged in relaxation techniques. (We will see how this approach applies to sexual arousal and crossdressing in Chapter 3.)

Aside from the relatively benign phobias, there were all sorts of fetish disorders, including people who got overly turned on by leather and or women's undergarments. The treatment at the time was aversion therapy in which the patient received pairings of leather garments and a drug that caused nausea. It appeared that such treatments were abandoned after a case in which the patient after the treatment started attacking leather baby carriages because they made him nauseous.

Then the course mentioned transvestites and classified them as fetishes or disorders motivated by sexual arousal. Similar attempts at treatment with nausea drugs as well as electric shock had been tried. They all had failed. The instructor did mention that transvestites were found all over the Western world, which seemed to me to indicate a biological cause.

Once I started working in Arlington, Virginia, in 1976, I did a tour of all of the local libraries, and to my surprise, the Arlington library had some transgender science books and a copy of *Conundrum*[8] by Jan Morris. Jan was an award-winning writer who published the story of her transsexual transition in this book. It was an autobiography, not a science book, but for the first time I understood what it truly meant to be a transsexual.

There was a period of time in the 1970s and 1980s when support groups were all the rage. The original support group was Alcoholics Anonymous (AA), which was formed in the 1930s to help people refrain from alcohol.

Unlike the original support groups like AA, the new support groups were formed to help people pursue their interests. Rather than try to get people to refrain from various behaviors, the new support groups encouraged them with how-to and safety information. Support groups for crossdressing formed all over the United States, usually on various topics. Some were networked and some were "franchised." Many of these still exist today. At some point in my life I decided that I was tired of crossdressing in private at home or in hotel rooms and decided to try out support groups.

The early mistake that I made was that I started attending support groups for **bondage, discipline, sadism, and masochism** or **BDSM**. I reasoned that if I had a fetish, then the logical place to go was where they practiced fetishes with a safe, sane, and consensual approach. How wrong I was! The people in these groups were tolerant of crossdressing, but they did not understand it and few practiced it. I did learn a lot about BDSM, but I had no desire to be a participant, and there were very few crossdressers in each group to interact with. However, on the positive side, the thing I did get from the experience was the address of the International Foundation for Gender Education in Boston. They published a monthly magazine, *Tapestry*, with a list of all of the support groups for crossdressers in the United States and the world. I wrote a letter to the Crossroads support group in Detroit and started going to their meetings.

When I started in Crossroads, it was a crossdressing support group, but it soon became a transgender support group. The word "transgender" had become popular and suited the group members more than crossdressing had. The group was diverse enough for me to meet transgender people of all sexual orientations and interests. I also attended support group meetings in Los Angeles at a group called Androgyny, where they had people who dressed in mixed gender items. I even met a gay male there who was in domestic relationship with another gay male. He was not transgender but dressed as a woman in order to maintain appearances as a heterosexual couple. At that point, same-sex relationships were not universally accepted. She was an interesting example of someone who crossdressed but was not transgender.

Gender fluidity is a relatively recent phenomenon and seems to be more frequent among millennials and younger people. I have met gender fluid people recently in support groups here in Atlanta and among those in the Lesbians Who Tech organization. There is very little science about gender fluidity, but one of the gender fluid people I talked to was a young person, going to college, who wanted to become an experimental psychologist like me. I hope she does so and does good research on gender fluidity.

DEFINITIONS GOING FORWARD

Definitions are all well and good but they are only the point of departure for understanding being transgender. As we move forward into the rest of this book, we should remember what Kate Bornstein had to say:

> Definitions have their uses in much the same way that road signs make it easy to travel: they point out the directions. But you don't get where you're going when you just stand underneath some sign, waiting for it to tell you what to do.
>
> —Kate Bornstein, *Gender Outlaw:*
> *On Men, Women and the Rest of Us*[9]

NOTES

1. Lewis Carroll, *Through the Looking Glass* (CreateSpace Amazon Publishing, 2000), 114. https://www.amazon.com/Alice-Adventures-Wonderland-Through-Looking-Glass/dp/1503250210/ref=sr_1_1?ie=UTF8&qid=1468593819&sr=8-1&keywords=through+the+looking+glass (confirmed July 15, 2016).

2. Michael Hurst and Robert Swope, *Casa Susanna* (Brooklyn, NY: Powerhouse Books, 2014).

3. I.W. Gregorio, *None of the Above* (New York: Balzer and Bray, Harper Collins, 2015), 56.

4. Virginia Prince, "Sex vs. Gender," in *International Journal of Transgenderism* 8, no. 4 (2005): 1.

5. Milton Diamond, quoted in D. Dean Kotula, *In the Realm of the Phallus Place* (Los Angeles, CA: Alyson Books 2002), 35. http://www.changelingaspects.com/Technical/A%20Conversation%20with%20Dr%20Milton%20Diamond.htm (confirmed May 19, 2016).

6. Janet Mock, *Redefining Realness: My Path to Womanhood, Identity, Love & So Much More* (New York: Atria Books, 2014), 21–22.

7. Calpernia Addams, "Burning Books, One Word at a Time," *The Advocate*, April 17, 2014; http://www.advocate.com/commentary/2014/04/17/op-ed-burning-books-one-word-time (confirmed May 19, 2016).

8. Jan Morris, *Conundrum* (New York: Harcourt, 1974).

9. Kate Bornstein, *Gender Outlaw: On Men, Women, and the Rest of Us* (New York: Routledge, 1994), 21.

CHAPTER 3

Biology

Nature chooses who will be transgender; individuals do not choose this.
—Mercedes Ruehl, Academy Award-winning
actress for *A Girl like Me*[1]

INTRODUCTION

Do not be afraid of a little biology. I promise not to get too technical. Fair warning, I will show you a few numbers so do not freak out because of them. As we discussed in Chapters 1 and 2, being transgender is a result of three things—biological gender predisposition; a binary, cisgender, and inflexible culture; and the ability of children to learn about gender behavior categories. Studies show that nearly all transgender children have this learning ability, so we will concentrate on biology and culture. This chapter deals with the biological factors that create gender behavior predisposition, at least as far as we know them today.

Because gender behavior predisposition is not under the control of a transgender person, they cannot be blamed for being transgender.

Being transgender, like being gay, tall, short, white, black, male, or female, is another part of the human condition that makes each individual unique, and something over which we have no control. We are who we are in the deepest recesses of our minds, hearts and identities.
—Linda Thompson, former wife of Caitlyn Jenner[2]

The biological evidence for establishing a gender behavior predisposition that results in being transgender comes from eight areas:

1. Being transgender is not rare and it exists in most of the societies of the Western world.

2. Awareness of being transgender occurs at an early age, so there is little time for nonbiological factors to work.

3. DNA genetics is a causal factor in being transgender based on inheritance studies. Deoxyribonucleic acid or DNA is the chemical we all receive from our parents that conveys the blueprint for structure and function of human beings. Evidence indicates that DNA inheritance provides the genes for being transgender.

4. There are biological differences in structure and function between the brains of transgender people and non-transgender people.

5. There are biological differences in body structure and function between transgender and non-transgender people that can be attributed to DNA differences.

6. Unfortunate "natural experiments" support the idea that gender behavior predisposition exists and cannot be changed by childrearing practices.

7. Epigenetics is a biological factor involved in being transgender, because the evidence seems to indicate that it modifies or blocks the expression of transgender DNA. Epigenetics involves non-DNA mechanisms passed on from parents and produced by the environment.

8. Other suggested nonbiological causes of being transgender are not supported by scientific evidence.

BEING TRANSGENDER IS NOT RARE AND IT EXISTS IN MOST OF THE WESTERN WORLD

The question of how many transgender people exist in the world is asked every day by not only reporters in the media but also by transgender people. Estimates before the beginning of this century were based on how many transgender people showed up at European clinics for help. The estimates we have now are far better, because they come from surveys of the population where large numbers of people can be asked. As people have become more open about whether they are transgender or not, the population numbers have continued to climb. Evidence from many countries indicates that transgender people are present, surprisingly in even the most repressive cultures and regimes.

So how many transgender people are there? Scientists try to establish a **population frequency** that will allow them to estimate the answer. We will define the population frequency is the fraction of people who are transgender expressed as a percentage. Sometimes you will hear it called the prevalence of being transgender, but prevalence is too closely identified with the frequency of diseases and diseased people in epidemics. I prefer to use the pure mathematical term "population frequency" and that is what I will use in this book. Being transgender is not a disease and should not be referred to with terms that connote disease.

In 2000, Lynn Conway, an accomplished engineer, decided that the estimates of population frequency from clinical sources were too much low based on her back-of-the-envelope estimates. While at IBM she was one of two engineers who designed the technologies in modern computers. She also happens to be a transwoman, so she was interested in the results. She did a rough calculation of how many people were in transgender support groups and how many transsexuals were being treated and found that it was many times higher than the clinical estimates. She proceeded to build a mathematical model for estimating the frequencies using engineering methods... Her estimate of the population frequency of being a transwoman was at least 1%, which was many times any clinical estimate. The clinical estimates were/ are low, because most transgender people do not go to clinics or see mental health professionals because they do not need to.

I gave a talk at the 2011 meeting of the World Professional Association of Transgender Health, the organization that sets guidelines for how to treat transgender people. In that talk I referenced Conway's estimates and to my surprise, it seemed as if no one there had ever heard of them. I keep a close watch on the published research in this area, and it is only in the past couple of years that I have seen her papers cited and then not in any detail. I presume that her estimates have largely been ignored, because she used an engineering mathematical modeling approach that is foreign to medical and mental health providers. However, in my opinion, they are still the best estimates for transwomen.

Conway's estimates for transwomen have been confirmed by later survey studies as shown in Figures 3.1 and 3.2. (If you are afraid of numbers, do not worry, because we will talk about what they mean in words.) Figure 3.1 shows Conway's results on MTF transgender (TG) frequency along with some more recent studies.

The figure shows the primary scientist who did each study, the year, the percentage population estimate, and the country from which the estimate was made. Estimates from Lynn Conway represent a lower bound for minimum population frequencies; the true frequency is probably higher. The Winter estimate is probably a little low because it only included transgender people who were out in public in Thailand, not those in the closet. The van Beijsterveldt estimates are for a population of children who have not experienced the rejection that comes with teenage years, so their rates are somewhat higher.

Since each study in Figure 3.1 used different rules for counting, they cannot just be averaged. So I made up a *rule of thumb of 1%* after considering all

Figure 3.1
Population Frequency Studies for Transwomen

MTF TG

Lead Scientist(s)	Year	Population Frequency (%)	Country
Conway	2001	2–5	United States
Winter	2002	0.60	Thailand
van Beijsterveldt	2006	3.20	Netherlands
van Beijsterveldt	2006	2.60	Netherlands
Olyslager and Conway	2007	1.00	United States
Reed	2009	1.00	United Kingdom
Clark	2012	1.20	New Zealand
Kuyper and Wijsen	2013	1.10	Netherlands
Shields	2013	1.30	United States
Flores	2016	0.7 (MTF+ FTM)	United States
Rule of Thumb		>1	
U.S. Population Transwomen TG		>1,540,000	

Source: Thomas (Dana) Bevan, *The Biopsychology of Transsexualism and Transgenderism* (Santa Barbara, CA: Praeger, 2014).

the studies. This means that for the United States, there are at least one and a half million transwomen and for the world it means that at least 1% of those born and designated as male in Western culture will be transwomen. Applying this frequency to the U.S. male population it means that at least 1,540,000 males are transgender. That is equivalent to the population of the city of Phoenix, Arizona, or Philadelphia, Pennsylvania.

Figure 3.2 shows some population estimates of being a transsexual (TS) transwoman. It shows Conway's estimates for 2001 and 2007 as well as more recent estimates. Brain's estimates are based on applications for passport changes but not everyone needs a passport, so the estimate may be a little low. To be conservative, the *rule of thumb estimate that we will use is 0.35%.* This means, that in the United States, there are at least 53,900 transsexual transwomen, which is reasonable because the vast majority of transwomen who have ever lived are still alive today. Widespread transsexual transition was only available in the last 40 years. Conway could account for approximately 40,000 MTF transsexuals in 2001, and 1,000 more per year is not unreasonable. Recent reports from the United Kingdom indicate that the current frequency of people requesting transsexual transition is

Figure 3.2
Population Frequency Studies for MTF Transsexuals

MTF TS

Lead Scientist(s)	Year	Population Frequency (%)	Country
Conway	2001	0.2	United States
Olyslager and Conway	2007	0.4	United States
Horton	2008	0.133	United States
Reed	2008	0.021	United Kingdom
Brain	2010	0.067	Australia
Rule of Thumb		0.35	
MTF TS Population in the United States		53,900	

Source: Thomas (Dana) Bevan, *The Biopsychology of Transsexualism and Transgenderism* (Santa Barbara, CA: Praeger, 2014).

approximately 0.2%, which includes both MTF and FTM. Most of these numbers reflect the number of transsexual transwomen who start transition; only approximately 25% of these eventually get genital plastic surgery.

In Figure 3.3, we do not have the benefit of estimates from Conway, because she only studied transwomen, but at least the estimates are in the same ballpark compared with the clinical estimates. The Horton estimates are based on clinical intake, so we would expect them to be on the low end.

Figure 3.3
Population Frequency Studies for Transmen

Transmen TG

Lead Scientist(s)	Year	Population Frequency (%)	Country
Horton	2001	0.036	United States
Clark	2007	1.200	New Zealand
Kuyper	2008	0.800	Netherlands
Rule of Thumb		0.5	
MTF TS Population in the United States		64,000	

Source: Thomas (Dana) Bevan, *The Biopsychology of Transsexualism and Transgenderism* (Santa Barbara, CA: Praeger, 2014).

Figure 3.4
Population Frequency Studies for FTM Transsexuals

FTM TS

Lead Scientist	Year	Population Frequency (%)	Country
Eklund	1980	0.00100	Netherlands
Eklund	1986	0.00200	Netherlands
Bakker	1993	0.00330	Netherlands
Weitz	1996	0.00100	Germany
Tsoi	1998	0.01200	Singapore
Wilson	1999	0.00130	Scotland
Gomez-Gil	2006	0.00210	Spain
Horton	2008	0.07140	United States
Veale	2008	0.00450	New Zealand
Brain	2010	0.02000	Australia
Rule of Thumb		0.015	
U.S. FTM Transwomen TS		2,400	

Source: Thomas (Dana) Bevan, *The Biopsychology of Transsexualism and Transgenderism* (Santa Barbara, CA: Praeger, 2014).

The rule of thumb I use is 0.5%. This means that there are at least 64,000 transgender transmen in the United States. These estimates may be low because females generally can wear clothes intended for men without rejection and need not present as women. They can crossdress without penalty. However, these results may also be high because they are based on self-reports of being transgender, not third-party behavioral observations.

Figure 3.4 indicates that there are fewer transmen seeking to transition than transsexual transwomen. The percentages are low because transmen transsexual genital plastic surgeries have not been offered as long as transwomen surgeries have been offered. They also do not account for the rapid improvement of genital plastic surgery techniques, particularly in the United States and Serbia that might encourage transition. The *rule of thumb that I selected was 0.015%* of the population, who are transsexual transmen, or about 2,400 in the United States.

By inspecting the last columns of Figures 3.1 through 3.4, you can see that transgender people exist in many Western countries. We know that they exist in other countries as well, but we do not have good survey data for them. Unfortunately, we know about the existence of transgender people in other countries mainly from the number who are attacked and/or murdered.

For example, we know that 95 transgender people were murdered in Brazil during 2015. Other countries leading in transgender murders (in descending order) are Mexico, Colombia, Venezuela, Honduras, Turkey, Philippines, India, Pakistan, and Italy.

AWARENESS OF BEING TRANSGENDER BEGINS AT AN EARLY AGE

Children know about gender behavior categories from an early age. Most know the fundamentals by age 2–3. They watch their parents and those around them who act as behavior models. They also get verbal education from their parents during contact, including face-to-face play. They see other people model gender behavior on the TV and other media. It is unlikely that they know about sex to any great extent, but they may have seen differences between mommy and daddy when they were undressed at home. By this age they know many of the gender behavior category rules and conventions, like pink is for girls and blue is for boys, even though there is no real basis for these rules and they are purely arbitrary.

I will never forget the day that I saw my first granddaughter running down the sidewalk when she was 2 years old. She was all in pink. She had pink shoes, pink stockings, pink tutu, and pink ribbons in her hair. She would not think about wearing any other color because she knew she was a girl. But her liking of pink was all due to what she had learned.

People may not give it much thought but the assignment of pink to girls is purely arbitrary. There is no biological reason why girls should prefer pink and boys prefer blue. Color-coding clothing for children is relatively new for human beings. It started in the early years of the 1900s, when merchants decided that they could sell more children clothing if they were color-coded. Before that, children generally wore white so that the clothing could be passed on to later brothers or sisters. If anything, blue was regarded as a girls' color because it was perceived to be delicate and pink was for boys. Males actually wore skirts until sometime in mid-childhood when they were "breeched," meaning that they now were allowed to wear breeches or pants. They started out in shorts and eventually were allowed to wear long pants. Clothing manufacturers together with their advertisers encouraged pink/blue differences. By World War II, pink was not only associated with being feminine but also with being homosexual, because some people believed that all homosexuals display feminine behaviors (which they do not). The badges that the Nazi made homosexual people wear were pink triangles.

Most transgender people realize that they are different starting at the age of 4–5. They know that their congruent gender behavior category is different from the one given to them at birth. The earliest report that I have heard from a responsible physician is that one transgirl told the doctor that she was really a girl at age 18 months or just as soon as she could form sentences.

Children may not be able to use the word "transgender," but they may say that they are really a boy or a girl when they have not been assigned to be in that gender behavior category. Just because they do not use the advanced word "transgender," it does not mean that they are not transgender. Some may not realize that they are transgender until later in life. Some children as early as 8 years old are certain that they are transsexual and want to prevent puberty and change their bodies as soon as possible. There are new pathways for such children, as we will see in Chapter 6.

I told my mother that I was really a girl when I was approximately 4 ¾. I know how old I was pretty closely because it was Christmas time. I remember a pretty pink Christmas balloon that made me feel feminine and triggered my telling her. She told me that I was "all boy" and not a girl because I ran around the house and yard and climbed on everything I could. That did not matter to me because there were girls in my neighborhood who were just as active as I was. She then tried to convince me that it was my duty to grow up as a man, to have children, and go into the military. She told me that I could not be a girl because I was not born that way. The word "transgender" had not been invented yet but I read about Christine Jorgensen, a famous transsexual, in the magazines. In her day, Christine was as famous as Caitlyn Jenner is now. I knew the relatively new word "transsexual" might apply. To this I replied that I had seen Christine Jorgensen in the magazines and knew that she had changed from a man to a woman. My mother rejected the idea that I was a girl but after some debate told me that when I grew up, I could decide whether to become a woman like Christine had done. I am sure my mother hoped that I would forget about Jorgensen.

Perhaps the most famous description of early recognition of being transgender comes from Jan Morris. She is famous for being an award-winning Welsh writer who wrote a series of travel books and a report back from the successful Hillary climbing party, which was first to scale Everest in 1953. In her autobiographical book, *Conundrum*, she wrote:

> I was three or perhaps four years old when I realized that I had been born in the wrong body, and should really be a girl. I remember the moment well, and it is the earliest memory of my life.
>
> I was sitting beneath my mother's piano, and her music was falling around me like cataracts, enclosing me in a cave ... My mother was probably playing

Sibelius, for she was enjoying a Finnish period then, and Sibelius from *underneath* a piano can be a very noisy composer.

—Jan Morris, *Conundrum*[3]

Although most transgender people cannot recall or write about it so well, these types of transgender realization in early childhood are typical. Some people struggle into their teens and adulthood with the feeling that something is wrong in the world but they cannot identify it. Some struggle with not only being transgender but also being gay or lesbian or some other sexual orientation. Some do not follow either gender behavior category and become genderqueer. Getting it all sorted out is the subject of Chapter 5.

Because being transgender begins at such an early age, it is likely that all children are born with a gender behavior predisposition. Early emergence of being transgender in childhood leaves little time for potential nonbiological causes. Potential nonbiological causes such as being taught to follow the "wrong" gender simply do not have time to take effect. There are also many studies that indicate that child rearing does not cause being transgender, and these are discussed further in "Biological Gender Predisposition and Two-Factor Theory of Being Transgender" section below in this chapter. The realization of being transgender at such an early age provides evidence to support the idea that being transgender is due to biology.

DNA GENETICS IS A CAUSAL FACTOR IN BEING TRANSGENDER

First a little DNA and genetics background. (Sorry but you need to know something about the science background to understand what makes people transgender and I will keep it short.) Then we will discuss the scientific evidence that supports the theory that DNA genetics is responsible for being transgender.

DNA is the genetic molecule that provides a blueprint for development and behavior of humans as well as all animals and plants. A molecule is composed of chemical elements joined together; in the case of DNA, it is composed of several elements that are joined into the shape of a helix or spiral. The DNA molecule is actually chopped up into 46 pieces called **chromosomes**. Humans usually have 46 chromosomes. There are two types of chromosomes, primarily for controlling body development (44 of them) and sex hormones (2 of them). The sex chromosomes are of two types, called "X" and "Y." The X chromosome molecule is longer than the Y chromosome. The information that chromosomes contain is divided into **genes**, which are laid out down the DNA molecule as the rungs on the spiral. Genes are "expressed" to provide instructions to cells. This means that the information from one or more genes is conveyed by "messenger" molecules to tell cells what to do. The outcome of this process is called a **trait**. The Y chromosome normally contains a gene (named the **SRY gene** for "sex regulation gene on the Y chromosome"), which is the trigger for male sex organ development. So in most cases a sex chromosome pair of XY will produce a male body and XX a female body. There are many exceptions to this rule that make it impossible to use sex chromosomes to determine biological sex.

Over the years, various athletic organizations have tried to use chromosomes and DNA to determine whether to put athletes with the male competitors or the female competitors. They have given up on using chromosomes and DNA because these approaches are unreliable. They subsequently have used a series of body structure and chemical tests to make this determination, but each test they have tried has failed to be reliable. Another reason is that differences cannot be correlated with athletic performance. The tests have failed because of human biological diversity. We are all different from one another at the DNA level.

Notice I defined sex in Chapter 2 as the presence of the organs of reproduction. How they get there is irrelevant. There are many genes that can influence sex organ development. But most are not on the sex chromosomes. The information used to determine the structure of sex organs is actually on some of the other 44 chromosomes.

For complicated body structures and behaviors, it usually takes several genes to produce a particular trait. For example, it takes over 15 genes to determine eye color. It takes many more genes to form a body with a male or female organ. We are just beginning to identify all the genes involved in a gender predisposition trait.

Scientists often use **twin studies** to determine if a trait can be inherited or passed on to children. At the moment of conception, the mother and the father contribute DNA to a cell that eventually becomes a baby. The original cell divides into many cells to start forming a child. Sometimes the cells will break off, forming two children. In this case, **identical twins** will be formed that start with exactly the same DNA. **Fraternal twins** can occur if the parents contribute information to form more than one cell. Fraternal twins do <u>not</u> share the same starting DNA. By comparing the traits of identical twins, fraternal twins, and other siblings, scientists can identify traits that can be inherited through DNA genetics. Scientists study the traits of fraternal twins and other siblings to be sure that the trait is inheritable and not something that is due to the environment.

Scientists run twin studies all the time to determine if a trait is **inheritable**, meaning that it can be passed on to future generations through DNA. For example, the strongest inherited relationship between identical twins is height. If one twin is a certain height, then the other is likely to be close in height. Psychologists use a statistic or number to give a number to the strength of this relationship. The number is called the correlation and ranges from 0 to 1. A higher number indicates a stronger relationship. In the case of physical height, the correlation is approximately 0.7, which is the strongest relationship we know of at this time. The relationship is not perfect as we will see because there is interference with the expression of the original DNA, either through changes in the molecule or through blockage of the information, which is supposed to go to cells.

There have been studies to measure the strength of the relationship. If one identical twin is transgender, will the other one be transgender too? The most recent measurement results for two studies were in the 0.62 to 0.7 range, which are very strong relationships. The study that produced the 0.7 result had over 14,000 twin pairs, which is a very large number for such studies. These studies also accounted for family environment because they also measured the correlation between fraternal twins and siblings in the family. A third study (which did not use the correlation measure) indicated that of 23 identical twin pairs, 39% were both transgender. All of these studies indicate that the probability of being transgender if you have a transgender identical twin is considerably greater than the population frequencies we estimated in the previous section.

Inheritance studies for being transsexual provided similar results. For MTF transsexuals, the two available studies reported 33% and 53% of transsexuals had an identical twin that was also transsexual. This compares with a study of nonidentical or fraternal twin studies that showed only a 1.3% relationship. Since fraternal twins do not start out with the same DNA, this latter study was a good control for the identical twin studies. Unfortunately, all of the published identical twin studies include very few people but that is to be expected because the frequency of being transsexual and the frequency of being an identical twin are both very low. These two studies indicate that the probability of being transsexual if you have a transsexual identical twin is considerably greater than population frequencies we estimated in the previous section.

The results for FTM transsexuals were similar with the results of two studies, indicating that 23% and 40% of identical twins had an identical twin pair that was also transsexual. The similar control study indicated that only 0.31% of transsexuals had a fraternal twin that was also transsexual.

So twin studies show that being transgender and transsexual are likely to be inherited from the DNA that transgender and transsexual people receive from their parents.

If being transgender is due to DNA genetics, then it is logical that there ought to be a place or places on the DNA of transgender people that differ from non-transgender people. Figure 3.5 summarizes results for studies that found DNA **genetic markers**. Researchers have found DNA genetic markers for being transsexual. Unfortunately, the researchers did not have enough financial resources or time to look across the entire DNA molecule, and they had to guess where to look with their available resources. That is unfortunate because for complicated traits, there are usually several DNA markers. Since then, the cost and time for a full DNA scan has greatly decreased. Some studies which did limited genetic scans have been unable to confirm these results; their authors point to differences in DNA from regional genetic heritage. The other possible reason is that identified genes only appear in their expected position about 65% of the time.

The researchers guessed that there ought to be markers on the places on the DNA molecule involved in sex hormone activity. For MTF, these were found in the estrogen receptor gene and the testosterone receptor gene, while for FTM, they were found in a location involved in formation of sex hormones. Receptors are the places where the hormones attach to the outside of cells in order to communicate with those cells. Receptors, like other body structures, are created by genes on the DNA molecule. The markers differed between MTF and FTM in terms of location and type. Because of the limitations of these studies, we do not know where other locations and genes on the DNA molecule can be found that correlate with being transgender. But the studies did prove the existence of biomarkers for being transgender. Since these studies were conducted, the price of a full DNA scan has decreased dramatically, and hopefully such studies will be conducted in the future. For now, these studies further support the biological involvement in being transgender, and together with the twin studies they point to DNA genetics as a factor.

Figure 3.5
DNA Markers for Transsexuals

Lead Scientist Author	Year	MTF/FTM	Gene
Henningsson	2005	MTF	Androgen receptor
Henningsson	2005	MTF	Estrogen receptor
Henningsson	2005	MTF	Aromatase enzyme
Hare	2009	MTF	Androgen receptor
Bentz	2008	FTM	Sex hormone formation

THERE ARE BIOLOGICAL DIFFERENCES IN STRUCTURE AND FUNCTION BETWEEN THE BRAINS OF TRANSGENDER PEOPLE AND NON-TRANSGENDER PEOPLE

Another way to know that being transgender is biological is to look for differences in brain structure and function between transgender people and non-transgender people. So far, many such differences have been discovered.

Figure 3.6 shows the structure of a section of the brain as you could see it if the eyes, skin, skull, and part of the brain were transparent until you got to about half way through the brain. The names of the structures in the brain may be foreign to you because they were invented by neuroanatomists who used Latin names in the belief that Latin would be a common neuroanatomical language, just as it is used in medicine.

The diagram is a drawing from the point of view of someone looking through your eyes and skull into the brain. The panel at the top of the figure is a view of the cross section of the brain as though sliced with a knife. The top of the figure indicates that the lower panel shows the middle of the brain. At the bottom of the lower panel is a structure called the optic chiasm, which is where the nerves from the eyes come together after entering the brain. This structure is just above the roof of your mouth.

In this figure, the right **Putamen, BNST, and INAH3** are groups of cells that have different sizes for transgender people than for non-transgender people. Do not bother trying to remember the Latin meanings of the words used for these structures; just remember they are places in the brain and they are important structures for behavior. The right Putamen is very active when the left hand is used, and as we shall see later, transgender people tend to use their left hand for more tasks than other people. The BNST and INAH3 are groups of cells that are important because they connect with a structure called the a**mygdala** (also shown) that processes information on emotions. If you are curious, *amygdala* is the Latin word for an almond because this structure has an almond shape. The amygdala is the place where information from the senses is used to trigger emotions. The BNST and amygdala connect with a group of cells that are known to mediate the experience of reward and pleasure through the release of the chemical dopamine. You have probably heard of dopamine in the context of drugs to avoid like amphetamine and cocaine, because these drugs stimulate uncontrolled release and activity of dopamine.

There are functional brain differences that support the idea that transgender brains are different from non-transgender brains. Because we can now watch the brain work in real time using scanners, differences in function have

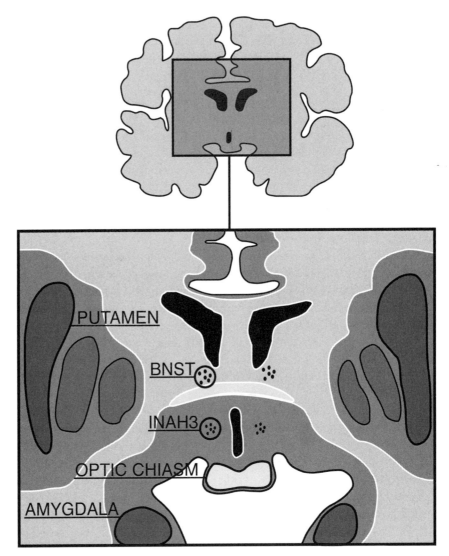

Figure 3.6
Brain Cross Section Showing Structures Associated with Being Transsexual
Source: Thomas (Dana) Bevan, *The Biopsychology of Transsexualism and Transgenderism* (Santa Barbara, CA: Praeger, 2014.)

also been observed. What these structural and functional differences mean is unclear, because we are just beginning to understand how the brain and nervous system work.

When I was in graduate school, I studied the region of the brain called the hypothalamus, where the BNST and INAH3 are located. At that time, I was interested in how this region functioned in eating and drinking regulation. That was because there was no financial support for exploring work on transgender people and the association of being transgender with the hypothalamus had not yet been made. But I dreamed of someday being able to watch brain function at work for transgender and other behaviors. Eventually I worked on a research program that included financial support for the first **MRI (magnetic resonance imager)**, which was later developed into a scanner that could watch the brain in real time. I did not conduct the research or I might have directed it toward exploring transgender behavior. But I never got to use these machines for research on being transgender. The availability and sophistication of brain scanning machines for research has greatly improved. But even now there is very little support in the United States for such transgender research and if it is done, it is done in other countries.

THERE ARE BIOLOGICAL DIFFERENCES IN BODY STRUCTURE AND FUNCTION BETWEEN TRANSGENDER AND NON-TRANSGENDER PEOPLE THAT ARE BELIEVED TO BE DUE TO DNA GENETICS

Body structure and functional differences between people are known as **biomarkers.** A summary of biomarkers between transgender and non-transgender people is shown in Figure 3.7.

Transgender people appear to be less right-handed than non-transgender people. Most people think that someone is either totally right or left-handed, but there are very few people who do all their tasks with either hand. Psychologists refer to **"handedness"** as the number of tasks performed by either hand. Transsexual people are less right-handed and do more tasks with their left hand than other people. We do not completely understand the mechanisms of handedness, but we do know that it is at least partially due to DNA inheritance. I do many things with both hands but I swing a baseball

Figure 3.7
Structural and Functional Differences from Other People

MTF/FTM	Difference
MTF/FTM	Both are less right-handed than non-transsexual
MTF/FTM	Finger length ratios
FTM	Teeth shape
FTM	Pelvic measurements and ratios
FTM	Higher blood levels of testosterone than non-transsexuals

bats and a golf club from the lefthander side. I do other things with my right hand.

When Bruce Jenner became Caitlyn Jenner, I went back to look at some of her old pictures when she was in the Olympics. Sure enough, Jenner threw the javelin and shot put with her left hand. I sent a picture to Diane Sawyer's producer who was interested in the science of being transgender. Maybe we will see it in the next interview.

There are various biomarkers that support the idea that being transgender is due to biological genetics. For both males and females, a prominent biomarker is the ratio of the lengths of the second and fourth finger. Transgender people have been shown to have different ratios from non-transgender people. Finger ratio differences are due to DNA genetics. They vary from geographic region to geographic region, and various ratios can be actually be bred in animals. We have even identified one of the most important genes that determine finger length, but it is not one of the genes that have been examined as potential transgender DNA markers. Some people claim that finger length ratios are associated with the influence of **testosterone**, a sex hormone, in the prenatal brain, but the evidence does not support this but instead supports a genetic correlation.

There are particular biomarkers for transmen. FTM transmen have been shown to have teeth shape and pelvic measurements that are different from non-transgender females. It is believed that these differences can be attributed to DNA genetics, because we know that the information for developing these structures is found in particular genes.

Pretransition transmen seem to have higher levels of testosterone in their blood than non-transgender females, but for most FTM, we do not know whether this is due to their normal biology or to taking hormones through do-it-yourself methods. We do know one cause of elevated testosterone levels in FTM. Some seem to have an increased incidence of **polycystic ovary syndrome (PCOS)**, which is a dangerous disease that greatly increases testosterone blood levels. These increased levels of testosterone in PCOS usually appear before transsexual transition. So the PCOS observed cannot be due to taking testosterone as part of the hormone therapy of transsexual transition.

UNFORTUNATE "NATURAL EXPERIMENTS" SUPPORT THE IDEA THAT BIOLOGICAL GENDER BEHAVIOR PREDISPOSITION EXISTS

Unfortunately there have been several "natural experiments" in which the idea of biological gender predisposition has been supported. They are unfortunate because they involve accidents or intersex births. A **natural experiment** occurs when biological changes are out of the control of the experimental scientist but the scientist observes their effects. The "experiments" of interest are cases where male babies have lost their penises due to surgical accidents or when male babies have differences in sexual development of their external genitals. In the past it was believed, particularly by John Money, that gender could be formed through child rearing. In some natural experiment cases, doctors and parents decided to create female-looking external genitals through surgery and raise the child as a girl. In most of these cases, as the natal male baby grew up, he eventually rejected being assigned to the feminine gender behavior category.

There is one particularly famous case that of John/Joan. John was not told of his circumcision accident by his parents or doctors, including John Money. He was given female external genitalia organs through surgery, being raised as a girl by his parents and given hormones. He had what appeared to be female external sex organs and breasts. Despite these things, John/Joan somehow knew that being a girl did not feel right and he rejected of his assigned feminine gender behavior category. Although John Money withheld the truth of his rejection, through his persistence the scientist Dr. Milton Diamond later found out. The final conclusion was that in the case of John/Joan, gender behavior predisposition could not be changed by child rearing. This case was documented in the best-selling book *As Nature Made Him*[4] by John Colapinto.

There are also cases of male children who had intersex conditions at birth and received surgery to give them external female genitalia. They are currently being raised in the feminine gender behavior category. Although the children did not know about their intersex conditions, at least half of 13 patients so far have declared themselves to be in the masculine gender behavior category. We await the results of how this group fares in the future. As a result of these and other cases, doctors and parents are now more likely to postpone plastic surgeries to alter external sex organs until an older age at which time the person can help decide which sex and gender behavior categories are best for them.

These cases provide further evidence for the involvement of biology in being transgender. It appears that people have a biological gender predisposition at birth that cannot be changed. Admittedly these cases are few in number and they only include children declared male at birth, so the results have to be considered with some caution.

EPIGENETICS IS A BIOLOGICAL FACTOR INVOLVED IN BEING TRANSGENDER

Although there is strong evidence for DNA genetics factor in being transgender, this factor does not explain all of the observed evidence. In particular, why do some members of an identical twin pair become transgender while others do not? Because of this, there is reason to believe that there is a biological **epigenetic** factor involved in being transgender. Epigenetic simply refers to non-DNA influences on development.

Most people do not realize it, but although identical twins start out with identical DNA at conception, by the time they are born, the twins differ in terms of many traits. This is due to changes in DNA or changes in how the DNA information is decoded and expressed. These changes occur due to epigenetic mechanisms.. For example, toxic chemicals and drugs work through such mechanisms to create changes in DNA, known as DNA mutations. DNA sometimes seems to change spontaneously without an identifiable mechanism. Some epigenetic mechanisms involve molecules that attach themselves to the DNA molecule and prevent or encourage expression of particular genes. There are even chemicals that are passed on by parents at the time of conception, which are not part of the DNA molecule that change DNA expression. The point is that some epigenetic mechanisms may prevent one twin of a transgender identical twin pair from becoming transgender even though that twin may start out with identical DNA.

There are two prominent epigenetic theories that say that being transgender might be due <u>entirely</u> to chemical exposure of a baby in the womb, but the current evidence does not support these theories. One theory involves exposure to the drug **diethylstilbestrol (DES)** that was given to pregnant mothers in the United States and used in the food supply from 1947 to 1973. The other theory involves exposure to too high or too low levels of testosterone and is called the **Prenatal Testosterone Theory of Transgenderism (PTTT)**.

DES was prescribed for pregnant mothers in the mistaken belief that it would prevent pregnancy complications and premature delivery. It was also given to animals to increase growth during the 1960s and 1970s. The reason for using DES for these purposes was that it was believed to be a similar drug to estrogen, because it resembles estrogen in its chemical structure. The use of DES for these purposes was halted when it was discovered that daughters who had been exposed to DES prenatally developed relatively rare tumors and cancers. Some effects were also observed for DES-exposed sons. The effects of DES have now been traced as far as the grandchildren of mothers who took the drug, indicating that DES is a toxic drug that changes the DNA molecule.

Subsequent research on DES indicates that although its structure may look like estrogen, it is quite different from estrogen in its actions. As indicated previously, DES mutates or changes DNA and causes predisposition to various types of cancer. It attaches to a different receptor site from estrogen. It generally penetrates the brain, whereas estrogen only penetrates at limited places. So if there is a case to be made for DES as a factor in being transgender, it could be considered a genetic mutation effect, not an epigenetic effect.

Although most of the attention about DES was given to female daughters because they had some rare forms of cancer, some DES sons decided to conduct research into the effects on males because they had been admittedly neglected by the National Institutes of Health (NIH) and Centers for Disease Control (CDC). They set up a website for DES sons to register and provide information about their medical or other problems. The website got about 500 DES sons to register online, and about 10% of these people reported being transgender and/or transsexual. Since the estimate of being a transwoman is 1%, you might conclude that DES had some effect but no formal statistical tests were performed or possible due to a biased sample. There is the possibility that those DES sons who were transgender were more likely to register and report being transgender than other DES sons. Additional evidence could be collected by the NIH and CDC, because they have a database of several thousand DES sons and daughters. They are supposed to do periodic surveys of these registrants. However, as far as I can tell, their investigators have never asked any of the people in this registry if they were transgender or transsexual.

As part of my scientific research, I called one of the NIH investigators who had done the most recent DES survey which was about sexuality. I had read the study and questioned them as to why they had not asked about being transgender. They replied that they had no knowledge that there was a theory that DES caused being transgender. It appears that they had not read all the literature, especially the online study and reports initiated by DES sons.

The second epigenetic theory is that the blood level of testosterone in the fetus causes being transgender. According to this theory, for transwomen the blood levels are too low and for transmen the levels are too high. Some endocrinologists have even suggested injecting pregnant mothers of males or transplanting testes into offspring to boost their testosterone levels in order to reduce any likelihood that the males would develop into homosexual and transgender people. This is the Prenatal Testosterone Theory of Transgenderism (PTTT). The theory was developed by endocrinologists in East Germany during the time when both the East German nationalists and the controlling Soviet government were seeking to rid themselves of both homosexuals and transgender people in a nonviolent way. After German reunification, these endocrinologists abandoned their contentions about homosexuals, with apologies, but the transgender theory lives on. The inspiration for this theory was derived from research on sexual behavior in rodents. The rodents (rats and guinea pigs) were treated with sex hormones in early development. Changes in sexual behavior were later observed for these rodents but it is doubtful that these results apply to human gender. There are several sources of evidence that refute the PTTT. Among them are as follows:

- The original research was on the <u>sexual</u> behavior of animals, not the <u>gender</u> behavior of humans. Sexual behavior and gender behavior are entirely different. Animals do not have gender systems like humans, with culturally defined gender behavior categories.
- There is no direct evidence that prenatal testosterone levels are too high or too low for transgender people in the womb. Measuring prenatal testosterone remains beyond the state of the art although 2D:4D finger length ratios are often cited as surrogate biomarkers. Transgender people do have different finger length ratios from non-transgender people, but this difference can be attributed to genetics, as was mentioned in the previous section.
- The animal behavior theory upon which PTTT is based has subsequently been revised to give DNA genetics a prominent role with regard to prenatal organization of animal sexual structures. Development of sexual structures starts with genetics and only later does testosterone effect development.
- There are males with an ailment called Kallmann syndrome who have very low testosterone levels from conception onward due to their genetics. The frequency of these people being transgender is very low, only one case reported in 50 years.
- There are females with **congenital adrenal hyperplasia (CAH)** who have very high testosterone levels from conception until their condition is detected. It is usually detected in puberty and can be easily treated once discovered with a drug that slows down production of testosterone in the adrenal glands. The frequency of these females being transgender is low and probably not different from the population. There are no known reports of CAH female transsexuals.
- There are people with **androgen insensitivity syndrome (AIS)** who have the genes to become male but they develop female bodies. This is because their bodies are insensitive to androgens, including testosterone. The part (gene) of the DNA molecule that causes this effect is also one of the places associated with MTF transwomen (see "DNA Genetics Is a Causal Factor in Being Transgender" section). People with AIS develop a gender behavior disposition that is congruent with the feminine gender behavior category, just like transgender people do.

- Testosterone only has effects in the brain and nervous system where a molecule called aromatase is present, limiting the possible effects of theoretically high testosterone levels. Aromatase is a catalyst that turns testosterone into estradiol and has been mapped to limited areas of the brain. It is actually estradiol that changes brain structures associated with sexual mechanisms in males. It seems odd but the female sex hormone, estradiol, actually triggers the development of male brain structures.

SUGGESTED NONBIOLOGICAL CAUSES OF BEING TRANSGENDER CAN BE RULED OUT

Nonbiological theories that have been suggested to cause being transgender include:

- Parental relationships and child rearing
- Sexual arousal due to crossdressing
- Many psychodynamic ideas

All of these theories can be ruled out at this time through analysis of the idea and/or the existing scientific evidence. Although there have been many studies attempting to establish a link between being transgender and parental relations or child rearing, none of them has demonstrated such a link.

There are studies that have established that the motivation for being transgender is not sexual arousal. While it is true that at the beginning of crosspresenting transgender people feel aroused, these feelings quickly go away. We will discuss this in more detail in Chapter 5, section "Acquiring Knowledge." There are about 20 psychodynamic ideas about inner thought processes thought to cause being transgender, but none of them qualifies as a testable scientific theory. They are vague and rely on internal processes that cannot be measured.

After moving to Atlanta in 1998, I starting looking for a psychiatrist or psychologist to help me with social problems associated with being transgender. I went to several before I found one that actually understood being transgender. One of them told me that my crossdressing was because I needed a comfort object, because I missed my mother. A comfort object is like Linus's blanket in the cartoon strip *Peanuts* that he always carries around. Another psychiatrist was a Freudian who never told me anything and just listened. I never once saw her smile. I called her the "ice maiden." I guess that was a reflection of repressed childhood feelings or transference or some other type of Freudian theory. Still another told me that I needed cognitive therapy because I had "mood disorders." It turns out he only offered cognitive therapy. It was like all of these folks I talked to had their own hammer and tried to use it on everyone who came through their door. I finally found a counselor who knew there was no treatment for being transgender and just asked how they could help me deal with my social issues.

BIOLOGICAL GENDER PREDISPOSITION AND TWO-FACTOR THEORY OF BEING TRANSGENDER

The biological evidence presented in this chapter supports the idea that we all have a biological gender behavior predisposition that develops from two factors: genetics and epigenetics. These factors are the ones involved in the **Two-Factor Theory of Being Transgender**. This biological gender predisposition is probably present at birth or shortly thereafter. It is certainly present by the time children start reporting being transgender at about the age of 4. Current evidence looks like the noncongruent predisposition involved in being transgender is associated with DNA genetics, but that epigenetics can block this predisposition, just like it can block other traits. Remember that identical twins start out with the same DNA, but epigenetics mechanisms cause them to have different traits at birth and thereafter.

Why do people have biological gender predispositions that are different? Differences in biological gender predispositions are due to the natural diversity of human beings. Biological diversity provides alternatives in times of crisis that have allowed human beings as a species to survive and evolve.

> Biology loves variation. Biology loves differences. Society hates it.
>
> —Milton Diamond[5]

As childhood develops, the conflict between a person's gender behavior predisposition and culture increases, as we will discuss in Chapter 4: Culture.

NOTES

1. Mercedes Ruehl (izquotes.com, 2015), http://izquotes.com/author/mercedes-ruehl (confirmed July 15, 2016).

2. Linda Thompson (Brainyquote, 2016), http://www.brainyquote.com/quotes/quotes/l/lindathomp714101.html (confirmed July 15, 2016).

3. Jan Morris, *Conundrum* (New York: Harcourt, 1974), 1.

4. John Colapinto, *As Nature Made Him* (New York: HarperCollins, 2000).

5. Milton Diamond, quoted in Nicholas Teich, *Transgender 101: A Simple Guide to a Complex Issue* (New York: Columbia University Press, 2012), 72.

CHAPTER 4

Culture

It was, I think, the eighteenth century which first imposed upon Western civilization rigid concepts of maleness and femaleness, and made the idea of sexual fluidity in some way horrific.... Certainly earlier centuries did not require the male to be unyieldingly virile or the female unremittingly demure, as Shakespeare's comedies happily demonstrate. There was more give and take in those days and the sexes mingled easily and freely....

Other cultures too, ancient and contemporary, have freely recognized a no-man's land between male and female, and have allowed people to inhabit it without ignominy.

—Jan Morris, *Conundrum*[1]

INTRODUCTION

In Chapter 2, we asserted that being transgender takes three things: (1) a biological gender predisposition; (2) a culture that is binary, cisgender, and inflexible with regard to movement between gender behavior categories; and (3) knowledge of gender behavior categories learned in early childhood. In Chapter 3, we discussed the evidence for a biological gender predisposition. In this chapter, we will take up the second requirement for being transgender that involves culture.

This chapter will cover aspects of culture that impact being transgender. There are four aspects that we will discuss:

1. Biological Theories of Gender Development
2. Diverse Gender Systems
3. Violations of the Rights of Transgender People
4. Hatemongers in the Culture

There is a lot of material to cover about these aspects, so to keep you from nodding off, here are some motivators for you to stay awake.

Biological theories of gender development are important because one of these theories forms the rationale for cultural rejection of being transgender. Most people in the culture are not even aware that this theory exists. The scientific evidence does not support this theory but there is a different theory that the evidence does support.

The binary, cisgender, inflexible gender system of Western culture is not the only gender system. Social anthropologists have studied a wide variety of diverse gender systems. The existence of such diverse gender systems means that culture can adapt to biological gender predisposition of its offspring. It also gives transgender people and their allies hope that Western gender system can evolve away from rejecting transgender people, which we will discuss in Chapter 9.

Transgender people have rights guaranteed by international and national ethical guidelines and treaties, which the United States has approved at least tacitly. These agreements were drafted to avoid atrocities against minorities of all types that Western culture experienced in the 20th century and the early 21st century. So even at the lowest level of government, if transgender rights are denied, it is a violation of international and national ethical standards. Although people who reject transgender people probably do not care about such agreements, they are not standing on the ethical high ground.

We will list the many types of violations of the rights of transgender people that exist, but do not get too depressed by the list because we will discuss how to cope with some of them in Chapter 5 and how we might stop them in Chapter 9. Such violations include violence, workplace discrimination, denial of healthcare, denial of accurate identity documentation, military discrimination, and public accommodation discrimination.

There are hatemongers in Western culture who earn their livings, as the name suggests, by selling hate to willing people. They attack being transgender using pseudoscience and distortions of clinical practice. In doing so, they reinforce cultural rejection of transgender people. Their media ratings, book sales, donations, political races, and public appearance fees support continuation of hate and cultural rejection. I would be among the last to advocate that their free speech should be infringed. The better solution is transgender people and their allies should be armed with the true science and facts to refute their arguments.

BIOLOGICAL THEORIES OF GENDER DEVELOPMENT

> A particularly insidious aspect of gender—our gender systems in the West, and perhaps for the planet as a whole—is that it is an oppressive class system made all the more dangerous by the belief that it is a natural state of affairs.
>
> —Kate Bornstein, *Gender Outlaw*[2]

In previous chapters, we have discussed that being transgender appears to have biological origins. The biological component is a DNA gender predisposition, and the cultural component is the inappropriate assignment of people to gender behavior categories based exclusively on birth sex, inflexibility, and limiting gender behavior categories to two. But how did this DNA predisposition evolve? There are two theories circulating in scientific circles that are important to know about. One of these, which we will call the **traditional sex-based evolutionary theory**, provides the intellectual underpinning for the Western gender system. However, the scientific evidence seems to support a different theory, the **kinship evolutionary theory**, which is consistent with gender diverse cultures. What is the natural state of affairs of gender from a scientific viewpoint?

"Traditional Sex-Based" Evolutionary Theory

The principle idea of this theory is that body differences between male and female resulted in a division of labor categorized by sex. So the theory goes, this division of labor provided the basis for gender behavior categories. The "traditional sex-based theory" of gender evolution involves the idea that natural selection in human evolution resulted in different gender behaviors for each sex. So the theory goes, gender behaviors emerged during the time when humans were organized into hunter-gatherer societies, primarily during the period 10,000–40,000 years ago. Proponents argue that this biological division of labor by sex has changed little since then. Many people cite this theory to justify the Western gender system without even knowing about it. They just contend that it is the "natural state of affairs."

So the "traditional" theory goes, behavior and therefore DNA supporting behavior were adapted to fit the human reproduction situation. The behavior of females primarily involved tasks related to pregnancy and child rearing and that of males involved hunting and group protection. Females were responsible for gathering food near home base camp, primarily vegetable in nature. The females were believed to stay close to home base camp because child rearing impaired their ability to run during hunting and to go far from home. Males on the other hand were responsible for hunting and protection of the society. Males ranged far from the home camp and brought back animal meat as a high-calorie source of food. Males defended the group from predators and other humans. For this reason, males evolved to have higher levels of androgens that facilitated muscle development, strength, and aggression. Since the males could not prove that they had fathered a particular child, they did not participate in child rearing but instead attempted to impregnate as many females as possible. According to these theories, female hormones such as estrogen and oxytocin evolved to encourage social bonding within the tribe or clan.

Particularly for the traditional sex-based theory, it was postulated that gender behaviors were passed on by parents through DNA genetic mechanisms. Some theorists believe that gender behavior is rigidly genetically predetermined by inheritance, while others believe that evolved attributes, predispositions, and temperaments interact with learning and the environment to produce gender behavior.

The most obvious criticism of the traditional sex-based theory of gender development is that we have witnessed a rapid change in gender behavior categories over the past century. These changes have occurred so rapidly that they could not possibly have been caused by natural selection through DNA changes. In contemporary culture, behaviors that were once considered by sex-based evolutionary theorists to be in only one gender behavior category are now performed in both categories. Both males and females are now customarily involved in child rearing, and some males have become dedicated homemakers. Marriage law has recognized the need to provide economic and legal protection for spouses who do not work outside the home. Due to technology advances, modern construction and warfare require less body strength allowing both males and females to participate in what used to be considered all-male jobs such as construction and the military. Due to technology, such jobs now provide economic opportunity for all people. Modern agriculture has largely supplanted the need for hunter-gatherer activities, resulting in a precipitous decline in personal hunting and fishing for food. Such activities are now pursued mainly for sport. Although movement between gender behavior categories is still frowned upon, transgender people are now being increasingly accepted.

Kinship-Based Theory

The second type of evolutionary theory of gender development is termed "kinship theory." The rationale for this theory is that early humans lived in family groups, tribes, and clans for cooperation and protection. Related by blood, much of the DNA information within group members was similar. Such theories say that it was the fitness of the group, not individual fitness, which was most effective in insuring survival. It was the "intrinsic fitness" of the group as a whole that was subject to natural selection and evolution. Natural selection also favored those groups in which survival skills and behaviors had redundant representation within the group. This meant that there was a natural advantage to spread critical behaviors across many members of the group. The groups with "backup skill" members had a better chance of survival. Individual behavior within the group can be seen in the short run as altruistic toward the group but in the long run as maintaining and improving group genes. This is sometimes called an "uncle" theory because even an uncle who never sired children of his own could pass on aspects of his DNA by contributing to the survival of his relatives in the group. The relatives of the uncle carried similar DNA to his own. Individuals might pass on their genes, not from direct involvement in reproduction but from facilitating group survival.

Much of the anthropological scientific evidence supports the kinship theory rather than the traditional sex-based theory of gender development. Social anthropological evidence has been acquired from contemporary hunter-gatherer societies starting in the late 1800s. It turns out that the evidence from such studies supports the kinship theory. Although some females may have stayed near base camp, they provided the majority of the calories for the group through gathering and hunting. When gathering sufficient amounts of food and game near the base camp declined, the group simply moved their base camp. Females also participated in group defense. Some males became artisans and developed weaving, pottery, and childrearing skills.

The societies that have been most extensively studied are the Native American tribes. (We will discuss them, along with other groups, in the next section.) Many of these tribes had three or four gender behavior categories, and some children were designated as **Two-Spirits**. These Two-Spirit people were permitted by their culture to move between categories at will, with accompanying changes in dress and presentation. There is a tendency to romanticize many of these cultures, even though many of their members lived near the subsistence level and they died at an early age due to malnutrition and disease. The pressure to survive was severe. We will discuss the social anthropological evidence for more flexible gender systems in the next section.

Most transgender people do manage to have children, even though their relationships may break up later because of being transgender. But the evolutionary pressure for gender diversity would be in the general population even if transgender people never reproduced. This is because it increases the probability of the survival of human DNA from successful groups. For this reason, we should expect that transgender people will occur spontaneously, without them necessarily having transgender relatives. And this is exactly what seems to happen. Although there are incidental reports of same-sex parent and children both being transgender, most transgender people do not seem to have transgender forebears. This finding may change as Western culture makes admitting being transgender more culturally acceptable.

So the next time you hear someone say that the Western gender system rejects being transgender because it violates the "natural state of affairs," you will know that they are using the traditional sex-based evolutionary theory. But the evidence does not support this theory. Rather, the human species has survived and progressed because of its diversity, including its gender diversity through kinship group survival and intrinsic fitness. Any gender system that seeks to reject transgender people on the basis that the traditional sex-based theory is the natural state of affairs is incorrect and ultimately interferes with our progress and survival as a species.

DIVERSE GENDER SYSTEMS

Other cultures and subcultures do not have the same gender system as we do in the Western culture. This is true both historically and even today. With the advance of the current Western culture, many of the cultures that existed historically have been erased. Those that remain have become subcultures that are struggling to survive and maintain their diverse gender systems in the broader Western culture. The gender systems of other cultures differ from ours in three respects:

- Some cultures have up to five gender behavior categories as compared with our two categories. Three and four categories are common.
- Many cultures assign children to gender behavior categories based not only on their birth sex but also on their behavior and reported spiritual experiences.
- Some cultures allow free movement between gender behavior categories depending on the needs of the tribe or group. The Native American Two-Spirit tradition honored those who were able to work and live in more than one category and many Two-Spirits became tribal leaders.

The importance of understanding gender systems of other cultures is that they reveal the biological diversity of human gender predispositions. Cultures must have seen the need in the behavior of their children for more than two gender behavior categories. <u>It is important to stress that the people in these additional categories were not transgender in the sense that we use the word today</u>. People who moved from one gender behavior category to another did not qualify as being transgender in these systems because such movement was sanctioned and/or encouraged by their cultures. To be transgender, one must move between categories when culture prohibits such movement. Being transgender will continue to make a transgender person into a cultural outlaw, outcast, and pariah until contemporary Western culture changes.

Native American Cultures

Figure 4.1 provides a summary of some of the cultures of interest that had nonbinary, non-cisgender, flexible gender systems. The first of these are the Native American cultures in the Northern hemisphere.

The Native American cultures were studied intensively during the late 1800s and early 1900s by social anthropologists. The intensity of their studies came from the realization that people in the Native American cultures were under pressure to conform to the prevailing Western culture and there was a limited time left to study their cultures before they disappeared or were tainted. These anthropological studies were so intense that the joke was told, "What is a typical family household like in the Zuni tribe?" and the answer was, "One husband, one wife, two children and one or two anthropologists."

It is clear from their gender systems that Native American cultures had acknowledged and continue to acknowledge the need for more than two gender behavior categories to deal with diverse gender predispositions. In more than 100 tribes, there were 3 gender behavior categories—2 categories based on birth sex and a third involving males taking on a feminine gender role. Over 50 of these tribes had a fourth category in which females were taking on a masculine role. Many of these cultures allowed and even encouraged movement between categories.

As can be seen in Figure 4.1, each of the tribes had names for the nonbinary gender behavior categories that they created. Some pertained to birth males assuming a third behavior category such as the Ojibwa *Agokwa* or the Lakota *Winkte* that was feminine in nature. Some pertained to birth females assuming a fourth category that was masculine in nature such as the Mojave *Hwame* and Sauk *Ickoue*. Some of the names referred to both the third and fourth gender category such as the Navajo *Nadleeh* and Paiute *Tubas*.

Some children in these tribes were designated as "Two-Spirit" based on their sex as well as their early childhood behavior and verbalizations of their dreams, spiritual experiences, and the product of their imaginations.

Figure 4.1
Diverse Gender Systems of Cultures

Culture Name	Subculture	Location	Time	Gender Behavior Category	Number in Category
Western	Transgender	Worldwide	Current	Transwoman	2
Western	Transgender	Worldwide	Current	Transman	1
Native American	Lakota	North America	Historical	Winkte	3
Native American	Ojibwa	North America	Historical	Agokwa	3
Native American	Mojave	North America	Historical	Hwame	4
Native American	Sauk	North America	Historical	Ickoue	4
Native American	Navajo	North America	Historical	Nadleeh	3 and 4
Native American	North Paiute	North America	Historical	Tubas	3 and 4
Native American	Zuni	North America	Historical	Lhamana	3
Native American	Zapotec	North America	Current	Muxe	3
Asian	Hijra	South Asia	Current	Hijra	3
Asian	Kathoey	Thailand	Current	Kathoey	3
Asian	Waria	Indonesia	Current	Waria	3
Asian	Bugis	Indonesia	Current	Calabai	3
Asian	Bugis	Indonesia	Current	Calalai	4
Asian	Bugis	Indonesia	Current	Bissu	5
Asian	Chukchi	Siberia	Current	Chukchi	3
Pacific	Hawaii	Hawaii/Tahiti	Current	Mahu	3
Pacific	Samoa	Samoa	Current	Fa'afafine	3
Pacific	Oceania	Tonga	Current	Fakaleiti	3
Pacific	Maori	New Zealand	Current	Whakawahine	3 and 4
Pacific	Western Pacific	Philippines	Current	Bakla	3
Middle East	Oman	Oman	Current	Xanith	3
Europe	Italian	Naples	Current	Femminiello	3

They were taught two gender behavior categories and allowed to move freely between them as needed. One day they might present in feminine clothing and pursue pottery making, and the next day they might present in masculine clothing and wage war or go on a hunt. Allowing members to express themselves in more than one gender category gave more people the valuable skills that facilitated the survival of the group. In such societies, both males and females of various gender behavior categories participated in child rearing, social relations, hunting, and defensive behaviors. Such cultures could not afford the luxury of a rigid division of labor, because as hunter-gatherers, they were at or near the subsistence level. Males in the tribes might take on Two-Spirits as spouses, which was taken as a sign that these males would prosper and move up in the tribe.

The Two-Spirit tradition indicates that Two-Spirits themselves became important people in the tribe, including becoming leaders, medicine men, or spiritual shamans. Legend has it that the most prominent chiefs, such as Sitting Bull, Crazy Horse, and Black Elk were Two-Spirits. One explanation given for their success was that they were able to understand people in multiple gender categories and mediate disputes. For example, Sitting Bull was a shaman who rose to be chief of his tribe. It has been reported that Sitting Bull had a sexy, pet Lakota *Winkte* nickname. All three of these chiefs led their tribes and nations into battle but also had a more feminine side.

Third gender behavior category and Two-Spirit Native Americans were misnamed **berdache** by Spanish invaders to the Americas. Berdache was the name given to them because the newly arrived Spanish did not understand the Native American cultures. Berdache referred to prostitutes in parts of Europe with which the Spanish had contact. No doubt some in the third gender category were homosexuals but they were not prostitutes, and their gender and sexual behavior were sanctioned by their cultures. The term "berdache" has a complex history. It started out in Persia and migrated to Catholic Spain through Muslim Spain. Unfortunately, social anthropologists used this word for several decades without knowing its history. They eventually recognized their mistake:

> But to American Indians, the institution of another gender role means that berdaches are not deviant—indeed they do conform the requirements of a custom in which their culture tells them that they fit. Berdachism is a way for society to recognize and assimilate some atypical individuals without imposing a change on them or stigmatizing them as deviant. This cultural institution confirms their legitimacy for what they are.
>
> —Walter Williams, *The Spirit and the Flesh*[3]

You should be aware that today the term Two-Spirit also encompasses all of LGBT within Native American circles and not just those who were assigned to multiple gender categories.

There is one surviving North American Native culture that has a third gender behavior category. It is the *Muxe* of the Native *Zapotec* culture who live in the southernmost part of Mexico. Because of the extreme isolation of this area, Western culture has not been able to extinguish this tradition of the Zapotec. The *Muxe* are males who live in a feminine gender behavior category but do not practice body modification because of their religion. The prevailing religion in this area is Catholicism, which has made accommodations for the *Muxe*. The *Muxe* are celebrated in festivals in several cities in the region and the church provides its blessings on them. Unfortunately there is limited anthropology information about the *Muxe*, because most available reports have been from newspaper and website reporters, not from social anthropologists.

Hijra

The *Hijra* is a third gender behavior category in South Asia. They have more members than any third gender category in the world, but their exact numbers are disputed. You will often see the *Hijra* entertaining at weddings and births according to some religious traditions but you may not see the behind the scenes extortion and pestering, which gains them these engagements. Most *Hijra* live in abject poverty because of discrimination. They are assigned to the lowest caste of societies. Historically, they have experienced discrimination and violence sanctioned by law and custom.

Estimates of their numbers range from 130,000 to several million. They are found mostly in India, Pakistan, and surrounding countries. The *Hijra* regard themselves as a third sex and have gained legal and political recognition in some countries. They are now able to get identification cards specifying their third sex in several countries, so more accurate population estimates will be available in the future.

The history of the *Hijra* goes back at least 500 years and is connected with the Hindu god, Vishnu, but today they practice many religions. They make a living largely by obtaining entertainment engagements such as weddings and baptisms. They also engage in begging and prostitution. In India they are organized in a hierarchical system with small groups called "communes" with guru leaders. Each commune is, in turn, affiliated with one of seven "houses," which are run by a *najak* leader. At the commune level, *Hijra* are directed by their gurus to earn money for the group. *Hijra* may be voluntarily castrated but many are not. Because of their relatively cohesive organization, they have developed their own language.

The *Hijra* are beginning to improve their economic and political situation because their numbers are too large to ignore.

Kathoey

In Thailand you will see **Kathoey**, sometimes called "ladyboys," on the street and even in regional and national televised beauty pageants. Apparently they seem to be an accepted part of the Thai culture and protected by Thai law. However, by custom their employment is limited to prostitution, entertainment, and lower level jobs. This limits their socioeconomic progress. The *Kathoey* are males who believe themselves to be a "second category of females" and who present in a feminine gender behavior category. Many take female sex hormones and get feminization and transsexual surgeries. The roots of the *Kathoey* reach back into even the rural regions of Thailand, but there are a large number in urban and tourist areas. In a study on the streets of Bangkok, over 17,000 individual *Kathoey* were counted by expert observers. It is believed that over 180,000 live in Thailand as a whole. For those in the world looking for prostituted sex, Thailand is a highly regarded sex tourism destination, particularly on the island of Phuket and the *Kathoey* are a feature of the sex tourism industry. The *Kathoey* have made some socioeconomic progress by disguising themselves as men during the day. They have obtained jobs in the retail and teaching areas and work in the masculine behavior category while on the job. Some Thai religions recognize marriages between *Kathoey* and males, but the marriages do not have legal recognition.

It appears that the *Kathoey* are tolerated by their larger culture because they represent big business for Thailand both in terms of national interest and sexual tourism. But they experience cultural discrimination that keeps them from progressing economically.

Waria

The **Waria** of Indonesia gained recent attention because one of them was a nanny for Barack Obama as a child and because of the 2011 film documentary *Tales of the Waria*. The *Waria* form a third gender behavior category that includes over 7 million people out of a population of 240 million. The *Waria* are males who openly present in a feminine behavior category. For Muslim religious reasons, they do not physically change their bodies to achieve feminization. As with Barack Obama's nanny, Evie, many of them are household workers and help with children. It is not clear whether Evie presented in a feminine gender category to child Obama. The *Waria* have achieved some visibility and success in the entertainment and beauty indus-tries. As with the *Kathoey*, some present in the masculine behavior category during the day to work in other industries. Also as with the *Kathoey*, the *Waria* are participants in internationally televised beauty pageants. However, it is clear from Evie's experience that life for the *Waria* can be miserable. It is important to note that the *Waria* should not be considered transgender peo-ple because they participate in a culturally sanctioned third gender category.

Bugis

The ***Bugis*** are a subculture of Indonesia which has the highest number of gender behavior categories I have found. They are a large subculture with approximately 8 million people. They have a total of five categories in their gender system. In addition to the Western masculine and feminine gender categories, their third category, the *Calabai*, are birth males who present in a feminine category. The *Calalai* are birth females who present in a mascu-line category. Finally, the *Bissu* may be male or female and represent a "gen-der transcendent" category. They typically present in *Bugis* religious garments. They provide religious guidance and counseling to the *Bugis* peo-ple. The *Bugis Bissu* have come to an accommodation with the Muslim church clerics, just like the *Muxe* did with the Catholic Church in Mexico. They negotiated an arrangement with Muslim clerics so that they do not infringe on the clerics' religious prerogatives.

Despite the *Bugis* having a different gender system from the rest of Indonesia, surprisingly they are accepted both politically and economically. The *Bugis* are predominately farmers, fishermen, and merchants. Several national leaders have been *Bugis* and they are free to engage in various eco-nomic areas.

Chukchi

The ***Chukchi*** is one of the last remaining Asian cultures that have a diverse gender system. They live in Siberia and follow the reindeer herds, which they use for food and hides. They have a third gender behavior category who are males and who adopt feminine presentations but, like the Two-Spirits, also participate in masculine activities such as hunting. Because they are so iso-lated and independent, they have been able to maintain their gender system despite numerous efforts at genocide by the Russian and Soviet military. They have done this mainly through using their knowledge of the land and cold weather military tactics. As far as I can gather, the *Chukchi* are so isolated that they have never been studied in detail by social anthropologists.

Pacific Islands

There are several Pacific Island cultures with nonbinary gender behavior categories as shown in Figure 4.1. These third gender behavior category people in these subcultures are males who present in a feminine category and primarily are involved in family care, although some engage in arts and fashion. With Spanish colonization and disruption by Western culture, including relocation due to military activity in World War II, the behavior of people in these categories has become westernized from its native state. About half of the remaining thousand or so of the *Fa'afafine* have moved from their native Samoa to New Zealand. The Maori peoples native to New Zealand, have a third gender behavior category, the *Whakawahine*, but they have all but disappeared. Their traditions have been merged into a GLBT group referred to as the *Takatapui*. The *Fakaleiti* of Tonga remain, although their historical status as shaman leaders in the Tonga culture has deteriorated under Spanish and American colonization. Some of them change their bodies using Western transsexual procedures such as sex hormone and surgical treatments. And they are mostly seen in beauty pageants.

The *Mahu* originated in Tahiti, but French nuclear testing displaced many from Tahiti to Hawaii. Traditionally the first male child of each family might become a *Mahu*. Each native community had a primary *Mahu* who was responsible for maintaining and teaching about their subculture. Janet Mock grew up in Hawaii; she describes the devolution of the *Mahu* as follows:

> What I later learned from by Hawaiian studies classes in Hawaii was that mahu defined a group of people who embodied the diversity of gender beyond the dictates of our Western binary system ... *Mahu* were often assigned male at birth but took on feminine gender roles in *Kanaka Maoli* (indigenous Hawaiian) culture which celebrated mahu as spiritual healers, cultural bearers and breeders, caretakers, and expert hula dancers and instructors. . . .

> But as puritanical missionaries from the West influenced Hawaiian culture in the nineteenth century, their Christian, homophobic and gender binary systems pushed mahu from the center of culture to the margins. *Mahu* became a slur, one used to describe male-to-female transgender people and feminine men who were gay or perceived as gay due to their gender expression.
>
> —Janet Mock, *Redefining Realness*[5]

The *Bakla* of the Philippines are a subculture of gender diverse people who are males who present in a feminine behavior category and are typically attracted to males. They have been present in Philippine culture for several centuries. They may undergo sex hormone therapy and feminization surgeries but rarely transsexual GPS. Although they are under cultural stress, they manage to have their own language, stores, and beauty pageants.

Middle East

Although many Middle Eastern cultures ban gender and sexual diversity, sometimes under penalty of death, there are some notable exceptions and interesting stories about these cultures. It may surprise you that although Iran has a highly authoritarian regime, it is second only to Thailand in the number of transsexual GPS operations performed. Although the country is dominated by a strict Muslim culture, as we saw with the *Muxe* and the *Bugis*, religious exceptions can be made on the basis of tradition and clerical declarations.

Until late in the 20th century, Oman was a relatively closed society and its rulers resisted changing tradition. For this reason the **Xanith**, a third gender category, continues to survive. The *Xanith* are males who present in a feminine gender behavior category. They do not wear a veil but dress in a composite of masculine and feminine clothing, leaning toward the feminine. They are subject to complicated cultural rules but have the same civil, political, and economic rights as men, and some are quite prosperous. They are permitted to have sex with males, which is forbidden in most countries in the Middle East. However, they also have sex with females and are permitted to marry females. Some are companions for males and some are prostitutes. Surprisingly, it is acceptable for the *Xanith* to revert back at any time to the masculine gender behavior category and continue their lives.

While traditional gender diversity in Iran has been erased by law, accommodations have been made to those willing to undergo transsexual transition, including GPS. Being a transgender person is illegal and subject to the death penalty unless that person completes transsexual transition. The government subsidizes transsexual GPS, and Iranian gender clinics have a large group of transgender clients.

The story about this exception to strict Muslim law is surprisingly simple. A transsexual advocate, prior to the Iranian Revolution, Maryam Molkara, persistently asked the Iranian clergy and then Ayatollah Khomeini for a ruling. Ayatollah Khomeini would later lead the Revolution to become the leader of Iran in 1979. Before the Iranian Revolution, transsexual treatments were tacitly allowed, but Molkara wanted a ruling that provided clerical legitimacy. After the Revolution, she met with Khomeini and got a *fatwa* or ruling that transsexual transition was permitted. The rationale was that a person needed a "clear sexual identity" to carry out religious practices. She also arranged for a state-sponsored religious charity to subsidize GPS operations.

The government now contributes to this charity and provides new birth certificates for those completing transition and GPS.

There is also a downside to the clerical exception for transsexuals in Iran. Since homosexuality is also subject to the death penalty, it is believed that many homosexuals are coerced into transsexual transition.

Femminiello of Naples

While most countries in Europe have adopted Western practices, which reject gender diversity, there is one traditional subculture that survives and is accepted—the *Femminiello* of Naples, Italy. They are males who present in a feminine gender behavior category and are generally accepted in their hometown. The *Femminiello* continue to assert that they are males, just ones who dress and act as women. Most of them are attracted to men and some are prostitutes.

Summary

The purpose of describing cultures and subcultures with gender systems that differ from our own Western system is to demonstrate that cultures can have more than two gender behavior categories; that people do not have to be automatically assigned to a gender behavior category based on sex alone; and that it is possible to have a system in which people can move between categories. Some cultures have recognized the need to accommodate diverse biological gender predispositions. <u>The people in these cultures are not transgender because they are following, not violating, gender system rules.</u> People in third, fourth, and fifth gender behavior categories achieve some degree of tolerance and acceptance by the larger cultures in which they reside, at least with regard to gender presentation. However, they often experience rejection when they try to improve their economic and political status.

VIOLATIONS OF THE RIGHTS OF TRANSGENDER PEOPLE

Transgender people suffer various violations of their human and civil rights because of cultural rejection. Rejection behavior is often culturally encouraged and can take many forms.

Rejection can be incorporated into discriminatory laws and regulations. A few years ago, passage of these measures might be attributed to ignorance of transgender people, but no longer. Transgender people are now too visible to ignore and information is readily available on being transgender. It is the duty of legislators to understand the effects of the laws that they pass. If they do not seek information or ignore it, they are shirking their responsibilities and undermining representative democratic government. Such legislative misbehavior is sanctioned and even encouraged by culture. Rejection can also take the form of social rejection that results from non-enforcement of protective laws.

Rejection through laws is very real to me. When someone in my wife's family died, they held a memorial service for him. I found that I could not attend because of newly passed state discriminatory laws in Mississippi, ostensibly passed to guarantee "religious freedom." The laws applied to hotels and all other public accommodations. And Mississippi and other states have actually passed laws forbidding cities and localities from setting their own protective laws. I could not be sure that I could get a hotel room or that I might not be evicted from one because I was transgender. I called the hotel designated by the family as the place to stay and, while they assured me that I could stay there, I could not be sure that I would be denied accommodation or subject to other discrimination in the small town where the memorial service was to be held. I finally worked out a plan to get a room in the adjoining state of Louisiana that did not have such laws, even though it meant driving an hour one-way to get there, including crossing the Mississippi. In the end I did not go to the service, feeling like I did not want to do business or socialize with people who hated me. I now cannot go into North Carolina as I will be subject to discriminatory restroom laws, which hopefully will be struck down soon. But again, I do not feel comfortable going into a place that expresses hostility toward me. So, sorry North Carolina, you will never again get my business.

There are numerous states that have introduced similar laws, particularly by Southern states. Living in Georgia, I am surrounded by many of these states that discriminate. I have been pouring over the roadmaps to see if there is some way I can drive my car out of the South to see my families in Colorado and in Virginia. Some states like Arizona and Illinois have recently refrained from having such laws, mainly due to the outcry of those who might lose business or corporations that did not want to lose their reputations. I expect and hope that the current batch of state laws which discriminate against transgender people will be struck down by Federal courts, but I foresee that new ones with minor changes will be intended to take their places.

Even if protective laws are in place, transgender people can experience social rejection which is sanctioned by culture. Influenced by culture, police may not enforce minor infractions of protective laws even if they

violate the letter of the law. There are often consequences of reporting violations, and corrupt police can use the opportunity to harass and take advantage of transgender people.

Violations of transgender human and civil rights may take many forms,
but for the purposes of this chapter, we will present them in seven categories.
The purpose of presenting them is to increase your awareness, not to discourage transgender people from expressing themselves in their congruent gender
behavior category. But first we will present some of the agreements that guarantee transgender rights both nationally and internationally. In Chapter 7, we will
provide some suggestions on how to cope with some of these violations.

Transgender Rights Guarantees

Because violations of human and civil rights have led to atrocities in the
past, many countries have adopted ethical standards for minority rights.
The founding fathers of the United States were well aware of European
abuses. Later, the international community established such standards after
World War II because of the atrocities committed on minorities during and
before the wartime period. Guarantees apply to Western culture as well as
dealings with non-Western cultures.

There are three statements of basic civil and human rights of particular
interest to transgender people in the U.S. The first statement of rights is the
U.S. Declaration of Independence. The reason for this declaration in 1776
was that the colonies were severing ties with England but even more important, the declaration put people around the world on notice of a new philosophy of civil and human rights. The new philosophy stated that governments
should be constituted to protect the rights of its citizens, not to protect the
rights of royalty or government. People were endowed with the rights to life,
liberty, and the pursuit of happiness. The founders established principles of
human and civil rights to keep culture and governments in check, being
knowledgeable of previous abuses. The U.S. Constitution elaborated on the
rights included in the Declaration. Since then, various rights laws have been
passed, including the *Civil Rights Act of 1964*, *Title IX of the Education
Amendments Act*, governing education, and the *Violence against Women
Act*, which has transgender protections. Transgender people have received
protection under these laws through court cases. The Equal Opportunity
Commission has recently taken legal notice of these cases as being the law
of the land.

In addition to the homegrown statements of human and civil rights in the
United States, there are international conventions of human and civil rights

that are generally consistent with U.S. rights but provide more detail. *The UN Declaration of Human Rights* was developed in 1948 after an international meeting was convened. The United States is a signatory to this document. Most recently, the *Yogyakarta Principles* were developed in 2013 at a meeting of international experts on human and civil rights. These Principles were intended to provide guidance to countries on laws and practices regarding GLBT rights.

Although few people are legal or ethics experts on transgender issues, at least you should know these standards exist and that the people of goodwill and high ethics recognized the problems that minorities and transgender people face.

Violence

Because their behavior is rejected by Western culture, transgender people are subject to various forms of physical and verbal violence. Most nations and states provide guarantees against violence for their people in the form of laws and policing. For transgender people, as well as other minorities, sometimes these guarantees are not realized because of culture and because the frequency of violence against transgender people is so high.

There are various forms of physical and verbal violence used against transgender people and they include, in order of severity: microassaults, microbatteries, bullying, and assault and battery crimes involving severe trauma. In our system of justice, assault refers to verbal threats and battery refers to physical aggression.

Microassaults are small verbal and non-physical acts that injure people because of the information and the physical threat they represent. For transgender people, the most common microassault is using the wrong pronoun, sometimes called **misgendering**. Sometimes it is inadvertent but sometimes it is deliberate. Next in severity are microassaults that are verbal attacks, which use such words as "tranny," "she-male," or pronouns such as "it" to refer to transgender people in order to injure them. The accumulation of such microassaults takes their toll on transgender people. The adage that "sticks and stones may break my bones but words will never hurt me" is untrue. Nonphysical injuries cause physiological reactions that may be just as harmful as physical attacks. **Microbatteries** are small physical acts of violence such as pushing and blocking peoples' movements. **Bullying** involves microassaults and microbatteries designed to coerce or dominate people. Bullying is often aimed at inhibiting expression such as preventing gender presentation and expression. Bullying has been recognized in schools, but it also occurs in the workplace and elsewhere. It contributes to transgender secrecy and depression. In the education domain, laws and programs have been set up to discourage bullying, although some scientific studies have shown them to be ineffective or to actually encourage school bullying. Essentially, the would-be bullies became well-trained bullies through these programs.

Finally, there are severe acts of assault and battery that rise to the level of criminal activity, given legal classifications as misdemeanors or, as more severe, felonies. These assaults may cause trauma resulting in bloodshed, broken bones, concussion, rape, or loss of life. Only 15 U.S. states have enhanced criminal penalties if a violent crime act is ruled a "hate" crime motivated by hatred or fear of transgender people. There are many examples of violent crimes against transgender people; the most notable examples in the past three decades include:

- The rape and murder of Brandon Teena in 1993, which was the subject of an Academy Award-winning movie *Boys Don't Cry*.
- The murder of Gwen Araujo, who was beaten and strangled in 2002 after making love and the subsequent revelation that she had male anatomy.
- The murder of Angie Zapata in 2008, which was the first transgender murder to be ruled a "hate" crime.
- The death of Vicky Thompson in an all-male Leeds prison in 2015, which brought further attention to the plight of transgender people that are not housed in prisons according to congruent gender behavior category. It is yet to be declared a murder.

Transgender murder is becoming more frequent around the world and is most frequent in Brazil with over 95 murders in 2015.

Violence against transgender people often begins in childhood. As noted in Chapter 2, many people recognize that they are transgender between the ages of 4–5, and children do not realize the danger they create by expressing their congruent gender behavior predisposition. Some parents reject children who reveal that they are transgender and some of those parents resort to violence. The violence is often sanctioned by culture, including family, church, and community. Although there are laws against parental abuse of children, they often go unenforced. As we have seen in Chapter 2 and will discuss further in Chapter 7, such violence or threat of violence forces many transgender children into a life of secrecy, which is corrosive.

Violence against transgender people intensifies in school during the period when cisgender children are most unsure of their gender and most sensitive about differences in presentation. Even small differences can be the triggers for rejection and bullying. Although some attempts to curb bullying occur in school, bullying can occur during non-school hours.

Some parents throw their teenage children out of the house because they are transgender, which constitutes the crime of child abandonment. Some children leave voluntarily to escape abuse. Many of these children end up homeless. They have limited job skills because of their difficult time in school and their age. In order to survive, many engage in the street crimes of prostitution and illegal drug sales. In one survey, 16% of transgender youth were found to be working in illegal street commerce. Because they engage in prostitution and intravenous drug use, they represent a reservoir of HIV and sexually transmitted diseases. One study found that transgender prostitutes practiced safe sex less often than cisgender prostitutes. Once they are convicted, these young transgender people are put on various sex crime registries. In addition to a criminal record, these registries further interfere with legitimate employment.

I live in a city that has a district known for its transgender prostitutes and street crimes. It is less than 10 blocks from where I live. The situation got so bad in this district that the city actually contemplated passing a law that would banish convicted prostitutes from the city, even though similar laws have been struck down because they violate the U.S. and state constitutions. Due to the efforts of local advocates, the city is now contemplating what is known as a "diversion" program that would prevent prostitutes from getting arrested if they are willing to go into programs that teach them about getting legitimate jobs. Other cities have set up housing programs that support transgender people so that they can get jobs and get out of criminal business. In order to keep transgender youth from becoming homeless and engaging in street crimes, the local culture needs to be changed to encourage parents to be more accepting, but that is a tough task.

For those transgender people with the qualifications necessary to hold a job, they still must face anti-transgender bullying and violence on the job. The U.S. Department of Labor has strict rules and laws against workplace violence and bullying, but they still occur and many incidents are unpunished. Many transgender people do not want to complain because it might affect their standing on the job. Although it is illegal, employers can always manage to find ways to lay off or discourage transgender workers if they believe that they have become "troublemakers." We will discuss this type of situation further in Chapter 7.

Most transgender people have suffered microassaults in public. This is especially true for transwomen. Transwomen receive catcalls and sexually harassing comments from people, usually males, in public just as birth females do. The difference is that transwomen suffer microassaults specific about them being transgender. Although sexual harassment is illegal, police seldom enforce the law for public comments. Transwomen are afraid to make police reports because there are numerous cases of police and government officials themselves committing violence against transwomen.

Violent acts against transgender people are common, but there are ways for transgender people to cope with the potential for violence, which we will discuss in Chapter 7.

> This pervasive idea that trans women deserve violence needs to be abolished. It's a socially sanctioned practice of blaming the victim. We must begin blaming our culture, which stigmatizes, demeans and strips trans women of their humanity.
>
> —Janet Mock, *Redefining Realness*[6]

Workplace Discrimination

Because of violations of civil and human rights, 25% of transgender people earn less than $10,000 per year. This is due to a combination of rejection at home, bullying and violence at school and on the job. In this section, we will discuss violations of rights due to workplace discrimination, which adversely affect the standard of living of transgender people. Many transgender people do not have sufficient income to pay for appropriate housing, medical care, and sustenance that are specified as human rights by international standards.

Workplace rights include freedom from workplace discrimination, the right for fair labor standards, and rules about workplace safety. We have previously touched on violence in the workplace in this chapter. All of these rights are often violated regarding transgender workers. The primary laws are Federal laws and policies against workplace discrimination are set and enforced by the U.S. Federal Equal Opportunity Commission. Workplace protection includes hiring, promotions, and assignments. Workplace safety standards are set and enforced by the U.S. Federal Occupational Safety and Health Administration (OSHA). Although there are some state and local laws that pertain to transgender rights in this area, they are seldom enforced. Local laws are often contradicted by state laws and precedents. There have been several Federal cases that were decided in favor of transgender people and the Equal Employment Opportunity Commission (EEOC) has now made these precedents into policy. But transgender people are still going to have to either complain to EEOC or sue their employers in cases of discrimination. No Federal law exists at this time protecting workplace rights for transgender people that would effectively require employers to follow it proactively.

The Employment Non-Discrimination Act was a proposed piece of federal legislation that Congress has not acted on since 1974, and transgender rights were only added to the proposed legislation in 2007. At the state level, only 18 states have laws that protect transgender people. Federal precedents and the EEOC support the workplace rights of transgender people, but the expense of lawsuits and formal complaints is a barrier to enforcement of rights. Outcomes are uncertain because such lawsuits are usually based on the EEOC prohibition on sexual discrimination, not on the right to transgender expression.

As to actual workplace practice, more than 47% of transgender people report losing their jobs because of their gender presentation. Transgender workers do not always report violations because they fear employer reprisals, so some violations are never counted in this statistic.

Until 2015, the Federal rule for workplace restroom use stated that "only reasonable restrictions" on restroom use be followed. The concern was that unreasonable restrictions violated worker human right to health and safety because withholding waste matter can result in urinary tract infections and other medical problems. Mental health professionals urge that transgender people use the restroom congruent with their gender behavior category for the mental health of their patients and to avoid stigmatization. Because of numerous complaints about requiring transgender people to go to faraway restrooms and those were not compatible with their gender, OSHA acted in 2015. They published guidance on "best practices" for use of restrooms by transgender employees. The policy also encourages employers to allow transgender employees to have access to restrooms that are congruent with their gender behavior category although it allows other arrangements such as single occupant restrooms with the consent of the worker for such procedures. We will see if this "best practices" document improves the situation of transgender employees.

I had some experience with OSHA, having managed a university unit that provided technology help to industry for safety hazards and I also cochaired a course for them. In general, OSHA does not act proactively because they have so few inspectors. Our unit was usually called in only <u>after</u> an accident or injury occurred. Employees do not want to report violations because they are concerned about employer retaliation. For this reason, I am skeptical that the "best practices" document will have far-reaching effects but it is on the right track.

Healthcare

Transgender people often have their right to medical care violated in the United States. Doctors and hospitals have refused treatment and medical professionals have committed microassaults against transgender people. Medical insurance companies refuse to provide coverage and continue to reject claims for transgender medical treatment. The situation has gotten somewhat better due to the Affordable Care Act (ACA) and Federal rulings regarding Medicare/Medicaid but at the state level, some states have deliberately been obstructive.

Physicians and other medical personnel sometimes refuse treatment to transgender people using the excuses that it violates their religious conscience or that they do not have sufficient knowledge of procedures for transgender medical care. Surveys indicate that 19–27% of transgender people have been denied healthcare. For those who do receive care, over 70% report verbal and physical microaggressions, including mocking comments and violations of HIPAA Privacy Rule. This is all in spite of the fact that the policy of medical professional societies is that medical personnel must accommodate transgender people. These include the American Medical Association and the American College of Obstetricians and Gynecologists under the Affordability Care Act (ACA), transgender people may not be discriminated against for treatment, although this still occurs in some states.

At one time, I was looking for a surgeon to do a breast implant operation for me. I decided that I would go to the local university healthcare service, since my family and I had always received excellent treatment there. So I called and made an appointment. About two weeks before my appointment, I received a voice mail from the appointment clerk saying to call her. I figured they just wanted to check out my insurance or change the appointment time. So I called and the clerk asked me why I wanted the surgery. Having always found this institution to be discrete, I told her that I was a male-to-female transsexual. She replied that they were unable to help me because I needed to have a team consisting of psychologist, endocrinologist, and medical doctor and that they did not have such teams at present. I assured her that I had such a team and told her who the members were. She then said that they could not treat me because they did not have the expertise to conduct breast implant operations on males. I found this laughable since they are a world-renowned medical center, and none of the other surgeons I consulted who mainly do the operation on females gave this excuse. She said that they were cancelling my appointment because they did not want me to come and then be turned away. I told her to have her supervisor call me. I got the same explanation. I told her I thought it was illegal under the ACA for them to reject me. She told me that unless I already was a patient, they could cancel my appointment at will. I messaged a transwoman who is also a lawyer and she wrote back, "This is the South, you are screwed," indicating that despite the law, the Southern culture would find a way not to treat me. Not wanting to be operated on by a hostile surgeon, I finally decided to get estimates from those in private practice who had "done" many of the transwomen that I know.

Even if they have medical insurance, transsexuals are routinely denied reimbursement for transition-related medical costs such as GPS. This is the case, even though studies have shown that it costs no more and may cost less to provide such care. The costs of transsexual care are more than offset by the costs of treating depression and attempted suicide which may happen to transsexuals if they are not treated. The ACA allows transsexual coverage but the problem is at the state level, since states make health insurance regulations. The great majority of state health regulations explicitly forbid reimbursement of transition treatments although the number of states forbidding this is decreasing. Eight states, like California, now require coverage. The momentum to change the policy comes from the American Medical Association, American Psychological Association, and the Veterans Administration, which have declared transition treatment a medical necessity. This position is supported by large corporations who want to retain their transgender employees and customers. At the Federal level, Medicare allows the full range of transition treatments, but GPS is only allowed on a case-by-case basis where medical need must be established. The U.S. Department of Health and Human Services (HHS) has recently started the ball rolling to get the Federal government to overrule state prohibitions.

Curiously, the Internal Revenue Service policy says that GPS is tax-deductible as a medical expense but not other surgeries such as breast implants. This is because of a lawsuit precedent in which the Federal court agreed that GPS was a medical necessity but the transgender plaintiff did not adequately prove medical necessity for breast implants.

Identity Documentation

The *Yogyakarta Principles* support the principle that transgender people should be able to get identity documents that are consistent with their congruent gender behavior category rather than with their birth sex. However, this principle has not been followed in both law and practice by many U.S. Federal and state government agencies, although reforms are progressing. Appropriate documents allow transgender as well as other people freedom to drive a car, take a plane trip, or enter government buildings. Sex markers "M" or "F" are used on many documents and may cause problems when it is at variance with expected cisgender presentation. This is true whether a person is transgender or not. Masculine-looking females and feminine-looking males often receive discrimination because people and law enforcement have stereotypes of what a female should look like. Such discrimination is occurring more frequently because of transgender restroom laws.

At the Federal level in the United States, many of the laws and practices for documentation have recently improved for transgender people to change passports and Social Security sex markers. However, the most commonly used identity documents, birth certificates and driver's licenses, are issued by the states. At the state level there is a hodgepodge of inconsistent and confusing laws and practices. Transgender people can easily get these documents changed in states like California and Florida but not in my home state of Georgia and other Southern and Midwestern states.

Improvements at the Federal level have helped transgender people get accurate documentation. Passport gender markers can now be changed with a doctor's letter saying that transsexual transition has started and no longer requires proof of GPS. The same is now true for Social Security cards. In 2015, the American Medical Association and the World Health Organization both urged that transgender people should not be required to have GPS for change of sex marker on identification. For a time, the Social Security Administration would send "no-match" letters to employers if sex markers were incompatible with employment records. This created embarrassment and employment problems for transgender people. But at the urging of some transgender advocates the Social Security Administration has stopped this practice.

At the state level, while there have been improvements, the laws and practices still are not compatible with the *Yogyakarta Principles* for birth certificates and driver's licenses. Most states allow changes to birth certificates (Tennessee is the exception) but both the allowed changes and the required proofs vary from state to state. Some states will change sex markers and names but others will only place an amendment on the birth certificate while retaining the original information. Amended birth certificates can cause problems for transgender people in getting driver's licenses and other types of identification based on birth certificates. The proof for changing birth certificates is different between states, some requiring proof of GPS while others only requiring a doctor's letter that transition has started.

In the United States, state-issued driver's licenses are the most frequently used identification document. In 2008, the Federal government passed the

REAL ID Act, which sets standards for state licenses. Compliant licenses are required for commercial aircraft travel, entry into Federal buildings, and voting in some states. However, not all states have complied yet; there are three remaining to do so. As with birth certificates, each license has a sex marker. Licenses can be changed with regard to sex marker in compliance with the REAL ID Act but, as with birth certificates, the required proof varies from state to state. Some states specify GPS, while others require a letter affirming that the transgender person intends to live in their new gender behavior category. Because of discriminatory laws requiring identification at the polls, an inaccurate driver's license can be used to prevent transgender people from voting. In the 2012 election, at least 27% of transgender people were ineligible to vote due to mismatches between gender presentation and sex marker.

There have been cases where driver's licenses have been denied because a government official did not think that a person's gender presentation matched their sex marker. A recent case was in South Carolina where a teenager, Chase Culpepper, passed their driver's test for a license but was denied one because Chase wore feminine makeup and hair and "did not look male enough." After complaints and threats of legal action, the state reinterpreted its policies.

Recently, the American Medical Association has joined the World Health Organization in taking the position that transgender people should not be required to undergo GPS in order to change legal identification documents, including birth certificates and driver's licenses. However, it remains to be seen whether the U.S. Federal and state governments will take notice of this declaration.

U.S. Federal and state laws and practices have improved, but they still do not fully comply with *Yogyakarta Principles*. The Principles only require proof of intended gender for changing identification documentation.

Military Service

For many years, transgender soldiers, marines, and sailors were expelled from the U.S. military if discovered as transgender, but this policy has recently changed. The change was important for transgender people because they join the military at a rate 20 times their peers. Now that the change has been made, the U.S. military will have to embark on a campaign to educate their doctors on how to treat transgender people and to educate their members on non-discrimination regulations. The United States now joins several NATO ally countries in allowing transgender soldiers and marines. The countries include Canada, the United Kingdom, and the Netherlands.

Public Accommodations

There are transgender antidiscrimination laws in many U.S. states and cities that guarantee access to public accommodations such as hotels, airports, restaurants, housing, and stores. But in many areas such laws do not exist or are being nullified by some states as in North Carolina, which nullified Charlotte, North Carolina, antidiscrimination laws.

In practice, the right to public accommodations access is often denied to transgender people in the United States. When surveyed, over 53% of transgender people report denial of public accommodations and harassment in hotels, restaurants, and airports. Over 29% report harassment and disrespect by police who are supposed to protect them in public areas.

Earlier in this chapter, I related my difficulties trying to go to Mississippi for a memorial service because they had recently passed one of the most discriminatory laws against transgender people. Mississippi merchants opposed the discriminatory law in their state and many now post rainbow colored signs saying, "We don't discriminate; If you are buying, we're selling." Since then, similar laws in Arizona and Illinois were passed but both governors sent them back to their respective legislatures to alter them. In both cases, pressure from business was applied to change the laws. The same process appears to be occurring now in North Carolina with a corporate boycott and threatened cutoff of Federal education money that has the potential to cost the state many millions of dollars. Recently the National Basketball Association cancelled plans for their next all-star game in Charlotte, North Carolina, because of the law.

Discrimination also occurs at transgender homeless and domestic violence victim shelters because many are run by religious organizations you certainly have heard of. One prominent case was that of Jennifer Gale who died while sleeping outside a homeless shelter during freezing weather. She was transgender and had been rejected by a religious shelter for overnight housing. The case made headlines because Gale was well known as a community leader and transgender activist in Austin, Texas. She also ran for public office several times.

Here in Atlanta, discrimination against transgender homeless people continues but transgender people are building not-for-profit capability to provide both temporary and permanent housing. The U.S. Federal government recently banned discrimination against transgender people in federally supported shelters. We will see if the situation improves or if we will continue to get stories like the story of Jennifer Gale.

HATEMONGERS IN THE CULTURE

In the past decade, the fabric of news coverage and commentary has changed with the huge growth in news outlets on cable television and on the Internet. Many of these now specialize in particular political interests and both news and commentary are slanted toward these interests. In order to fill airtime, these sources have hired hatemongers to stir up controversy in order to compete for viewers. Hatemongers attack any group that might not be able to defend themselves, whether religious, ethnic, or social group. Since transgender people have become more visible, advocating that people should hate transgender people has become a growth industry.

In addition to the current breed of "journalists" who are focused on ratings and Internet "hits," hatemongers have all sorts of specialties. They are billed as experts in mental health, medicine, religion, law, and science. Some hatemonger mental health "experts" deny that being transgender exists, that it is an illusion, or that it is a dark illness, disorder, fetish, or perversion. Medical "experts" claim that transgender people are homosexuals (some are but there is nothing wrong with that), claim that transgender people crossdress to get sexually aroused, or claim that transsexual transition does not help transsexual people. The science says that all of these are untrue.

Certain psychiatrists provide armchair diagnoses of prominent transgender people, which violate the American Psychiatric Association (APA) ethics code. The code specifies that diagnoses require an in-person examination. And if a psychiatrist does examine someone, the resulting diagnosis information cannot be revealed under Federal HIPAA privacy law and the Hippocratic Oath. It is significant that the most prominent of these hatemongers has had to resign from the APA. Lawyer hatemongers claim that granting transgender rights or bathroom access will somehow infringe on the religious or privacy rights of others. People who claim to be scientists spout pseudoscience or "cherry pick" the results of research to show that transsexuals frequently revert back to their birth sex and gender behavior categories after completing transition. Of course, most of the hatemonger claims are nonsense, but people watch these hatemongers and pay for the experience through advertisements and cable subscriptions. In Chapter 10: FAQ, we will provide some "intellectual jujitsu" suggestions to counter hatemonger arguments with science and fact.

NOTES

1. Jan Morris, *Conundrum* (New York: Harcourt, 1974), 43.

2. Kate Bornstein, *Gender Outlaw* (New York: Vintage, 1995), 105.

3. Walter Williams, *The Spirit and the Flesh: Sexual Diversity in American Indian Culture* (Boston, MA: Beacon, 1986), 74.

4. Kimberly Pierce (Director), *Boys Don't Cry* (Fox Searchlight, 1999).

5. Janet Mock, *Redefining Realness* (New York: Atria, 2014), 102–103.

6. Ibid., 161.

CHAPTER 5

Sorting It All Out

See, I was a lonely, frightened little fat kid who felt there was something deeply wrong with me because I didn't feel like I was the gender that I had been assigned. I felt there was something wrong with me, something sick and twisted inside me, something very bad about me. And everything I read backed that up . . . .

The hard part was sorting it all out. The hard part was taking a good look at everyone else and the way they looked at the world, which was a lot different from the way I looked at the world.

—Kate Bornstein, *Gender Outlaw*[1]

The very first task that Psyche had to accomplish in her search to be reunited with her lover, Eros was to sort, by type, a roomful of seeds. According to the myth, these seeds covered the floor, and rose to nearly the height of the ceiling. I spent the first thirty years of my life sorting out the cultural seeds of gender and sexuality.

—Kate Bornstein, *Gender Outlaw*[2]

INTRODUCTION

Later in her wandering, Psyche has a similar task but a kindly ant colony saw her plight and took care of the sorting. Let us see if knowledge of science can help with the sorting. Nothing against ants, of course.

This chapter is about providing tools for making decisions about being transgender. Because decisions come up quickly, transgender people must become knowledgeable in advance of decision situations. They must become "students of the game" and learn all they can about being transgender and about themselves. The decisions often come up quickly, and the transgender person feels that they must be made soon, leaving little time to go through an extensive decision-making process. The transgender person is often under time pressure to make a decision either because of social pressure, biological forces, or self-pressure to resolve a crisis. Counselors can help by getting transgender people to talk about the decisions and provide knowledge. But decisions about being transgender are highly personal and should be made by transgender persons themselves. Because there are so few trained and experienced counselors, a transgender person typically must often educate their own counselors about being transgender. In any case, the responsibility for the decision belongs to the transgender person.

WHAT ARE SOME TRANSGENDER DECISIONS?

There are many decisions that a transgender person must make, and this section describes some of them. We will discuss various life pathways that these decisions create in Chapter 6 in greater detail. Some of the transgender decisions that we will discuss in this section are:

- Am I transgender?
- Am I going to continue transgender behavior?
- Should I go into secrecy in the closet?
- Should I start a social transition?
- Should I take blockers to delay puberty?
- What is my sexual orientation?
- Should I start transsexual transition?

The earliest decision that a transgender person must make is <u>whether they are transgender or not</u>. This decision often occurs in childhood and is often reconsidered in later life. Children may not know the word "transgender" but they know about the two gender behavior categories, boy or girl, at an early age (2–3 years). They know that their behavior fits better with one category or another. They also know which category they were assigned at birth and if it fits. Because they do not know the word "transgender," they will say, "I am really a girl" or "I am really a boy." These phrases or similar ones indicate that they know they are transgender based on observations of their own behavior and their feelings about the gender behavior categories. Given the choice, they prefer to behave in a category that was not assigned at birth and they know it. Transgender children are under pressure to decide whether they are transgender to resolve it in their own minds and to meet the demands of others. They see everyone else declare their gender behavior category and feel social pressure to do the same.

Chronologically, the next decision transgender children usually make is to decide whether to <u>continue their transgender behavior in the open, to only do it in private or to stop altogether.</u> This decision is often forced by cultural rejection of their behavior by family, other children, or community that increases in frequency and intensity as they enter elementary school. The pressures are enormous to go "into the closet" to avoid rejection. Some children may stop their transgender behavior altogether, but transgender behavior may emerge in later life. This also means that they need to learn about two gender behavior categories, the one that fits them and the one that they have to follow to avoid rejection. It is very much like an actor having to learn two roles at the same time.

Adopting **secrecy** causes transgender children to be burdened with telling lies and playing two gender roles. It creates a high mental workload. It also gets in the way of close friendships because a friend may discover the secret. It has other negative effects, as we will discuss in Chapter 6.

Some transgender children sense that they are under time pressure to delay puberty, which they know will cause unwanted body changes. Unwanted body changes feature breast development for FTM and voice change for MTF. Some of these changes can be reversed in later life, but some changes cannot easily be addressed. In order to delay puberty, two decisions must be made. The first is whether to pursue **social transition** that qualifies transgender children to make the decision about hormone blockers. Social transition involves living in your congruent gender behavior category. For children, this often requires close coordination with school officials and for some it means moving to another school district. A successful social transition is often required by medical doctors and mental health professionals to qualify the child for puberty blocking hormones. The second decision, around the ages 8–9, involves transgender children in coordination with their families and healthcare providers to decide whether they should take **puberty blocking hormones** (blockers). Blockers can be effective in reducing some of the unwanted effects of puberty even if they are begun in teenage years.Some children try to "tough it out" by continue their transgender behavior without mental health or medical advice. They encounter increasing cultural rejection, including bullying and extreme physical violence. They may later adopt secrecy or stop their transgender behavior altogether.

Children are increasingly labeling themselves as **genderqueer** or **gender fluid** in late childhood and adolescence. Genderqueer people feel that they do not fit into either gender behavior category and may dress and present themselves in a mixture of masculine and feminine characteristics. Because they dress and present in a category that they were not assigned at birth by sex, they are a subset of transgender people. Labeling oneself as genderqueer requires knowledge of the concepts of gender and being genderqueer, which are not usually mastered until adolescence.

As transgender people mature, they may also need to sort out their **sexual orientation**, which often becomes entangled in their transgender behavior. There is increasing pressure for transgender adolescents to label themselves with regard to gender and sex. They might be able to confirm their transgender label through social transition, but they cannot really be sure about sexual orientation until they have had various sexual experiences. This type of sexual experimentation can be dangerous and should not be undertaken until adulthood. But transgender people should be prepared for the potential entanglement of gender and sexual orientation and be knowledgeable about what they both involve.

> But the need for a recognizable identity, and the need to belong to a group of people with a similar identity—these driving forces in our culture, and nowhere is this more evident than in the areas of gender and sex.
> —Kate Bornstein, *Gender Outlaw*[3]

After 16 years old, decisions on **transsexual transition** are common, although a very few decide to transition at an earlier age. Transsexual transition really involves a series of decisions as to body modifications. Transsexual transition can emerge early in life or from recreational transgender behavior.

These are the most common transgender decisions, but there are many more that we will discuss in the next Chapter 6.

WHAT FACTORS TRIGGER TRANSGENDER DECISION-MAKING PROCESSES?

There are three factors that trigger most transgender decisions: biology, existential crises, and advancing age. A transgender person should be aware of decision triggers and recognize them so that they can realize what is happening to them.

Biological **gender behavior predisposition** underlies all transgender decisions because when it is in conflict with assigned gender behavior category, it results in transgender behavior. The evidence for a biological predisposition was presented in Chapter 3. The biological clock can also trigger transgender decisions. As indicated in Chapter 6: "Puberty Blocking" section, some transgender children and their parents realize that puberty represents a biological deadline to decide whether to get hormone blockers. This triggers decisions regarding social transition to support the blocker decision and the blocker decision itself. To be maximally effective, hormone blockers should be started at age 8–9 but are still effective in blocking some puberty effects until about age 15. (The idea that females start puberty before males is turning out not to be true. If anything, males start a little earlier.) If the deadline is not met, puberty can cause unwanted body changes.

The second factor that triggers transgender decisions involves one or more of four **existential crises**. An existential crisis begins with an event that threatens a person's view of themselves and causes them to reconsider their behavior. For example, a person's spouse or one of their loved ones may die and the person realizes that they will also die someday. Most people put their mortality and certainty of death out of their minds unless something like this happens. The event creates an unpleasant state of mind that people feel they must resolve as quickly as possible to relieve unpleasant feelings. Such crises frequently cause decision-making under time pressure and facilitate changes in behavior. These behavioral changes may or may not be related to the cause of the crisis. Transgender people who have been putting off making decisions about being transgender are suddenly thrown into a crisis, because they realize that they may only have a few years left to express their congruent gender. They have a limited time to experience being true to their authentic character and personality, which they have been hiding. For transgender people, existential crises can provoke decisions about their transgender behavior, some of which are listed in the previous section.

The four existential crises that transgender people should look out for are the realization of:

- Death and mortality
- Meaninglessness
- Isolation
- Personal freedom

(I actually have these written on a card in my wallet and I frequently remind myself of them.)

Realization of death means realizing that someday you will die. A crisis may be triggered that starts us to think about mortality. Such crises often result from the deaths of spouses, loved ones, and friends, but it also can also result from people taking the time to think about what is ahead. This crisis changes behavior because you suddenly are aware of all the things you wanted to achieve in your lifetime but have not yet addressed. Psychotherapists know this trick and sometimes provoke an existential crisis of mortality in their patients by reminding them of the death of people close to them.

This usually causes a change in behavior, which is what the psychotherapist and the patient ultimately want to achieve.

Realization of meaningless pertains to the realization that life has no inherent meaning. We must all choose a meaning or meanings for our own lives. In my case, I was a Cold War warrior either in the Army or in the technology business for over 30 years. For me, this started when the Russians launched the first orbiting satellite and our technology leadership was questioned. In 1961, I was a junior in high school and the National Science Foundation shipped me off for an eight-week summer crash course on computer science, physics, math, chemistry, science, and the social sciences. When the Berlin Wall fell on November 9, 1989, what had given meaning to my life for many years went away. The Cold War was over. I even remember where and when I realized this. It was after delivering a plan for future Cold War technologies that I suddenly realized would never be followed. I had stayed up all night for two nights preparing the plan, delivered the plan, and was sitting on the tarmac at Dayton airport. It changed my behavior because I decided then to come out of the deep closet. I started to go to support groups. Eventually, I felt comfortable expressing my gender behavior openly.

Realization of isolation means that one comes to understand that we can never really appreciate what others are experiencing. We cannot really get into other peoples' heads. The school solution to this crisis is to find someone to love—to come as close as possible to a human being. A crisis occurs when you lose your lover through death or indifference. Sometimes you do not experience isolation from a spouse because it is gradual. It is like the proverbial frog that will stay in a pot of cold water as it heats up to boiling and not jump out until it is too late. A common situation is for a person to lose one's spouse due to death, in which case that person might experience two crises simultaneously, both realization of death and realization of isolation. Transgender people see this happen to friends all the time, and a likely result will be an increase in transgender behavior such as coming out.

Transgender people also experience isolation in two other common situations. The first is that isolation is one of the results of secrecy. It becomes impossible to get close to someone if you are trying to keep your transgender behavior a secret. The second is when transgender people are abandoned by their spouses because their spouses reject their transgender behavior. This situation involves a contest between love on one hand and acceptance on the other. It used to be a rule of treatment and in some countries a law that in order to go through transsexual transition, a transgender person had to divorce their spouse. Many stayed together anyway, and today it is no longer a requirement for transition in most countries.

Realization of personal freedom means that you are responsible for all the things in the world. You realize all the things in the world that you would like to change and that you have the freedom to change them (or at least some of them). This means that you are responsible for all the things that need changing! The realization is overwhelming and has been described as peering into a black hole or abyss by existential writers. Transgender people experiencing this crisis often come to realize that they are free to engage in transgender behavior rather than staying in the closet.

To summarize, the four existential crises concern the realization that you will die, that people require a meaning for their lives, that people are isolated from one another, and that we are responsible for everything wrong in the world because we could do something about these wrongs.

The third factor that triggers transgender decisions is **advancing age**, which reduces the pressure to keep being transgender a secret. Let us add to the above example that we used to explain the realization of death as an existential crisis. What can happen to a transgender person who loses a spouse at an advanced age is that they may greatly increase their transgender behavior. These changes may include coming out or starting transsexual transition. In addition to realization of mortality and isolation, there are other factors that may encourage older transgender people to increase their transgender behavior. With advancing age, the number of family members and others who would object to their transgender behavior decreases over time because of death and physical separation. In addition, people of advanced age sometimes retire to live on pensions, Social Security, savings, or other assets. As a result of this financial independence, the transgender person is no longer exposed to cultural objections at work, which might threaten their job.

It was probably no accident that I started transsexual transition after my mother and father had both died and I could start my own business. Since the time at age 4 ¾ when I told my mother that I was really a girl and not a boy, she had watched me like a hawk for behaviors that violated my assigned gender behavior category. For many years, I had managed to keep my secret and avoid any signs of femininity. I played intercollegiate football, joined an Army mountain and winter warfare unit, and eventually served on active military duty. I even continued athletics by becoming a football official and coaching soccer teams. To her satisfaction, I put in a good appearance of being "all boy" as she would say. But occasionally she would flip her lid when she detected feminine behavior. Once I joined her and my wife at lunch and inadvertently carried a cosmetic tote bag (which ironically belonged to my wife) that contained financial papers. She started criticizing me for carrying the feminine bag but was interrupted by my wife who knew all about me being transgender and my mother's objections to it. While I was reeling from my mother's attack, my wife managed to change the subject of the conversation.

I eventually left the big businesses that I had worked for to pursue my own business with one employee (me). That meant that I could transition without caring about who saw me because I was my own boss.

DECISION-MAKING PROCESSES

Science knows a lot about making decisions. The U.S. Department of Defense and other government organizations have spent many millions of dollars to try to identify the best ways to make decisions. They developed complicated processes aimed at making effective and accurate decisions. The processes that they developed take plenty of time and one can study a problem to death and never reach a decision. In fact, sometimes a process takes so long that the problem may go away. That is the reason bureaucracies like these processes. However, by continuing their research, the Department of Defense (DOD) eventually found that most decisions on the battlefield are made with an entirely different, simpler process, particularly when the decision has to be made under time pressure.

What the DOD found is that most decisions are made using what is called a **naturalistic decision process** that was discovered by a psychologist named Gary Klein. This simple process involves:

- Identifying alternatives;
- Creating a mental model of what will happen under each alternative; and
- Choosing between the alternatives.

This process requires that people already have most of the knowledge to make the decision beforehand. It is sort of like the old "come-as-you-are" parties where people are only notified about the party time, as it is about to happen.

Decision Alternatives

This chapter and the next one are aimed at giving you some hints at what the decision alternatives might typically be. One example is the first decision transgender people might face is typically about labeling themselves. The alternatives are transgender, non-transgender, and maybe genderqueer. For transgender children, the alternatives might be to begin social transition or not. But there also might be other variations, such as should "I wait until I change schools so I can start in a new school with my congruent gender."

Mental Models

Creating a mental model of what will happen under each alternative requires some imagination. We create mental models of behavior all the time, although we may not be aware that we do this. Probably the earliest mental models that humans formed were about the behavior of animals of importance to them. It was vital to have such models because animals provided food, shelter, and transportation. These early humans passed this knowledge on to their descendants through oral traditions and wall paintings, which can still be seen today. Military people create mental models of their enemies through careful study. General Patton kept a book by Erwin Rommel on military tank tactics on his bedside table. For a time, Rommel led the German Army in Africa and Patton was his adversary. We create mental models for modern things as well. We have mental models about the behavior of computers, cell phone apps, and the family dog or cat. These mental models may not reflect the inner workings of the computer or the brain of the dog, but they allow us to predict their behavior.

Creating mental models for transgender decisions requires visualization of decision alternatives. "What would being transgender look like? What would genderqueer look like? There are the positive feelings of authenticity but could I stand the cultural rejection of being transgender? What could I do to prevent me from being bullied or attacked?" Chaz Bono imagined mental models for his coming out decision as:

> For me, it was never a question of whether or not I was transgender. It was a question of what I'd be able to handle transitioning and having to do it in the public eye. One of the issues that was hard for me to overcome was the fear of that.
>
> —Chaz Bono[4]

Mental models require various forms of knowledge that we will discuss in the "Types of Knowledge" section later. You should also understand how the brain selects from alternatives, which we will cover in the following section "Choosing between Alternatives in Transgender Decisions".

Acquiring Knowledge

The naturalistic decision process uses "come-as-you-are" knowledge and some imagination. Because many transgender decisions come up fast, we typically use a naturalistic method. This means that we need to increase our knowledge of being transgender <u>before</u> such decisions are required. Even though they currently reject transgender kids, the Boy Scouts are right about one thing—their motto "Be Prepared" applies to transgender decision-making. Transgender people need to be mentally prepared with knowledge and experience when the time comes.

As we saw in the previous section, transgender people are often forced to make decisions in a hurry because of biology or because of internal realizations that are based on unpredictable external events. Because some decisions may come unexpectedly, transgender people should try to reduce the panic and stress of those decisions by proper preparation, which involves getting knowledgeable about being transgender. We are not just talking about knowledge gained from "book" learning but also knowledge that can only be gained through experiences.

The brain gathers knowledge through four separate brain systems that allow people to retain and recall information. These knowledge systems are subconscious in nature, so we have limited access to them. Acquiring, accessing, and integrating the information from these brain systems require some tricks, which we will discuss in a later section. The most important factor in transgender decisions is the behavior of the transgender person, so transgender people must become expert observers of their own and others' behavior, which accomplished through a particular brain system that is involved in movement. Some transgender people need to unlearn their sexual arousal, which is mediated by a different, emotional memory system. Otherwise sexual arousal can get in the way of decisions. These transgender people have to "unlearn" these interfering emotional reactions, which occur during cross-dressing and crosspresentation. We will talk more about the four separate brain systems in the next section.

Because I am a scientist at heart, I have spent my entire life trying to acquire knowledge relevant to being transgender. Some of my earliest memories are reading magazine stories about Christine Jorgensen. This was immediately after World War II, and Christine in her male body had been somewhat of a war hero. She was one of the first to undergo transsexual transition, including GPS. At that time, I knew that I was a girl and wanted to be like Christine. Later, when my family got the *Encyclopedia Britannica* (in book form), I poured over any transsexual-related article I could find. But these articles left me confused. They led me to believe that some people would think that I was diseased and send me off to the "loony-bin," as the local mental hospital was humorously called. But I never really believed that I was diseased, after all, I was not hurting anyone by crossdressing and then there was Christine. When I got to proper libraries in college and graduate school, I continued to be disappointed. The books I wanted were never in the stacks, probably because they had been stolen or held underneath the librarian's desk because they were controversial. I did manage to read Jan Morris's book *Conundrum* in the Arlington County (Virginia) Library and a couple of science books. She found being transgender as curious but not pathological which gave me hope.

> It had occurred to me that perhaps mine was a perfectly normal condition, and that *every* boy wished to become a girl. It seemed a logical enough aspiration, if Woman was so elevated and admirable as being as history, religion and good manners combine to assure us.
>
> —Jan Morris, *Conundrum*[5]

The Dartmouth and Princeton libraries were useless, so I would go to the Boston Public Library or Rutgers Medical School Library. Eventually, the Internet started providing information although its holdings increased painfully slowly. The accuracy of the Internet information also was/is sometimes a problem. Now I can get all the scientific articles I need online or at the nearby university medical library online and I have read over 3,000 of them.

Types of Knowledge

So how do we acquire knowledge? We know from neuroscience that there are four basic systems in the brain that acquire and update knowledge. Each one of these makes a contribution to the knowledge needed for making decisions. The four types of knowledge systems are:

- Declarative
- Experiential
- Motor
- Emotional

Declarative knowledge is formed by book learning, the Internet, and from facts provided by other people in verbal or written form. (You are doing this now.) Transgender people should learn as much as they can about being transgender, gender behavior categories, gender systems, and the biology of gender. It used to be hard to find such information on being transgender, now the problem is that much of the information out there on the Internet and in publications is inaccurate. So transgender people allies and all people have to make up their own minds about what is correct. With regard to scientific studies, remember to ignore what the researchers say and make up your own mind from the results.

Children hear a lot of declarative knowledge about gender behavior categories from their parents and others, but it may not fit well with their biological gender behavior predispositions. Adult transgender people need to talk to each other and possibly counselors to acquire and test information. Knowledgeable mental health counselors used to be rare, but more are becoming available because school and continuing education training programs are increasing. My daughter's medical school now has integrated information about treating transgender people into their courseware. There are several not-for-profits and schools that now do the same. For example, recently I went to a WPATH training course for mental health and medical practitioners here in Atlanta. This was the second of its kind for WPATH, but more are on the way.

The second knowledge system is that of **experiential memories**. These memories are formed through experiences, which one gets through support groups and outings. Transgender people need to undertake such experiences only if they are safe and do not endanger their well-being and their families. Support groups' meetings are often followed in the evening by outings deemed safe by the groups. Transgender people can look back on their experiences when making decisions, paying particular attention to their own behavior.

The third knowledge system is that of **motor knowledge** or **memories**. We are familiar with the automatic motor aspects of being able to ride a bicycle, or putting on a bra, or applying makeup, but there is more to this learning/memory system. It turns out that when we watch other people do things, the patterns in our brains begin to resemble those of the doers. We learn from these patterns. This is sometimes called **modeling**. Children are expert observers of gender behaviors and learn by carefully watching other children and adults. Transgender children are even keener observers because in many cases they cannot read yet. Their skills are also sharpened because they often have to learn two gender behavior categories, the one congruent with their gender behavior predisposition and the one to which they were assigned by birth sex.

The fourth knowledge system involves **emotional memories**. These are of particular importance to transgender people, because emotional memories that trigger sexual arousal get in the way of transgender self-assessment. Pairing a sensory stimulus with a physiological state forms emotional memories. In the case of sexual arousal, various stimuli become associated with sexual arousal through this process. This can occur by pairing the stimuli associated with your congruent gender with sexual arousal, which is most frequent during puberty and early adulthood. During this period, sexual arousal frequently occurs spontaneously, so the conditioning process goes on nearly all the time. In my day the Sears catalogue provided the stimuli but today the Internet and mass media mostly provide them.

People who realize that they are transgender often are aroused by stimuli associated with wearing clothes and makeup associated with their congruent gender. In fact some people used to believe that this arousal was the reason for being transgender. That is, that being transgender was a fetish. But sexual arousal fades with time and exposure to the stimuli. Such arousal learning can be unlearned by repeated stimulus exposure without arousal. Until such time that it becomes "unlearned," such arousal gets in the way of nonsexual emotions that transgender people have. Once the arousal subsides, transgender people often report that they feel relaxed, authentic, and happy when crosspresenting. For me, after 64 years of presenting as feminine, the sexual arousal from crossdressing has long since faded.

We will discuss how to deal with sexual arousing emotional memories in the "Emotional Learning: Extinguishing Learned Sexual Arousal" section.

How to Acquire Knowledge about Being Transgender

The most obvious way to acquire <u>declarative knowledge</u> is to read everything about being transgender that interests you. There is a lot of hatemongering and misinformation out there, so you need to develop trusted sources. I will give you a starter set of websites and books in this chapter. They are sources that have stood the test of time as to accuracy for me. There are several websites and reference books that I trust including:

- The WPATH website[6]
- The Endocrine Society website[7]
- The Transsexual Roadmap[8]
- Lyn Conway's web page[9]
- Zinnia Jones's web and video pages[10]
- National Center for Transgender Equality website and reports[11]
- My book, *The Biopsychology of Transsexualism and Transgenderism*[12]

Each of these sources is described below. URLs and citations for these information sources are contained in the Notes section of this chapter.

You will recall from Chapter 2 that WPATH stands for World Professional Association for Transgender Health, and this organization sets standards for medical doctors, mental health professionals, and others who treat transgender people. Although they tend to talk in "medicalese" and may use some pathologizing language, the information they provide is highly trustworthy. WPATH has a statement in their policies that being transgender is not pathological. The WPATH standards have all the details of how a transgender or transsexual person should be treated by medical and mental health professionals.

Lynn Conway's website has a wealth of information on being transgender and on those transgender people who are outstanding in their fields, whether it is music, science, writing, or other areas. Lynn Conway is to be trusted because she is an MTF transsexual who has wide and historical experience with transgender matters. She is a professor emerita at the University of Michigan in engineering and continues to receive many honors for her work. In my opinion, she has done the best research on estimating the frequency of MTF transgenderism, using, of course, an engineering estimation model that we described in Chapter 3.

The Transsexual Roadmap is a site put up by Andrea James and it has a lot of resource information for transsexual people as well as non-transsexual transgender people. It is pretty well kept up, although Andrea is now heavily involved in the movie industry and transgender advocacy.

Zinnia Jones is an up-and-coming young blogger who has used scientific evidence in her posts, which is pretty accurately portrayed. She is outspoken as an advocate for secularism, but you will get the straight scoop from her on science and a lot of other transgender issues.

The National Center for Transgender Equality (NCTE) has the best up-to-date information on legal and political issues. If you want to know how to currently change your birth certificate in your birth state or what the U.S. Transportation Security Agency (TSA) is planning to do to you when you try to get on an airplane, it is all on their website. Mara Keisling leads NCTE, and she and her staff have become expert on transgender politics. They have managed to get the Federal government to reform many of its practices to take transgender people into consideration.

Finally, there is my previous book, *The Psychobiology of Transsexualism and Transgenderism*, which I do not mean to shamelessly promote. However, I did write the book because it was the book I would have wanted to read before making transgender decisions in my life, especially my decisions on transsexual transition. Even today, I go back to the book for answers. I wrote it to be readable for anyone who is interested enough in transgender science to deal with all the scientific conventions. I also blog monthly at www.tgforum.com. You can ask me questions there as Dana Bevan.

There are a lot of other websites and sources for transgender people, but many of them are commercially oriented. This starter set should start you in the right direction. After that you will have to make up your own mind as to accuracy.

We move next to gaining **motor knowledge** of being transgender. Acquiring such knowledge requires careful observation of people in both gender behavior categories. As long as you are safe when you do it, learn how people dress, do their hair, and present themselves. Children are particularly good at this because that is one of the primary ways they learn about gender in the first place before they are capable of talking.

Teenagers are also good at detecting differences in gender behavior, particularly teenage girls. Such groups literally have chased me through several shopping centers. They get excited because they saw me as someone who is at variance with what they are currently learning about gender and sex. When I was dating my current wife, I used to carefully watch women and how they present themselves. She got pretty jealous of them until I explained that it was part of the process of learning about being feminine, since I never went through female puberty in my teens. Then she would join in and we would both watch and compare notes because she wanted to know what was in fashion and how to look as well.

There actually is a science of behavioral observation called "task analysis." I make my living as a human factors' psychologist and use this science to capture information on what people do in critical jobs like nuclear power plant operators and airplane pilots. Then human factors psychologists can better design computer systems for these jobs.

It is not too complicated; just try to break down behaviors into manageable tasks. You can even make lists of them. The tasks will vary with various environments, which is something you should know about in order to fit in. You do not want to wear ball gown or the wrong makeup to a barbeque. It will help you to understand what is appropriate for various environments. This is important for being transgender in public. If you are still in the closet, it will help you understand what you have to do to successfully present in both gender behavior categories.

Remember that, as you carefully observe gender behavior, the motor system in your brain is going through the same motions as what you see. You are training your motor system to know about gender. You can do this anywhere, but be sure to be in a safe place where you can be inconspicuous. Sunglasses help to prevent people from feeling self-conscious when you watch them.

As to gaining **experiential knowledge**, you must start going out to public places and presenting in your congruent gender behavior category, but do so gradually. Support groups are there to give you a safe start. Some even let you dress on-site where the meeting will be held, and so you never have to be outside the building, which might be a church or hotel. Transgender support groups allow you to realize that you are not alone, to make friends, and to have positive experiences. Many adult support groups go out to safe restaurants or bars after each meeting. You should not take this next step until/unless you feel comfortable. Some meet-up groups do not even hold formal meetings but meet at restaurants and go out later to bars and nightclubs. For those in counseling, a transgender person might go to their counselor's office crossdressed. Buildings with family restrooms are convenient for this. I did this many times and the only exposure was to a few people in the elevator because the family restroom was in the basement. When one is ready, the next step is to go to a transgender convention. There are many conventions around the country. The biggest are Gender Odyssey in Seattle and Southern Comfort in Fort Lauderdale. Conventions provide the opportunity to crossdress in a safe environment for several days. They usually have safe outings at night and during the day. If you have a counselor, they will want you to try being transgender for increasing amounts of time, and many transgender people continue doing that by attending conventions.

I first heard of transgender support groups when I had seen an article in a prominent magazine. It featured a crossdressing support group called "Crossroads" in Detroit. There was a picture of one of the crossdressed participants on the front cover of the magazine. Since I was often in Detroit on travel, I decided to try it. By going to a local support group, I managed to get their address. I wrote a letter to them (this was before email) and, with some nervousness, called the telephone number I got back in return mail. The leader of the group said that she would help me. I was panicky because I could not go to the regular weekend meetings very often because of my schedule. She solved that problem instantly and in doing so reassured me. She invited me to the couples' meetings, which were held on Thursday evenings once a month. The couples were older but adopted me as a young person to be educated. I began to learn about being transgender, a word that had just become popular. I was amazed at how diverse the group was. It included executives, factory workers, postal workers, teachers, farmers, and their wives. Transgender people with all sorts of sexual orientations were welcome. I will never forget listening to a questioning person who was not sure of their gender category or their sexual orientation. This was Detroit and their main job was demonstrating automobiles at car shows, sometimes with masculine presentation and sometimes with feminine. For many years, I seldom missed one of those couples' meetings and the leader that I had talked to at the beginning became my mentoress. I still keep in touch with her.

For children, there are special transgender camps, which help children to know that they are not alone and to make friends. Gender Odyssey holds such a camp in conjunction with their convention, and there are day camps in El Cerrito (Camp Rainbow and Camp Kickin' It) and elsewhere. In addition to urban camps, there are camps like Camp JRF in Pennsylvania and Camp Raman in the Berkshire Mountains in the country and mountains. Children may also be able to go to a school exclusively for GLBT students. The Pride School has recently been opened in Atlanta for GLBT children.

At some point a transgender person might go out in public with friends or by themselves in order to increase their knowledge. In some places you might encounter staring people or catcalls, but a transgender person needs to get used to that sort of immature behavior. Again, try to go to safe places and do not do anything you are not comfortable with. For several years I used to go out by myself crossdressed by keeping culturally safe clothing in the trunk to change into. Because I live in the South, I have learned to dress all in feminine exercise gear, which most people might overlook as being feminine. With a stroke of lipstick and a pair of earrings, I can feel better instantly. By the way, dressing down in your non-preferred gender in order to pass or be ignored is to know dressing as *en drab* as opposed to *en drag*. **Drag** refers to the theatrical instruction to players to "Dress As A Girl." It later was adopted by theatrical feminine impersonators.

The next step in gaining experience is to take a trip while totally presenting in your congruent gender behavior category. It takes some considerable courage to load a suitcase with all feminine or all masculine dress and go on a trip for the first time. And if you are flying, TSA inspection represents an additional gender hazard. We will talk about how to deal with the TSA in Chapter 7.

After public living in one's congruent gender behavior category for increasing periods of time, the next step is to go full time. Transsexuals do this, of course, but even some non-transsexual transgender people do this as well. As part of transsexual transition, mental health and medical professionals will expect you to go full time to convince yourself that you feel comfortable doing it.

We will discuss emotion learning in the next section.

Emotional Learning: Extinguishing Learned Sexual Arousal

The primary emotion that transgender people have to learn about is sexual arousal. There is a separate system in the brain for learning and unlearning sexual arousal centered on the *amygdala*, which we encountered in Chapter 3.

Sexual arousal is learned through a process known as Classical or Pavlovian conditioning. If previous "neutral" stimuli are repeatedly paired in time with sexual arousal, the neutral stimulus will come to trigger sexual arousal. The other side of this learning is that if this stimulus is presented repeatedly without sexual arousal, it will no longer have the ability to trigger sexual arousal. This is known as extinction or unlearning. Russian scientist Pavlov demonstrated this kind of learning and unlearning not with sexual arousal but with the arousal accompanying food in dogs. He would pair a bell sound with the dog being fed and soon the bell made the dog start to salivate without the food. Likewise, by exposing the dog to the bell sound without the food, unlearning or "extinction" would take place. Most animals have similar learning mechanisms, including humans.

How does this apply to transgender decision-making? The ability to learn sexual arousal emotions explains why crossdressing and crosspresenting trigger sexual arousal in transgender people. Such arousal can interfere with making transgender decisions by triggering brain mechanisms that find sexual arousal pleasurable. However, since the sexual arousal in this case is learned, it can be unlearned. Crossdressers who initially get aroused will extinguish the response with repeated crossdressing. In fact, psychologists use a similar technique to unlearn phobias and other emotional phenomena. It is called "flooding desensitization." Crossdressing is ideal for flooding desensitization because all the arousing stimuli are there at once. The emotional system will eventually come to ignore these stimuli.

So in order to be prepared to make decisions without the distraction of sexual arousal, a transgender person must increase crossdressing time and frequency. Some of the experiences described in the previous section apply here. Support groups and increased crossdressing in public can provide the needed "extinction." Depending on sexual orientation, transgender people may acquire new learned sexual arousal triggers.

Choosing between Alternatives in Transgender Decisions

Although people think that they are making decisions with their conscious mind, in fact, there is good scientific evidence that all decisions are really made by subconscious mechanisms. The science indicates that decisions are made by these mechanisms before conscious awareness occurs. It is important to realize this when you organize and use the information that you acquired about being transgender. These subconscious mechanisms seem to vote on decision alternatives, with the "loudest" votes contributing more to the decisions than others. A mechanism can become "louder" by more frequent nervous system activity as if it was "insisting" on a particular decision outcome.

Subconscious mechanisms do not communicate well, so information gained by one mechanism or type of memory does not automatically transfer to the others. For example, motor memories like riding a bicycle do not always translate to declarative memories without a person writing them down or verbalizing them. So it is important to get the memories out of all your various memory systems by keeping a journal, writing a blog, or talking to someone you trust like a professional counselor or friend. In this way, the one memory type will "hear" what the others have to say. This can also be done in support groups during the typical "open discussion" or social part of the meeting. Support groups are also a place where you should be able to ask general questions about being transgender. Motor memories that occur from watching other people model gender behavior can be turned into declarative memories by talking about them.

Experiential and emotional memories can also be associated and captured. How did you feel during your first public crossdressing episode? Put it in declarative memory by writing it down or talking to someone about it. Declarative memories from book learning and instruction can be analyzed in light of all the memory systems' contents. Did I observe and sense the unlearning of sexual arousal due to crossdressing in past experiences? Verbalization through speech can be accomplished by going to a counselor or just by talking to transgender friends and allies. This is another benefit of partially coming out of the closet and go to support groups. Writers call this process "making explicit what is implicit" in memory, which allows subconscious parts of their brain to share information.

During this process of "sharing" information between subconscious memory systems, it is important to pay particular attention to one's behavior because <u>gender is behavior</u>. You can make lists of behavior to see how your behavior fits with cultural gender behavior categories. You can chart it over time, determine what behaviors you like or do not like, and what works for your biological gender predisposition. As a prelude to potential transsexual transition, transgender people should also observe which body parts they need to modify to conform to cultural expectations.

Understanding one's behavior should always come before a transgender person assigns identity labels. If a person is not crossdressing or crosspresenting, it is unlikely that they are transgender. Genderqueer represents a mixture of behaving in both gender behavior categories. Likewise a person should not rush into declarations of sexual orientation without analyzing their own behavior. Identity labels originally came out of the history of being transgender because mental health professionals needed labels as a way to remember their patients' behavior. Since their other patients may have had diseases, they fell into the trap of inventing pathological labels for being transgender. At that time they did not understand that being transgender is a perfectly normal biological phenomenon.

The best way to label yourself as a transgender person is to say that you are transgender and a transman/transwoman. If someone asks you how you know that, you can tell them about your crossdressing sessions. If you say you identify as woman or man, tell them that it indicates the gender behavior category that you follow. A person should be proud to use the label transgender and if need be to declare that my gender is feminine or masculine to label yourself as a transwoman or transman. I prefer that you not say your "gender identity" is a woman or man because that ignores your objective behavior and puts it into the realm of inner thought, which cannot be so easily defended.

There is a character in the *Matrix* movie series (incidentally co-written and directed by Lana and Lilly Wachowski, both now MTF transwomen) called the Oracle who counsels the hero Neo on deciding whether to try save his love interest, Trinity, or risk the end of all human civilization. She tells him:

Neo:	Then why can't I see what happens to her (Trinity)?
The Oracle:	We can never see past the choices we don't understand.
Neo:	Are you saying I have to choose whether Trinity lives or dies?
The Oracle:	No, you've already made the choice. Now you have to understand it.

—The Wachowskis, *The Matrix*, 2003[13]

In this case, Neo's subconscious mechanisms have already voted on the decision. Now it was his task to understand why he made the decision that he did. Often enlightenment and understanding occur long after a decision has been made. The best that a transgender person can do is to cram all the knowledge they can into those subconscious mechanisms and hope for the best. But the need for transgender people and others to make good decisions never ends. The next decision will be coming up before they know it. Time to learn all one can about being transgender.

NOTES

1. Kate Bornstein, *Gender Outlaw: On Men, Women and the Rest of Us* (Vintage, 1995), 7.

2. Ibid., 5.

3. Ibid., 3.

4. Chaz Bono, Brainy Quote, http://www.brainyquote.com/quotes/quotes/c/chazbono437966.html (confirmed July 17, 2016).

5. Jan Morris, *Conundrum* (New York: Signet, 1974), 21.

6. World Professional Association for Transgender Health (WPATH), (2016), http://www.wpath.org (confirmed May 1, 2016).

7. The Endocrine Society (2016), https://www.endocrine.org/search?q=transgender (confirmed May 1, 2016).

8. TS Roadmap, Andrea James, http://www.tsroadmap.com/index.html (confirmed May 1, 2016).

9. Lynn Conway (2016), http://ai.eecs.umich.edu/people/conway/conway.html (confirmed May 1, 2016).

10. Zinnia Jones (2016), https://www.youtube.com/user/ZJemptvhttps://www.patreon.com/zinniajones?ty=h (confirmed May 1, 2016).

11. National Center for Transgender Equality (NCTE) (2016), http://www.transequality.org (confirmed May 1, 2016).

12. Thomas (Dana) Bevan, *The Biopsychology of Transsexualism and Transgenderism* (Santa Barbara, CA: Praeger, 2014).

13. The Wachowskis, *The Matrix* (Warner Brothers, 2003).

CHAPTER 6

Transgender Pathways

INTRODUCTION

As far as we know, the biological predisposition for being transgender continues throughout all of life, but transgender behaviors change over the life span of a person. Figure 6.1 shows these pathways. We will describe each of them in this chapter. For now, the point must be made that there is science to show that these behavioral patterns or pathways exist, although we do not know the exact numbers of people traveling particular pathways. Most transgender people go into secrecy after realization in childhood that they are transgender. A few brave souls try to "tough it out" by continuing to show transgender behavior through childhood and adulthood. Clinicians have tried to track this latter group without much success. Studying a population of transgender children through to adulthood is fraught with all sorts of problems, and currently their results are not generalizable. However, it is studies of this latter group that you will hear about in the news in regard to whether openly transgender children grow up to be homosexual, transsexual, or discontinue being transgender. We do know the bottom line from surveys described in Chapter 2 where secrecy is now less of an issue, and the numbers reveal that there are approximately 1–2% transgender people of which approximately 0.36% are transsexual people. This is the result of all the people in the pathways at the bottom of Figure 6.1.

REALIZATION OF BEING TRANSGENDER

The **realization of being transgender** generally occurs between the ages of 4 and 7, with 50% of the realizations by age 6. There are reports of transgender children coming to realization as early as age 18 months, although these are rare.

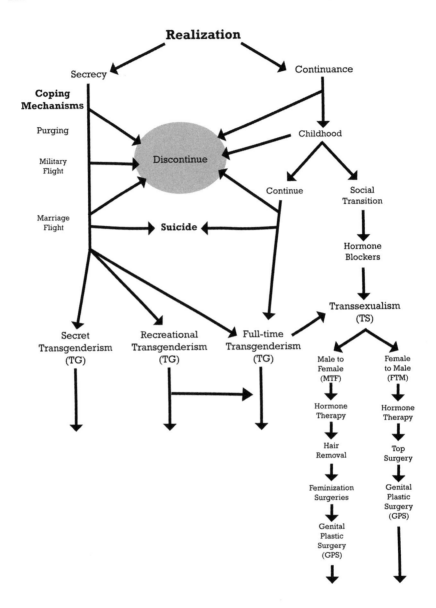

Figure 6.1
Transgender Pathways

Most children do not know the word "transgender," but they refer to themselves in their congruent gender behavior category as boy or girl. Most do not use the word "transgender" until they are about 9, but the age of use has been steadily decreasing from late teenage years for the past 50 years since the word became popular.

The initial realization of being transgender is that "God has made a mistake" or that there is "something wrong." Children know about gender behavior categories and they know that they have been wrongly assigned. Culture allows females to behave as "tomboys" during childhood but will not tolerate "sissy" boys. Transboys are allowed to publicly present as boys about a third of the time but transgirls are allowed only 2% of the time by their parents. This double standard continues into adulthood. But it allows many transmen to express themselves without being labeled as transgender.

Realization gives way to two pathways; many children express their preferred gender in secrecy, while only a few continue to express it in public. The next section describes the secrecy path and the following section describes what we will call the "continuing" path.

SECRECY

Because they realize that they are violating cultural norms, the overwhelming response of children to realization of being transgender is to express their preferred gender in secret. We do not know how many do this as children but we know that at least 1% of males and 0.35% of females partially or fully emerge from secrecy to later declare themselves transgender in support groups and surveys. Children become expert at finding ways to express themselves in secret and "covering their tracks" afterward.

Caitlyn Jenner reports marking her mother's closet so that she could replace borrowed clothes without suspicion after a crossdressing session. My experience was similar, although I also dabbled in secret makeup and perfume sessions that were harder to hide. Because I had been made up for a Sunday school minstrel show, I knew exactly how to put on and take off makeup successfully. During the show, I wore makeup so that I could be seen dancing on the stage with my female partner who was similarly made up. I would later go into our home bathroom, lock the door, put makeup, perfume, and lipstick on, and look at myself in the mirror. I learned all about cold cream and makeup remover. I remembered to scrub where I had applied perfume and place all of my mother's makeup back in the same location. I am sure that my mother could smell something wrong, laughed to herself, but never said anything to me.

Secrecy about being transgender may continue long beyond childhood, but it has so many negative effects that it is hard to maintain for a lifetime, although this does happen. For example, Billy Tipton was a relatively well-known jazz musician who was discovered to be a transman upon his death. He hid the fact that he was transgender from the public and from several female girlfriends, although he never married. Virginia Prince, a well-known transwoman who started a national support group, carried on a bicoastal life for a time in which she presented as a businessman on one coast and transwoman on the other. There are undoubtedly cases in which transgender people die with their secret and the families dispose of clothing and other property in order to cover up this fact, but we may never know about these.

Secrecy is painful and hard to maintain for long periods of time. It has many negative effects including:

- Increase in mental workload that interferes with work and relationships
- Isolation
- Loss of authenticity
- Loneliness
- Depression and negative body changes
- Suicide
- Prevention of access to mental health professionals

Hiding the secret of being transgender results in high mental workload that interferes with work and relationships and is highly stressful. Hiding the fact of being transgender results in cover-ups and lies. This produces intense mental concentration to the exclusion of other mental processes. A survey has reported that over 70% of transgender people do not tell people at work about being transgender. This means that they constantly have to lie when answering innocent questions like "What did you do this weekend?" The transgender person may have crossdressed at home, or driven to a support group meeting in a different state, or gone out with their transgender friends, but they have to lie about it at work. Even simple mental tasks like picking the "right gender" pronouns that would not arouse suspicion becomes cumbersome. If you are cisgender, to get a sense of how difficult this is, try talking about what you did last weekend and using the "wrong" pronouns for your friends. High mental workload from being transgender results in lower performance on the job and in awkwardness dealing with people, both of which cause stress.

Professor Jennifer Finney Boylan, best-selling transgender author, expressed her feelings about secrecy:

> I was sitting on top of a mountain of secrets so high it was almost impossible to see the earth anymore. For one thing, now that I lived alone, I was living as a

woman half the time. I'd come home and go female and pay the bills and write
and watch television, and then I'd go back to boy mode and teach my classes.
I did not venture out into the world much en femme, although I did get out
now and then. It was unbelievably frightening . . .

   At every waking moment now, I was plagued by the thought that I was living
a lie.

   —Jennifer Finney Boylan, *She's Not There: A Life in Two Genders*[1]

Keeping a secret results in social isolation. Transgender people in the
closet isolate themselves from others because of the fear that they inadvertently will say or do something that reveals their secret. This means that they
deliberately avoid making friends and keeping up with friends in order to
keep people at a distance. One way of reducing the stresses of secrecy is to
be able to confide in friends, but transgender people deprive themselves of
these opportunities.

   I spent over nearly 40 years totally in the closet and 10 partially in the
closet going to support groups. Now I find that I never really learned how
to make friends and establish a social support network. I realize now that
I constantly moved away from my family and from the friends that I had at
schools as a deliberate strategy on my part to isolate myself. I went to high
school in the Philadelphia area, and although I was accepted to go to the
nearby University of Pennsylvania, I decided to move away from home and
go to a remote college in New Hampshire. We will talk about "flights" aimed
at dealing with being transgender, like my college flight, in the "Purging,
Military Flight, and Marriage Flight" section.

   Being transgender and in the closet causes loss of authenticity. Authenticity simply refers to being oneself and doing the things that seem natural and
allow one to explore talents and preferences. In addition to the frustration
of not being able to express one's gender predisposition, loss of authenticity
also occurs when transgender people construct "cover stories" to convince
people that they are following their assigned gender behavior category.

   Transgender people pursue certain activities not because they want to but
because they feel that they have to. Transwomen may take up athletics not
because they are particularly good at them, but because they are expected
to do so. No one would have expected an athletic he-man like Bruce Jenner
to be transgender; she suffered in secrecy all during her athletic career. I mentioned that I went far away from my friends and family so that I could be
going to New Hampshire. I did not mention that the college I went to was
all male at the time and emphasized masculine behavior. It also had the
advantages that I could play football there and join the mountain and winter
ROTC detachment. The Reserve Officers Training Corps (ROTC) allows

students to obtain military training during college and receive officer commission upon graduation. What a cover story! I was going to an all-male college, playing intercollegiate football, and learning to ski as the military does. But it was not authentic for me. I would much rather have played soccer, which was then falsely regarded as a sissy sport. I learned about soccer when I went to National Science Foundation's science summer camp, in my junior year in high school. Many of the kids there were from New York City and played soccer as part of their culture. After dinner, we would play until dark. Soccer was fine with me after I learned that it was acceptable for girls to play it too. There was much lost time and opportunity.

The inevitable result of self-isolation and loss of authenticity is loneliness. Being transgender in the closet is a lonely existence. Being unable to have close friends and being unable to be with those who have similar interests result in loneliness. As Lee Etscovitz a transgender person, wrote in the poem *Loneliness*:

> Loneliness stalks me
> in the darkness of my bed,
> in the crowdedness of a bar,
> and when I walk the fields.
> It presses in upon me
> when I wish to be alone,
> smashing my solitude,
> drowning my days,
> wrecking my weeks,
> and punching me
> in the stomach of my existence.
> —Lee Etscovitz, 1985 Renaissance Education
> Association, quoted by Transgender Forum[2]

Increases in mental workload, isolation, loss of authenticity, and loneliness all contribute to depression in transgender people. It is estimated that at least 60% of transgender individuals show signs of depression. This is not the kind of depression that originates from malfunction of the brain that is termed "organic"; it is what is called "reactive" depression. It is a perfectly normal reaction to the effects of secrecy and cultural rejection that transgender people experience. Secrecy also causes other negative physiological effects such as suppressed immune system response.

All of the above effects of secrecy contribute to a high rate of attempted suicide among transgender people. Estimates of attempted suicide range from 31% to 43%, depending on the study. This is much higher than the general population frequency of 1.6%. Many successful suicides probably go undetected, so the rate is probably higher. It is not just the closeted transgender people included in these statistics, but transgender people who are out also contribute to the high transgender suicide rate, including those unable to have GPS.

Of course, the same secrecy that precludes normal family and social relations also prevents transgender people from seeking help from mental health professionals. In fact, most transgender people never see a mental health professional, unless the situation is extreme or they decide to pursue transsexual transition. There are probably several reasons for this. First, there are not many mental health professionals experienced in counseling transgender people, although now more counselors are in training. To be qualified to counsel transgender people it is recommended that the counselor not only take courses on the subject but also intern with an experienced professional for at least a year. Unfortunately, some mental health professionals try to treat transgender people using psychotherapy or other therapies that they have been taught but which do not "cure" them of being transgender. Second, transgender people are afraid of the stigma of going to a mental health professional. In the past, transgender people in the military or with a security clearance have been expelled from the military or lost security privileges if they admitted that they went to a counselor. Transgender people in those situations can now obtain counseling without penalty. And third, some transgender adolescents who are not yet of legal age do not want their parents and families to know about or to be involved in counseling because of family rejection.

It should be noted that secrecy does not just have negative effects on the transgender person; it affects all those who share the secret of the transgender person. It is like a toxin that spreads to others who, in turn, experience all of the same negative effects of keeping the secret that we have described in this section.

PURGING, MILITARY FLIGHT, AND MARRIAGE FLIGHT

Purging, military flight, and marriage flight are attempts to cope with the toxic effects of transgender secrecy but are usually unsuccessful in the long run. They are shown in Figure 6.1 in the upper left corner. I have tried all three and do not recommend them to anyone.

Purging involves getting rid of any article of clothing, makeup, computer files, or other sign that the person is secretly a transgender person. It is a major problem of transwomen because they must acquire and hide the things they need to present in the feminine behavior category; it is still a problem for transmen but there are usually fewer things to hide. Transwomen hide dresses, makeup, wigs, undergarments, and breast forms. Transmen hide breast binders and "packers" that simulate the male genitalia. Such items must be acquired and hidden from family and others, which creates fear of discovery in the transgender person. Transgender people sometimes rent storage lockers to keep their items hidden. Transgender people who travel for business are likely to keep a suitcase with their gender presentation items in a storage locker or the trunk of a car for quick access. Some transgender clubs and organizations actually provide temporary storage for purged transgender items, knowing that the person will reclaim the items in a few months after the purge cycle is complete.

Purging tends to occur in cycles. The transgender person comes to believe that if they get rid of all the things they have hidden, they will get relief from the fear of discovery. Even though they may have purged before, some may think that if they get rid of the hidden items, they will be "cured." All is well for a few weeks and then the transgender person gradually starts reacquiring things. They may also start visualizing how they want to look at support groups or other social events. In a few months, the transgender person will again have all the things necessary to follow their congruent gender behavior category. This completes a purge cycle but purge cycles are likely to reoccur. Personally, I purged at least a half dozen times.

It used to be that purging only involved physical items, but now computer systems get purged as well. Computer files, email messages, and browsing histories may betray a transgender person, particularly to someone close to them who has physical access to their computer.

I found that I had a need to crossdress every six weeks or so, which meant that my purge cycles lasted a maximum of six weeks. The maximum for others may be different. I have even encountered a person at a support group who had purged several years ago and went to a meeting without any presentation items. The transwomen in the group were easily able to outfit her with spare clothing and makeup. Sure enough, she was crossdressed at the next monthly meeting and at subsequent meetings for as long as I knew her.

I kept a bag in my garage or car for business trips and became an expert on how to get through the baggage process and inspection procedures of the time. My favorite place to purge was the Minneapolis airport. I would frequently fly through Minneapolis to the West Coast, since the flights were cheaper and arrived earlier in the day. I always carried my transgender bag as carry-on and checked my boy clothes bag. It was safer that way because if questioned I could always say that the carry-on bag belonged to my wife. This avoided the risk that a checked bag might be misdirected and delivered to my home or workplace. My heart seemed to stop when a coworker once out of kindness actually delivered my bag to a secret government installation. No one seemed to suspect anything, even though I could clearly see the outline of my heels in the garment bag. On the legs to Minneapolis back from the West Coast, I would start to get the urge to purge. I was not looking forward to the stressful process of hiding my secret transgender bag, and I was afraid that someone in my family would discover it. So upon landing in Minneapolis, I would find an isolated trash container and dump the bag. It makes me heartsick to remember the jewelry, makeup, and clothing that I dumped, but it seemed like the right thing to do at the time. For a few days at least, I was relieved of physical evidence of my secret.

A second way that closeted transgender people try to cope is through **military flight**, meaning that they join the military in an attempt to flee from being transgender. Transwomen go into the military in the belief that they will be "cured" by being forced to practice being masculine. Transmen get a chance to participate in military culture, which is still quite masculine in nature. The science on military flight is solid, thanks to Dr. George Brown who courageously counseled transgender people in the military and now transgender people in the Veterans Administration healthcare system. Transgender people join the military at 20 times the rate that other people do, which means, by my estimate, that there are currently at least 20,000 transgender people in the U.S. military. The military provides an absorbing environment that occupies one full time. It distracts transgender people from expressing their gender behavior category. The military also requires social contact and bonding, which help alleviate the loneliness and isolation. Being in the military used to limit the opportunities for crosspresentation, although transgender people are now allowed to do this while not on duty. Because of the recent legitimization of being transgender in the military, transgender people now should be able to serve openly, although there are undoubtedly issues to work out.

I joined the military for several reasons, including the desire of my family for me to serve. My father had not been able to serve in World War II due to childhood Scarlet fever and osteomyelitis that resulted in one leg being shorter than the other. It was one of the reasons my mother gave for rejecting my revelation at age 4 ¾ that I was a girl, not a boy. Staying out of Vietnam was the second reason, because joining the reserves in ROTC meant that I would not be drafted, although if things got really bad I might be called up. I reasoned that if things got worse in the war, I would be in the military no matter what. The third reason was the challenge of learning about mountain and winter warfare, a real manly endeavor. Although I got good grades in ROTC particularly with regard to military history and technology, the military trainers somehow knew that I was not gung ho enough to be a student leader in the unit, so I was relegated to being the unit "treasurer." I went to graduate school believing that I would owe the military a commitment to serve for two years, but as the Vietnam War and military forces were quickly winding down, they change my commitment to three months of training. This was unexpected; I had not applied to any college for teaching, so I was without a job. I quickly volunteered to work in a military medical laboratory. I spent nearly three years on active duty working on pharmacology projects. Not much of a macho assignment but I did get to continue biopsychology research.

A third way that transgender people cope with being in the closet is **marriage flight**. Marriage flight means that a transgender person, usually a transwoman, deliberately marries in hopes that the negative impacts of secrecy will be reduced. Some think that it might "cure" them but that is not the case. As Jennifer Finney Boylan wrote:

> I did love her, though, for a little while anyhow. That was the thing: I still believed on some fundamental level that love would cure me. That if only I were loved deeply enough by someone else, I would be content to stay a man. It wouldn't be my authentic life, but it would be all right. It was better, in any case, than coming out as a transsexual, taking hormones, and having some gruesome operation and walking around like Herman Munster. An authentic life wasn't very appealing. And so I allowed myself to be lifted off the ground by the levitating properties of romantic love.
>
> —Jennifer Finney Boylan, *Stuck in the Middle with You: A Memoir of Parenting in Three Genders*[3]

Marriage usually just raises the stakes for transgender secrecy and makes the secret harder to protect. Inevitably the secret is shared with the spouse or the spouse discovers evidence of being transgender. The spouse feels bad because they have been deceived and may question their own gender and sexual orientation. They wonder whether they are gay or lesbian. After learning more about being transgender, they may come to fear that the transgender person will change sex and leave them. If the spouse gets through all these emotions, the marriage may have a chance. Increasingly, marriages persist despite one of the partners going through transsexual transition.

SECRECY OUTCOMES

A transgender person living in secrecy may continue throughout their lifetime. More likely than not, they will partially come out and participate in support groups or make friends and socialize with them. This type of transgender pathway we will call the <u>recreational transgender</u> one. Partially coming out increases the risk of exposure, but in most situations there is a "balance of fear" that keeps transgender people from outing other transgender folks. Most transgender people feel better about themselves with this partial outing, which may continue throughout their lifetime. A few transgender people actually crosspresent full time but do not go through supervised transsexual transition. They may take do-it-yourself hormones because there are countries that do not require a prescription for sex hormones. This is a dangerous thing to do because a person taking hormones may overdose and should be regularly monitored by a medical doctor in accordance with WPATH guidelines. Herbal medicines purporting to have sex hormone effects do not work.

Some non-transsexual "full-timers" may get operations to modify their bodies like breast augmentation in the case of MTF or breast removal in the case of FTM. There are no guidelines or standard medical practice that ethically requires mental health professional's authorization for such operations outside of WPATH-supervised transition. However, in order to get transsexual GPS, they need to follow the procedures set out in the WPATH guidelines. Most reputable surgeons will not perform GPS without the appropriate letters from mental health and medical authorities, which are required by WPATH. And some surgeons require more documentation than WPATH. We will discuss the WPATH guidelines and transsexual transition process in more detail in the "Transsexual Transition" section of this chapter.

Some transgender people who have followed a life of secrecy for many years will come out of the closet and seek transsexual transition procedures, either through a period of partial coming out or directly coming out. This was the situation with Bruce, now Caitlyn Jenner, who came out partially to friends and support groups and then started the transition process. Caitlyn evidently started transition, then stopped for a few years and then started again. My situation was similar; I was 40 years totally in the closet, 10 years partially being out, and 9 years as a transsexual. I started transition, then stopped for a few months and then started again. I completed transition last year.

CHILDREN WHO CONTINUE BEING TRANSGENDER

Referring to the upper right of Figure 6.1, some courageous children continue being transgender and do not adopt a strategy of secrecy. This occurs despite increasing rejection from parents, family, and community as they grow up. Although families are now more accepting now than a few years ago, they still experience rejection from outside of the family. There are three pathways for them. The first is to continue to be transgender no matter what. The second is to go through a "social transition." The aim is to demonstrate readiness for endocrine treatment before age 8 in the form of blockers to prevent puberty with a later decision on transsexual transition at age 16. The third is to discontinue being transgender as social pressures mount in school and social activities.

CHILDREN/YOUNG ADULTS BEING TRANSGENDER WITHOUT SOCIAL TRANSITION OR ENDOCRINE TREATMENT

There are some children/young adults who just tough it out and continue to pursue transgender behavior despite cultural rejection. They "tough it out" in the face of bullying and verbal/physical violence. This pathway contains two categories of children/young adults. The two categories consist of those who are able to stay with their families until the age of majority and those who cannot.

The first category, those who can stay with their families, includes courageous transgirls and transboys who continue to present in their congruent gender behavior category. They risk verbal and physical rejection. Transboys have a somewhat better time of it because culture initially recognizes the phenomena of "tomboys." The conventional wisdom is that such tomboys who are known to temporarily reject the feminine gender behavior category will "come around later," so their cultural transgressions are tolerated.

Transboys and transmen also have it a little easier because females have more latitude in dress, particularly in modern times when wearing pants is acceptable. But even transgender people in this category are rejected by their families and communities. They are still rejected by those who have been taught by culture to fear and hate people who are not like themselves, particularly when it comes to gender presentation.

We know that transchildren exist in this category because of the numerous lawsuits aimed at allowing them to express their congruent gender, while at school this pertains particularly to participation in school activities, including proms and graduation in which culture and dress codes reject their congruent gender crosspresentation. We are also beginning to see "restroom" and "locker room" lawsuits and actions because Federal laws prohibiting sexual discrimination in education have now been interpreted to protect transgender people. We do not have accurate records of how many "tough it out" until they are of legal age, but we know they exist.

The second category consists of transgender children and young adults who must leave their homes, typically because of rejection of their transgender behavior. Surveys show that over 57% of transgender children and adults have experienced rejection at home by parents or family. They may be thrown out and disowned by their parents, as sanctioned by culture, or they may leave to avoid verbal and physical rejection. Most of them end up homeless on the street where in order to survive they engage in street economies such as prostitution and drug dealing. They also are likely to take drugs. More than 16% of transgender people report on surveys that they have engaged in illegal street business.

Although some may disregard the health of homeless transgender people as being irrelevant to their lives, the fact is that transgender prostitution creates a reservoir of HIV and sexually transmitted diseases that create a public health danger to everyone. Worldwide, transgender prostitutes on the street are 49 times as likely to have HIV as other people. Even worse, there are statistics that seem to show that transgender prostitutes for some reason are less likely to take prophylactic precautions when having sex than non-transgender prostitutes.

Transgender people on the street disproportionately contribute to transgender poverty. Transgender people are four times as likely to have incomes under $10,000 and this rate increases if the person is homeless. Because of homelessness, dropping out from school, economic discrimination, and other factors, the rate of unemployment of transgender people is at least 40%.

Homeless transgender people are often rejected by shelters, particularly those with religious ties. We talked about one death in Austin, Texas, that can be directly tied to such rejection, as the transgender person died from cold exposure outside of a religion-sponsored homeless shelter after having been rejected because she was transgender. There are probably more deaths and illnesses that could be attributed to such rejection, but we do not know exactly how many. The predicament of homeless transgender people has gotten so bad that it has received Federal attention. According to recent Federal regulations, any shelter receiving Federal support money must accommodate homeless transgender people. There are also initiatives by cities and private organizations to provide housing notably in San Francisco and Chicago. For example, the Transgender Housing Atlanta Program (of which I am a member) seeks to provide temporary and permanent shelter to transgender people here where I live.

Transgender prostitutes face another problem. If arrested and convicted, the transgender person is put on various sex crime registries, which essentially preclude getting a regular job. In many cities, so-called diversion laws have been put in place to deal with this problem. Under these laws, if detained for prostitution, a person can elect diversion, which consists going into a program that provides housing, counseling, and reeducation rather than arrest and prosecution. The goal is to get these transgender people into legitimate jobs.

The root cause of transgender homelessness is needless rejection by parents and families. Culture sanctions such rejection through religious philosophies, community norms, and political posturing. Some subcultures are particularly hypocritical, because they ostensibly believe in forgiveness but do not grant it to transgender people. Transgender people are not homeless, engaging in prostitution, or engaging in the drug trade because they want to. They do so because it is the only way they have to survive, given cultural rejection.

There have been some studies to determine the numbers of transgender children who continue through childhood and young adulthood, but they have significant scientific flaws. Most of these studies were conducted to provide support for the contention that transgender children will grow up to be gay or transsexual adults, but these studies do not demonstrate this convincingly. The studies are fraught with methodological problems as described later. The vast number of transgender children go into secrecy, which means that they are not available for surveys.

The studies of transgender children in question were performed on populations of children who were referred to clinics or psychiatrists for severe and multiple problems. In the scientific terminology, we can refer to such children of being part of "clinical sample" and the studies are referred to as "longitudinal" because they seek to follow the children into adulthood. In the case of these particular studies, there are several reasons for doubting their generalizability to the larger population of transgender people including:

- Small sample size
- Sample not selected to be representative
- Longitudinal study dropout rates are high
- Co-occurrence with actual illnesses

The samples tend to be small, far smaller than 1% of males and 0.5% of females who I estimate are transgender. Most of them involve less than 100 people. The sample is an available sample and not one representative of the larger population. Many children in these groups were selected by their parents to go to clinics, because they believed that transgender behavior was something that needed to be "fixed." Whether deliberate or not, some mental health professionals encourage such biased selection by telling parents about other flawed studies of the same type. It is a vicious circle. The fact that the children have been referred to gender clinics may reflect their parents' concern that "there is something wrong with them" based on the prevailing culture that tends to reject transgender behavior. It is likely that the children are selected more on the basis of their parents' cultural biases than on the behavior or needs of the children.

These studies are called longitudinal because the idea is to follow the person for a long time from childhood to adulthood. This type of study is fraught with all sorts of biases. As they mature, children and young adults in the sample tend to drop out for various reasons, sometimes over 50%. In the case of being transgender, it is likely that some children and young adults have gone into secrecy or do not want to admit that they are still cross-presenting or that they are indifferent to the success of the study.

Finally, the participants in such studies are usually extreme cases who have more than one problem. There is evidence that about 40% of those appearing at a gender clinic are not just transgender, which is not pathological, but also have actual physical illnesses. Clinical people refer to such patients with a co-occurrence of more than one problem as having "comorbidity." This is a scary pathological word, but it means nothing more than having more than one problem. Since being transgender is not an illness, the term should not be applied to transgender people, although in mental health circles it is still used out of habit. Some hatemongers have used this statistic to imply that transgender people have or are more likely to have mental illnesses. The people in these studies are not representative of transgender people as a whole.

TRANSGENDER CHILDREN TREATMENT

Increasingly, children with understanding parents or family are turning to new treatment methods for dealing with being transgender. These include a process involving counseling, social transitioning, and drugs that block puberty. The process leads to a subsequent decision whether to start **hormone therapy (HT)** at age 16, although some start earlier.

Counseling

Transgender children are receiving counseling at increasingly earlier ages. This is because of a greater awareness, recognition, and acceptance of parents with regard to being transgender. It is also, in part, because of the availability of puberty blocking drugs that need to start at age 8–9 in order to have their maximum effects in preventing unwanted body changes from puberty. Such body changes interfere with future gender presentation.

Puberty is occurring in the population at large at younger and younger ages. In order to be eligible for puberty blockers, WPATH recommends that the child complete a **social transition** in their congruent gender behavior category. This is similar to the Real Life Experience (RLE) recommended for adult transsexuals (see "Real-Life Experience" section later in this chapter). The aim is to demonstrate that the child can successfully live in their congruent gender behavior category. The onset represents a deadline for completing social transition to the satisfaction of the transgender child, family, and counselor. Counseling has to start before social transition.

Counseling may be all that is necessary particularly for children who want to "tough it out." The WPATH guidelines recommend that a qualified counselor should (paraphrase):

- Find out whether the child has any problems or issues at home, school, or elsewhere that need to be addressed by counseling.
- Find out if the child has any health problems that could interfere with social transition and later with hormone blocking. (The child's medical doctor should also be asked to do this.)
- Make psychotherapy available (although there is no proof that it "cures" being transgender).
- Encourage everyone around the child to accept their transgender behavior.
- Do not attempt to change the child's gender behavior.
- Provide support for decisions on social transition, administration of hormone blockers, and sex hormone therapy.
- Not encourage irreversible body changes through sex hormone therapy or surgery until the child is at least 16. (This is not a hard-and-fast rule because the situation of some children makes it necessary to start HT at an earlier age.)

Notice that the guidelines explicitly say that no attempt should be made to change the child's gender behavior. Some mental health professionals have attempted to do this but such, so called, **reparative therapy has** been shown to be unsuccessful and may injure the child. In the United States, many states have passed laws forbidding such activity and a similar federal law has been proposed.

The decisions of when and where to start social transition depend on several environmental factors, including acceptance by schools and the community. Some children and their parents decide to wait until they can move locations in order to make a new start in the child's congruent gender behavior category.

Whether or not the decision is made to take hormone-blocking drugs or start transsexual transition, a mental health counselor should be available. A counselor is needed to prepare the child to cope with the cultural rejection, bullying, and violence that the child is likely to encounter and assist the child to deal with such problems.

Puberty Blocking

Normal puberty causes body changes that interfere with desired gender presentation in childhood and adulthood for transgender people. Drugs have recently been used that can block puberty, and they have been used successfully in the small number of cases where they have been tried. The procedure is still experimental but, so far, the results have been good.

The primary purpose of blocking puberty is to give the transgender child time to "sort it all out" as we phrased it in Chapter 5, with minimum risk. It gives the transgender child about seven to eight years of extra social transitioning experience before a decision must be made on hormone therapy at age 16.

The blocking hormones interfere with normal puberty by changing the brain mechanisms that control **gonadotropin-releasing hormone (GnRH)**. GnRH is responsible for starting and continuing puberty in both males and females. The concentration of this hormone is sensed by particular cells at the base of the brain in the hypothalamus. As we indicated in Chapter 3, if you put your tongue on the roof of your mouth, the hypothalamus is less than an inch above it. If the levels of hormones in the blood stream are too low to cause puberty body changes, more GnRH is released. It flows into the pituitary gland where the two hormones that act on the body to cause puberty are stored and released.

Hormone blockers actually overstimulate the cells that release GnRH, causing them to be more sensitive to blood hormones and "fooling" them into stopping the release of GnRH. There are several blocking drugs, including leuprolide, histrelin, and triptorelin, which are administered by injection or implant and nafarelin, which is taken in a nasal spray. All of these drugs are expensive (at least $1,000 per month). They were originally approved for children who started puberty too early.

Blockers should be approved and ideally administered by an endocrinologist who is working with a child's counselor and medical doctor. This is because the child should be periodically monitored through blood testing and examination. Endocrinologists believe that puberty blocking hormones can impact body growth and height, although they believe that these effects are small.

Recent studies have shown that blocking drugs can have positive effects even if started later, up to age 16. In particular, the supraorbital rim or "eyebrow overhang" that is prominent in postpuberty males can be reduced in size by administration of blockers even if started at age 16. Many MTF who transition late in life have had to have this bony structure ground down in size during facial **feminization surgery**. Blockers can reduce the need for such surgeries.

I wish that transgender puberty blocking procedures had been available when I was a child, and probably many other transgender people feel the same way. I would have jumped at the chance for social transition and blockers, but I am pretty sure at that time not many parents would have accepted the idea. Frankly I would not have minded a little less height, which currently interferes with my gender presentation. But I have seen plenty of transwomen at conventions who are tall and stand nearly seven feet in heels who do not seem to mind being tall at all. If there is ever an opportunity to have a transgender basketball team, I want to coach them.

Sex Hormones

WPATH guidelines recommend that hormone therapy not be given to children until they are 16 years old and have successfully completed social transition. However, there are cases in which hormone therapy has been started earlier. One of the best-publicized cases was Kim Petras who started sex hormone therapy in Germany at age 12. She is now a singer, model, and performer. She did not take blockers because they were not generally used at the time for transgender children but went directly to sex hormone therapy. She also completed GPS at age 16, although the earliest currently recommended age is 18. Then there is the case of Jazz Jennings who has been telling her story on U.S. national television since she was 6 years old, first on Barbara Walters's interviews and later on her own reality television show. When she was 11, she started blocking drugs and also taking estrogen. These two public cases as well as others illustrate that WPATH guidelines are only recommendations that can be adjusted in cases where it is in the best interest of the child.

If a child starts sex hormones, it means that they have begun transsexual transition, which we will discuss in next section.

TRANSSEXUAL TRANSITION

As shown in Figure 6.1, people starting transsexual transition arrive through four pathways. They typically do not arrive until they reach the legal age of maturity, but as we saw in the previous section, some start at the age of 16 (minimum WPATH recommendation) and some even earlier. One pathway consists of those who "tough it out" from childhood and continue to go full time in their congruent gender behavior category as legal adults. This includes the children who tough it out and/or go through social transition and hormone blockers. The second pathway comes from those who are still in secrecy about being transgender and decide that they want to go full time through transsexual transition. The third pathway is from the partially out or recreational-transgender path. For example, Caitlyn Jenner went from being totally in the closet to partially out before she emerged publicly to follow the transsexual path.

I know these pathways exist; they are documented in the literature, and I have met transsexuals who came through all three pathways. However, I cannot tell you scientifically how many people follow each pathway because the data simply are not available. I can tell you that the United Kingdom has done surveys for their national health services to project how many doctors, counselors, and endocrinologists they may need in the future to treat transgender and transsexual people. So they thought that counting then current numbers of transgender people gave them a handle on what their needs will be. They regard transgender people as being a reservoir of potential transsexual people and mention these three pathways for those who arrive at transsexual transition. However, their estimates were low and they have not kept pace with the demand, so there is a long waiting list for even transgender counseling.

Those who have started and those who have completed transsexual transition are currently all over the news. This has happened before, back in the early 1950s with the emergence in the United States of Christine Jorgensen as someone who had "changed sex." She had been in the military in World War II but after surgery became an instant celebrity, performing as actress, model, and lecturer. The current interest with transsexuals is a result of many transsexuals gaining prominence in acting, writing, journalism, and reality shows. The coming out of Caitlyn Jenner as a transsexual capped it all off.

There are numerous misconceptions about transsexual transition. The first is that going through transsexual transition is some sort of mountain climbing expedition in which the goal is to get to the top of the mountain, meaning that one has to complete transsexual GPS in order to succeed. So the misconception goes, anything else is a failure. Only about 25% of transsexuals actually get GPS. Transsexuals may have a general idea at the outset of what body parts they want to change. However, the actual decisions are made sequentially and separately that makes transgender decision making a critical skill, as we discussed in Chapter 5. Transsexual GPS is not necessary for a successful transition. Due to ignorance of these facts, many states have laws requiring GPS for change of name, driver's license name, and sex marker change or birth certificates. Legislators who passed these laws clearly have not done their due diligence.

The second misconception is that transsexual transition cannot change sex. We defined "sex" in Chapter 2 as involving sex organs. We can change external sex organs such as breasts, genitalia, and the face with hormones and surgery. We can change the brain and nervous system with HT and create functional vaginas. We can remove hair from the face and elsewhere and perform hair transplants. We can grow hair with hormones in the right male patterns, including male pattern baldness. I believe that such changes are sufficient to declare that the person has changed sex.

Changes in our capabilities are on the horizon. Medical science has already been able to transplant functional uteruses and penises, but it has not been done yet for transsexual people. Last year there were two births by women that resulted from uterine transplants. Penis transplants are being tried for those with genital mutilation and wounded male soldiers, and the U.S. military plans transplants for at least 60 male soldiers. Surgical voice operations are still regarded by most transsexuals as risky and need to be perfected. There are some things that we cannot yet do, like transplant ovaries, testicles, but medical science will probably be able to do them in a few years.

We cannot do chromosome or gene alterations but remember, we put the rabbit into the hat in Chapter 2. We confined sex in Chapter 2 to sex organs, regardless of how they got there. So chromosome or gene alterations do not count as sex changes. Attempts to use them as sex determinants by the Olympics and international athletics have failed miserably. There is too much natural variation in them.

The third common misconception of transsexual transition is that all MTF or FTM must go through exactly the same procedures in the same order. WPATH guidelines are just that—guidelines and the processes they describe can be altered to fit patient needs. There is only one exception and that is the procedure for getting transsexual GPS for which WPATH requires two permission letters and even more are required by some surgeons. Some transsexuals skip hormone treatment and go right to breast implants, believing that their genetic ancestry will result in unsatisfactory low breast growth from

HT. Some get electrolysis hair removal after hormone therapy and some before, believing that hormones will increase their sensitivity to pain.

It is true that the transsexual person should put off irreversible changes until later in transition so that they have time to change their minds and thus limit potential harm. For example, many plastic surgeries on the body are reversible. Breast implants can be removed and breast reductions can be performed for transwomen. But transsexual GPS is very difficult to reverse, so it is usually undertaken toward the end of transition. It is done near the end, not because it is the culmination of transition but because it should not be performed until the transsexual is sure.

A fourth misconception is that only transsexuals undergo the procedures included in transsexual transition guidelines. For safety reasons, the guidelines of professional organizations should be followed with help from qualified mental and medical health professionals. WPATH is the primary professional organization with guidelines but there are others, including the Endocrine Society, the Royal College of Psychiatry, American College of Obstetricians and Gynecologists and the Canadian affiliate of WPATH, which is CPATH. While decisions about transsexual transition procedures are usually up to the person, every transsexual should have a group of mental health and medical "lifeguards." Unfortunately many transgender people undergo procedures on a "do-it-yourself" basis. Breast implants outside of the guidelines are often performed on transgender people because they do not require permission letters.

Some procedures are dangerous on a do-it-yourself basis. Sex hormones and sex hormone blockers do not require prescriptions in some countries, and transgender people can get them cheaply through mail order. Taking hormones on your own is a risky business, because transsexual hormone therapy requires constant medical monitoring to adjust dosages and to look for early indications of potential side effects. It is also dangerous because you do not know what you are getting in the pills or injections. They can be and are counterfeited and the dosages can be irregular.

While I strenuously believe that no one should take sex hormones without medical supervision, unfortunately some transgender people do take them on a do-it-yourself basis. I have to admit that I actually legally obtained such drugs from other countries, including Canada and Vanuatu. I had valid prescriptions but my purpose was to avoid my local pharmacy to preserve my privacy. But I would not do it again. And the drugs were not any cheaper. I was curious about the source of the drugs and discovered that, from their online pill guides, the primary countries were the United States, New Zealand, and Australia.

That gave me some confidence that they were good but they still could have been counterfeit. Pill-making machines are not controlled technologies. All this do-it-yourself medication also sets up a problem when seeing doctors or going to emergency rooms because most such drug takers do not report taking the hormones. This can complicate diagnosis and treatment of whatever medical problem they have.

One of the most dangerous procedures, which is not approved by any guidelines, are silicone injections, which are life threatening. Some transgender people get them to get bigger breasts or other body parts from quacks. The silicone is usually not medical grade and is the same material used to caulk your bathtub or house. By the time medical problems develop, the quacks are gone to another part of the country.

A fifth misconception is that all doctors, mental health professionals, and endocrinologists know about transsexual transition. If you are a transgender person, be sure that you find knowledgeable, experienced professional help. The truth is that most doctors know nothing about treating transsexual patients, but they are still legally allowed to prescribe hormones. However, because of increased visibility of transgender people, the number of knowledgeable medical doctors is slowly increasing. Until this year most medical schools gave no instruction to doctors on transgender people. At most they had eight hours of instruction on all of GLBT. Some medical schools have begun to add instruction on dealing with transgender people, including the etiquette of politely asking which pronouns transgender people prefer and other issues. WPATH and others have started holding continuing education courses for healthcare providers. That is a start. But WPATH also recommends that providers "intern" for a year with those experienced in treatment of transgender people.

Motivation for Transsexual Transition

While you may see all kinds of psychobabble in the news about why people start transsexual transition, the practical reason is that transsexual people see the need for body modification. They want to look and feel authentic and also to be attractive to other people. They want to do this to express their congruent gender behavior category. As Jan Morris expressed it:

> I regarded sex as a tool of gender, and I believed that for me as well as most people the interplay between the two lay very close to personality, not to be measured by blood tests or Freudian formulae .... To myself I had been woman all along, and I was not going to change the truth of me, only discard the falsity. But I *was* about to change my form ....
>
> —Jan Morris, *Conundrum*[4]

Jan Morris described Dr. Harry Benjamin who started the organization, which is now WPATH:

> Dr. Benjamin, an endocrinologist, had come later in life to the study of sexual anxieties, and by the 1950s was deep in the problem of gender confusion ... He had explored every aspect of the condition (being transsexual) and he frankly did not know its cause; what he *did* know was that no true transsexual had yet been persuaded, bullied, drugged, analyzed, or electrically shocked into an acceptance of his physique. It was an immutable state.
>
> —Jan Morris, *Conundrum*[5]

Transgender people have trouble feeling authentic while wearing wigs, breast forms, gaffs, binders, and packers. Wigs are a pain to take care of and hot, particularly where I live in the South. Breast forms you probably know about because women who have had surgery for breast cancer sometimes wear them to have a good shape in their clothes. Transwomen sometimes use them for the same reason. The others you may not know about. Gaffs are compression garments for the external genitals, which many transwomen use to prevent their genitals from showing. Binders are tight fitting garments designed to minimize the shape of the breasts, which transmen often use unless they have had "top surgery" to reduce their breast size and construct a male-like chest. Packers are male genitalia replicas that transmen use to fill out their crotch area and provide a birth male shape. All these artificial appliances are uncomfortable and reduce feelings of authenticity. Part of loss of authenticity is the fact that other people in the culture expect certain body shapes in each gender behavior category.

Remember that we said in Chapter 2 that transgender homosexuals exist as a subset of transgender people. No doubt some of these people go into transsexual transition in order to have the right genitalia and bodies to have relationships with same-sex people (who will become the opposite sex after transition). This may be particularly true for FTM homosexuals who change their sexual orientation at the start of transsexual transition. About 40% change their sexual orientation. They will want the musculature and facial hair to attract females.

MTF Transsexual Transition

Procedures for MTF transsexual transition include:

- Mental health assessment
- Hormone therapy

- Voice therapy
- Facial hair removal
- Facial feminization surgery
- Real-life experience
- Transsexual GPS

Each of these will be described, in turn, in the following sections.

Mental Health Assessment

Before starting transsexual transition, it is advisable to get a mental health assessment from a qualified psychologist, psychiatrist, or social worker. It is important to establish a relationship with the mental health professional, because a person needs to have support readily available to help deal with all sorts of problems, which accompany any big change. A professional, with your permission, can also explain and help family and others affected by the change. For some procedures, permission letters are necessary either because WPATH requires it or because some prospective doctor or surgeon requires it. It is best if the transsexual establishes a prior relationship with the mental health professional so that they will be able to respond to the needs of the transsexual.

The mental health professional has a duty under WPATH guidelines to be sure that some mental health or other problem will not interfere with transition. This may not preclude proceeding with transition, but any such problem needs to be recognized and dealt with.

The mental health professional can act as a guide for the transsexual and can provide a sounding board to discuss transition procedures. So it is important that the professional have knowledge and experience in dealing with transsexual transition. The professional should be knowledgeable about local facilities that transsexual people need like transgender-friendly hair salons, electrolysis shops, and clothing shops. There actually are a few custom tailors who cater to MTF transgender people like Bindle and Keep in New York City and Zuit Suit in Atlanta. By providing such information, the professional is engaged in what is called "patient management." Before embarking on transition, the professional and the transsexual should develop a plan for making sequential decisions about transition procedures. The plan does not have to be followed precisely but it is a place to start.

Of critical importance is discussion of how the transsexual will make a social transition and begin to increase their time publically expressing behaviors in their congruent gender behavior category. This will not be a problem for those who are already "going full time." But for those who are not, this social transition involves gradual increases in the duration of congruent gender presentation.

Hormone Therapy

Hormone therapy for MTF transsexuals involves administration of sex hormones and blocking drugs to feminize the body by changing its structure. You may hear this referred to as "hormone replacement therapy" or HRT but that term is incorrect. WPATH guidelines simply refer to it as "hormone therapy" or HT. There actually is such a thing as HRT. It is a treatment procedure in which hormones are replaced when they are no longer being secreted by the body. For example, it is sometimes used in those females who have had hysterectomies or in dealing with menopause. Transsexuals do not receive HRT; they receive HT because the sex hormones they receive are those that would typically be very low in birth males. So for MTF transsexuals, there is no hormone loss to "replace."

MTF HT is nearly completely reversible. Most of the effects reverse themselves after HT is stopped. Breast growth can be reversed since breast size reduction operations are readily available. For this reason, HT is usually the first thing that transsexuals do in transition.

Endocrinologists vary in exactly what drugs and dosages they prescribe, depending on their clinical experience and the needs of the patient. Guidelines for use of the drugs are provided by WPATH and the Endocrine Society. The drugs usually prescribed for MTF HT in the United States are:

- Estradiol valerate (2–6 milligrams (mg) daily oral)
- Methylprogesterone (5–10 mg daily oral)
- Spironolactone (100–400 mg daily oral)
- Finasteride (2.5–5 mg daily oral)

The drugs may have various brand names depending on the manufacturer and distributor. They can also be given by injection, patch, and some under the tongue.

I actually take all of these medications every day as well as a baby aspirin, some Lipitor, and a weekly vitamin D pill for a total of 9–10 pills. It is not easy trying to down all these, and it takes me a couple of hours to get the job done.

Estradiol valerate is a synthetic estrogen-like drug that has a direct feminizing effect on tissue, for example, breast tissue. It also blocks testosterone production in male testes by blocking release of GnRH. It should not be confused with estradiol ethinyl, which was used in the past but was found to encourage dangerous blood clots that estradiol valerate does not do. Along with other forms of estradiol, estradiol ethinyl should not be used for HT but it is out there in the marketplace. Estradiol valerate stimulates estrogen receptors in various cells around the body that results in feminization. To explain further, some cells in the body have places on their outside membranes that fit estrogen molecules because of their shape, like a lock and key. When the estradiol lands on these places, there is a chemical reaction that attaches the estrogen molecule to the cell's outer membrane and that sends a message to the cell. While the most important target organs for estradiol in HT are the breasts, it also has other effects, primarily on the body and facial skin. Estradiol valerate stimulates development and enlargement of one kind of breast tissue called stromal tissue that gives the breast structure.

Estradiol valerate blocks the release of gonadotropin releasing factor in the hypothalamus of the brain. We encountered the GnRH mechanism with respect to the use of hormonal blockers in transgender children. In MTF, estradiol valerate in the blood stream tells this mechanism that no more testosterone is needed. The mechanism no longer secretes GnRH, which would trigger the pituitary gland to release hormones that would otherwise cause the testes to manufacture and secret testosterone. Lower testosterone levels reinforce the feminizing effects of estradiol valerate.

The endocrinologist for the MTF transsexual will typically measure both estradiol and testosterone to see if the drug regimen is working. I have a big body, so I need 6 mg per day of estradiol valerate to have good effects and register good levels of estradiol in my blood stream.

The second drug that is commonly used in MTF transsexual transition is medroxyprogesterone, which is a synthetic drug that mimics the effects of the naturally occurring hormone progesterone. Similar to estradiol, medroxyprogesterone feminizes the body and also blocks testosterone release by blocking release of GnRH. It also acts to develop and enlarge the lobular tissue of the breast, which is responsible for milk secretion. Estradiol valerate and medroxyprogesterone thus act to develop and enlarge both types of tissue in the breast. Some physicians prefer not to give medroxyprogesterone because they believe that estradiol along with drugs that block formation of testosterone is sufficient. Some are also concerned about breast cancer, although the rate of this disease is relatively low in transwomen. It also occurs in non-transgender males although at a very low rate.

The third drug prescribed in the United States for MTF HT is spironolactone that blocks the manufacture of testosterone and blocks the testosterone or androgen receptor. Testosterone, like estrogen, has its own receptor sites on the outside membrane of some cells and spironolactone occupies these sites and prevents testosterone from getting to them.

Spironolactone is also prescribed for high blood pressure and it has the effect of increasing potassium levels. In my case, I take 300 mg of spironolactone daily because of my body size and because I also have high blood pressure. I was taking a separate blood pressure medicine but it is unnecessary with a higher dose of spironolactone. Spironolactone acts to increase growth of hair on the head that helps older MTF like us with male pattern baldness.

The fourth drug often prescribed in the United States is finasteride, which is a drug that prevents testosterone from being converted into Dihydrotestosterone (DHT). DHT is an active form of testosterone that causes body growth in males. It has a chemical attraction to testosterone receptors, which is stronger than testosterone itself and it stimulates them. Synthetic versions of DHT are the notorious anabolic steroids that people illegally take to build muscle, which have side effects similar to MTF HT, including breast growth.

These MTF transition drugs are usually given by mouth, but some physicians prefer to deliver them by injection because this route is less stressful to the liver and because some patients do not reliably take their medication.

The main effects of MTF therapy are shown below:

- Breast and nipple growth
- Decreased muscle mass and strength
- Body fat redistribution to hips and butt
- Softening of skin and dry skin
- Decreased growth of facial hair
- Decreased male organ sexual function and infertility
- Increased sense of touch and smell
- Increased emotionality

Although some MTF would like to raise their voice pitch and shrink their Adam's apple, HT will not do these things. There does not seem to be a good way of predicting HT breast growth success at this time. Some endocrinologists add medroxyprogesterone to try to increase growth by giving this drug either daily or at a schedule that mimics the female menstrual cycle, but the results of such procedures have not been reported in controlled studies. The alternative method for breast augmentation is breast implants, which about 50% of MTF end up getting them because of unsatisfactory HT results. These carry with them the near certainty that surgery will be required again after 7–10 years because the implants harden. Breast implants are less risky than they used to be but they may harden prematurely or leak. It is clear that bigger breasts are more attractive and make clothes fit better. MTF should only get implants after two to three years on HT in order to give HT a chance to have its effects and so the implants will fit properly.

There are some potential risks of MTF HT, but it is normally safe and effective. The most important risk to discuss is that of blood clotting in the lung or thrombosis. Estrogen has an effect on blood-clotting chemicals in the blood that encourage clotting. But since doctors have switched from estradiol ethinyl to estrogen valerate in the past two decades, the risk from thrombosis appears to have decreased markedly. Those with existing blood clotting problems may not be able to take estradiol until the problems are resolved. Transsexuals taking estradiol should still be aware of the potential danger of clots and immediately seek medical help in the case of unexplained pain in the legs or shortness of breath. All other potential risks are low and have gradual onset, so they can be detected in regular medical appointments.

MTF transsexuals on HT should have regular medical appointments and be monitored for blood testosterone, estrogens, progestins, prolactin, and potassium. They should do monthly breast exams and get mammograms at the same recommended intervals as birth females. The current recommendations are yearly until age 70, then every other year, but recommendations keep changing with new science, so ask your doctor.

I started MTF HT somewhat by mistake. My counselor encouraged me to try a low dose of hormones because doctors in the local university hospital had had good results in calming transwomen patients. So I went to a local endocrinologist to get them. The endocrinologist refused to take my insurance, probably because she had been burned too many times before for treating transgender people. And that was fine with me because I did not want anyone to know that I was a transgender person at the time. I also did not claim insurance for the drugs but paid directly. At the time I did not know the recommended doses and did not pay much attention to them.

When I started taking the hormones, I got scared to death. It was so wonderful! All of a sudden I felt very different. My mood improved, my nipples started to become sensitive and grow, and immediately started to gain weight. Turns out, I was not getting the low dose of hormones; I was getting the full HT treatment. So with one interruption caused by my cold feet, I continued HT.

Until I started HT, I did not realize that breasts grow from the nipples outward. It surprised me when they popped out. They develop first and then the rest of the breast. I again checked with the medical literature and suddenly realized what I should have known, which was that I was experiencing what birth females go through at puberty. It felt good but I also suddenly realized how much I had missed during my teenage years. I also realized how much I had lost through male puberty, including my soprano singing voice of which I had been so proud.

Living in the South, I have not had good experiences getting mammograms. Under Medicare Part B, I am supposed to get free screening tests every year but neither of the two facilities that I have gotten mammograms from seemed to be able to bill the insurance company correctly. No one had experience with "males" coming in for screening tests. The experience of explaining that I was a transsexual in front of all the technicians was embarrassing and unpleasant. I think they did this because of rejection of transgender people by the Southern culture and because it was new to them. Now I am proud to be a transsexual and tell everyone I know. Compared to the embarrassment they created, the actual mammogram test was a breeze.

I also learned from my HT research that there are only a few testing laboratories that can accurately measure estradiol and testosterone blood levels. An experienced endocrinologist or medical doctor will know that there are only a few testing laboratories that are certified for accuracy by the Centers for Disease Control (CDC). The listing of which labs have CDC certifications are on their website. Results from other laboratories are erratic and should not be trusted. Inexperienced doctors and endocrinologists may not know this unless they have "interned" with those experienced in treating transsexuals.

Voice Therapy

MTF HT treatment does not change voice pitch or inflection, but voice therapy is taken by many transsexuals so that they sound more like natal females. Voice therapy is completely reversible, although it sounds very strange if you are used to a way of speaking coming from a particular transsexual person and they go back to their original way of speaking. Transsexuals try never to do this.

At puberty, the voice of the birth male will change to go lower in pitch or frequency. That cannot be reversed with HT but male and female voices have some overlap in pitch. If MTF transsexuals can talk in that overlap range or above it, they will likely be recognized as having female voices. Voice therapy can help MTF transsexuals talk in that higher range with an appropriate sound through practice and feedback. There are many experienced coaches for transsexuals and even software is available to help. I have an app on my cell phone that helps with voice practice.

Pitch is not the only difference between male and female voices. Word choice and word emphasis are different as well. Birth females will use certain words and not others and make some of their statements sound like questions by raising the emphasis at the end of a sentence.

I have tried voice therapy but I have found that my voice that went from soprano to baritone at puberty is now in the bass area. I just try to talk a little softer and prettier, and it comes as a shock when I use my military "command voice" if the public address system fails. However, I am not done trying.

Facial Hair Removal

Most MTF transsexuals have the hair removed from their faces to avoid having a beard "shadow." Beard hair can show right through even heavy makeup and as the day goes on, it keeps on growing and will eventually show through.

There are two methods for permanent facial hair removal—electrolysis and laser. Both attempt to kill off the hair follicle beneath the surface of the skin. Electrolysis is the old, tried, and true method for removal. In electrolysis, a very narrow needle is inserted next to the hair follicle cells and electricity is passed through the needle that destroys the follicle about 50% of the time. The hair is then pulled out with tweezers. Transsexuals with heavy beards sometimes have to spend hundreds of hours on this process and it is not pleasant.

Laser hair removal is a relatively recent development, and it radiates intense light into the follicle to kill it. The process is faster and less painful but more hair follicles recover than with electrolysis. Laser works best on dark hair because the dark hair absorbs light better.

Before starting transition as a non-transsexual transgender person, I tried to cover up my beard shadow using a number of methods. Water-based pan makeup like they used to use in the early movies was effective because it could be applied in a thick coat. Then I tried the pan stick makeup that worked almost as well. I learned that whatever makeup one uses, it is getting the right concealer under the makeup that makes the difference. If you look closely, beard under makeup has a somewhat green tinge. So the solution, which is unexpected, is to use a red-orange concealer before applying makeup. A cheap red-orange lipstick does okay but the best is made by Kryolan (not Krylon) that caters to drag queens and theatrical makeup artists. Although it is relatively expensive, it does not take much to work and a small container lasts for a long time. I still have plenty in my original little pot that I got in 2006. It looks really weird to put red-orange lipstick or the Kryolan concealer on your face before you apply makeup but it works really well.

I went through several hundred hours of electrolysis to remove facial hair. Since I am older, most of my hair is now white or grey, which means that laser removal would not have been effective. That is the bad news; the good news is that now that I have completed electrolysis, most stray grey or white facial hair will not leave a shadow once shaved or tweezed. I got to know my electrolysis technician really well and am grateful to her but I will never return. It was painful, particularly under the nose. Some transsexuals actually get a dentist or doctor to give them a local injection to deaden the pain, but I managed to get through without it.

Facial Feminization Surgery

There are many plastic surgeons who specialized in plastic surgery for MTF transsexuals. Several can usually be found at the transgender conventions to market their services and are happy to do free consultations. They can do a wide range of surgeries to make transsexual look more feminine, including chin reduction, cheek and lip augmentation, scalp advance, eye overhang reduction, and tracheal shaves. Scalp advance is a procedure to reduce the apparent size of the forehead, which seems to increase in size due to male pattern balding. Tracheal shaves reduce the size of the Adam's apple. Many of these are standard plastic surgery procedures that birth females have done. Transsexual people should ask their counselors and former patients about the reputations and results of these plastic surgeons.

Real-Life Experience

In order to get permission from mental health professionals and medical doctors to get GPS, many require a real-life experience (RLE) period of at least a year. The purpose of the RLE is to demonstrate that the transsexual can live and work in their congruent gender behavior category. Although the RLE can be waived for particular patients, it is a good idea for transsexuals to do an RLE because many of the problems that they may have after GPS will surface and can be dealt with. RLE is important because GPS is close to being irreversible, and the transsexual should not do it unless they are sure that they can cope with work and social relations.

MTF Transsexual GPS

Transsexual GPS refers to having external genitalia be reshaped to make them more like the sex expected by culture of their gender behavior category. For MTF they desire to have genitalia that look more like female genitalia. Kate Bornstein, transsexual writer, expressed the need for FTM GPS this way:

I never hated my penis; I hated that it made me a man—in my own eyes, and in the eyes of others.

—Kate Bornstein, *Gender Outlaw*[6]

In order to do this, the surgeon repurposes much of the tissue of the male genitalia. MTF GPS works well and the technique is constantly improving. Many medical doctors are unable to distinguish the anatomical results from those of a birth female.

In order to reduce its cost, many MTF transsexuals travel abroad to have the operation done, primarily in Thailand. Thailand has the distinction of being the second leading provider of such operations after Iran. The Thai clinics help their patients with trip planning and making them feel at home. The clinics encourage transsexuals to socialize and make friends with the other transsexuals who are there. Many transsexuals become lifelong friends through this bonding process.

Postoperative care is the responsibility of the MTF transsexual who must regularly dilate her new internal structures to prevent them from narrowing. They should continue to have periodic medical checkups and be on the lookout for any signs of urinary track blockage or infections. They can occur but can usually be treated easily.

The science shows that almost all GPS are successful and contribute to improvements in quality of life for transsexual people, reducing depression and the risk of suicide, and provide better feelings of authenticity. You will see people in the press, politics, or social media trying to make the argument that many transsexuals revert back to their previous gender behavior category, but this is extremely rare, occurring less than 0.3% of the time. They use this argument in an attempt to demonstrate that children and adult transsexuals should not be allowed to live in their congruent gender behavior category or use the restroom associated with that gender. The argument is false; there are very few transsexuals who revert back. However, that does not mean that transsexuals who complete transition will live without problems for the rest of their lives, so counseling should be readily available. Transsexuals still face cultural rejection and social problems even after they are done with transition.

People sometimes attach stigma to being "pre-op" GPS transsexual rather than a "post-op" GPS transsexual. This sometimes occurs even in the transgender community. Increasingly, transsexuals are refusing to talk about their "private parts" because it is irrelevant to their gender and none of other peoples' business.

For MTF transsexuals, about 25% change sexual orientation after completing transition. They become attracted to males. Some who were homosexual before transition will remain attracted to males and by definition become heterosexual. Some stay attracted to females, which technically makes them lesbians. About 10–15% are asexual.

Caitlyn Jenner was caught off guard by questions about her sexual orientation in his TV interview with Diane Sawyer. Caitlyn tried to dodge the question but finally recovered by saying that she was asexual. This made me believe that he (it was his preference to use masculine pronouns in the interview) had learned a little transition science from his mental health professionals. In my case, I have completed transition and remain attracted to females, which makes me a proud lesbian. I recently joined "Lesbians Who Tech" because I am a technologist and a lesbian. I received a warm welcome at the first meeting, even though I did not hide that I was transgender.

FTM Transsexual Transition

Procedures for FTM transsexual transition include:

- Mental health assessment
- Hormone therapy
- Top surgery (Mastectomy)
- Masculinization surgery
- Real-Life Experience
- Voice therapy
- Transsexual GPS

Each of these will be described, in turn, in the next section.

Mental Health Assessment

Just as with MTF transsexuals, it is advisable for FTM before starting transsexual transition to get a mental health assessment from a qualified psychologist, psychiatrist, or social worker. It is important to establish a relationship with the mental health professional because a person needs to have support readily available to help deal with all sorts of problems, which accompany any big change. A professional, with your permission, can also explain and help family and others affected by the change. For some procedures, a permission letter is necessary either because WPATH requires it or because a prospective doctor or surgeon requires it. It is best if the transsexual establishes a prior relationship with the mental health professional so that they will be able to respond to the needs of the transsexual.

The mental health professional has a duty under WPATH guidelines to be sure that some mental health or other problem will not interfere with transition. This may not preclude proceeding with transition, but any such problem needs to be recognized and dealt with.

The mental health professional can act as a guide to the transsexual and can provide a sounding board to discuss transition procedures. So it is important that the professional have knowledge and experience in dealing with transsexual transition. The professional should be knowledgeable about local facilities that transsexual people need like transgender-friendly barbers, endocrinologists, dermatologists, and clothiers. There actually are a few custom tailors who cater to FTM transgender people like Bindle and Keep in New York City and Zuit Suit in Atlanta. By providing such information, the professional is engaged in what is called "patient management." Before embarking on transition, the professional and the transsexual should develop a plan for making sequential decisions about transition procedures. The plan does not have to be followed precisely but it is a place to start.

Of critical importance is discussion of how the transsexual will make a social transition and begin to increase their time publically expressing behaviors in their congruent gender behavior category. This will not be a problem for those who are already "going full time." Public exposure of the gender presentation of FTM should be increased gradually.

Hormone Therapy

Hormone therapy for MTF transsexuals involves administration of sex hormones, primarily testosterone to masculinize the body by changing its sex organs. You may hear this referred to as "hormone replacement therapy" or HRT but that term is a misnomer. WPATH guidelines simply refer to "hormone therapy" or HT. There actually is such a thing as HRT for males. It is actually a treatment procedure in which testosterone is not being secreted in sufficient levels and is augmented. For example, it is sometimes used in those males who have had traumatic loss of their testes. Transsexuals do not receive HRT; they receive hormone therapy or HT because the sex hormones they receive are those that would typically be very low in birth females. Birth females do have a little testosterone, but it is made by the adrenal glands, not by sex organs. So for FTM transsexuals, there is no hormone loss to "replace."

MTF HT is not completely reversible, but it is usually the first procedure in FTM transition because it is more reversible than some other transition FTM transgender procedures. In fact, some FTM have actually conceived and delivered children by temporarily stopping HT, when they had not received transsexual GPS.

Endocrinologists vary in exactly what drugs and dosages they prescribe, depending on their clinical experience and the needs of the patient. Guidelines for use of the drugs are provided by WPATH and the Endocrine Society. The drug usually prescribed is testosterone cypionate, which is usually administered by injection into a muscle. The typical dose is 5–100mg every two weeks. There are many other injectable testosterone drugs, and there are gels and gel patches generally applied to the legs and armpits. There are no reports about their use in FTM HT. You probably have seen commercials to sell the gels to "men with low T." Mostly these commercials are used for actual HRT in non-transsexual people who have low testosterone for some reason. For a time, I actually took testosterone by gel patch when I was trying to cure myself of being transgender. Some of the patches burned my thighs and the skin still gets irritated from time to time. (It did not cure me.)

FTM transmen tend to have higher testosterone blood levels than birth females before HT begins, so the endocrinologist should perform blood tests before giving testosterone to get a baseline. There are several possible explanations for this, including individual differences, do-it-yourself administration, a medical condition called polycystic ovary syndrome, and stress. If pre-HT testosterone is elevated, the physician should pursue all three of these explanations. The physician may decide to start with a lower dose.

Many physicians miss the diagnosis of **polycystic ovary syndrome** (**PCOS**), which is a relatively common (5–10%) genetic disease of females. It results in the ovaries secreting testosterone into the blood stream at unusually high levels for birth females. There is no cure for PCOS but it can be treated, and if the FTM transsexual has it, they need to be monitored and testosterone dosage carefully controlled.

Stress results in release of testosterone from the adrenal glands, so elevated levels could be caused by psychological or physical stress. If stress is the problem, then the FTM needs to explore this with their counselor.

The effects of FTM HT are the following:

- Permanent voice change
- Permanent male pattern scalp hair loss
- Beard/body hair increase
- Increased muscle mass and strength
- Increased libido
- Cessation of menstruation
- Protection against osteoporosis

Of these effects, the first two are irreversible, while the others will decline if HT is stopped. Testosterone changes the shape of the voice box for FTM, just like it does for birth males who go through puberty. Sometimes, endocrinologists give oral finasteride to FTM with male pattern baldness or topical minoxydil/finasteride.

Risks of FTM HT are the following:

- Increased red blood cells
- Weight gain
- Acne
- Sleep apnea

These risks do not pose severe problems if the FTM transman is carefully monitored. Elevated red blood cell (RBC) counts can easily be detected and they can be treated. The FTM should be aware of the symptoms of elevated RBC, which are shortness of breath and skin itching after baths or showers. Sleep apnea may also occur which involves disruption of breathing and therefore sleep. This can be diagnosed in sleep studies and treated with a CPAP device that maintains external positive air pressure.

There is evidence that at least 40% of FTM change their sexual orientation after HT begins. Those that change become attracted to females, making these FTMs heterosexual by definition. It is not clear whether the HT drives the change or whether the FTMs were oriented toward females to begin with.

Top Surgery (Mastectomy)

After HT starts, FTM start to schedule themselves to have their breasts removed and plastic surgery performed, called **top surgery**. This is important for FTM because they want to have male-looking chests. Until surgery, they are forced to wear breast binders that compress the breasts and are extremely uncomfortable. The procedure is actually one that is well understood because many aging males develop breast tissue because their testosterone levels decline. This condition is known as **gynecomastia**, and the operation to reduce breast size and make the chest look male is fairly common.

Masculinization Surgery

Just as MTF alter their appearance through plastic surgery to become more feminine, some FTM have **facial masculinization surgery** to make their faces look more masculine. But many FTM avoid such surgeries simply by growing facial hair.

Real-Life Experience

Prior to FTM GPS, many providers recommend that the FTM have a year-long real-life experience (RLE) to demonstrate and build confidence that they can work and live in their congruent gender behavior category. This should not be a problem for FTM because they typically have already completed a social transition. The adjustment to RLE also may not be easier because culture allows females to dress and present in masculine clothing and because of HT, the FTM transsexuals may already have grown facial hair and have a masculine voice.

Voice Therapy

Although HT will lower the pitch of FTM voices, it will not erase speaking habits of inflection, word choice, and timber. For this reason, some FTM get voice therapy, but it is not as popular for FTM than MTF.

Transsexual GPS

Many FTM have their ovaries and Fallopian tubes removed, but only 40% have transsexual GPS performed on their external genitalia. This is probably due to dissatisfaction with the results of current procedures, although they are improving rapidly. It is not now possible to construct a fully functioning penis, although cosmetically some look very male-like. As we indicated in the introduction, one penile transplant has already been successful and the U.S. military is planning to conduct 60 more for male wounded warriors as soon as their technique can be perfected. It is not clear whether the plastic surgery or the penile transplant approach will win out, but it is good that both are in the pipeline.

Risks for FTM and MTF Transitioners

MTF mortality risk for transitioners has been greatly reduced by the substitution of estradiol valerate for ethinyl estradiol, which had increased the risk of blood clots and sudden death. Studies have found that mortality risk for MTF and FTM transitioners is the same as for other people, but in the past the risk for MTF from ethinyl estradiol was 6–8% higher than natal females. Some studies have found a small increase in mortality for both MTF and FTM transsexuals due to suicide, drug overdose, and HIV/AIDS. This increase is not believed to be due to the physiological effects of FTM transition procedures. It is clear that transsexual transition does not cure all of the problems that transsexuals experience, so it is important that they have counseling available even after the end of transition.

Transition and GPS Regret

You have probably already read or heard from critics of transgender people that transsexual transition regret is common. Nothing could be further from the truth. They are using one study, taken out of context. The vast number of studies report no or very little transsexual transition regret and general satisfaction with HT. Taken together, the reports indicate that less than 1.3% of transsexuals experience regret and that percentage is declining. The conclusion is that transsexual transition is an effective treatment that improves the well-being of the transsexual. But transsexual transition will not solve all social or medical problems, so it is clear that transsexuals have ready access to their counselors.

NOTES

1. Jennifer Finney Boylan, *She's Not There: A Life in Two Genders* (New York: Broadway Books, 2013), 70.

2. Lee Etscovitz, 1985 Renaissance Education Association, May 8, 1985, cited in Transgender Forum.

3. Jennifer Finney Boylan, *Stuck in the Middle with You: A Memoir of Parenting in Three Genders* (New York: Broadway Books, 2014), as quoted in Goodreads quotes, https://www.goodreads.com/author/quotes/30973.Jennifer_Finney_Boylan (confirmed May 19, 2016).

4. Jan Morris, *Conundrum* (New York: Harcourt, 1974), 114.

5. Ibid., 52.

6. Kate Bornstein, *Gender Outlaw* (New York: Vintage, 1995), 47.

CHAPTER 7

Coping with Transgender Issues

INTRODUCTION

I obtained a "D" class soccer-coaching license by virtue of a training course I took in order to coach my children's teams. The person who taught the course was John Ellis who had played in top English leagues and coached some national teams before coming to the United States. Not to name-drop but John's daughter is Jill Ellis who is the current coach of the U.S. woman's team that just won the World Cup, the most prestigious soccer tournament in the world. To get to the point, John never told players what to do, unlike so many "mechanical" coaches in the United States who did not really understand the game. His approach to improve a player was to make suggestions in techniques or tactics, which he told them that they were free to use or not. All he asked from them was to try the suggestions in practice and games. His goal was to allow players to make their own decisions. To do otherwise stifled their creativity in solving problems. Soccer presents players with unique problems, because the game has many moving players and parts, which require creativity. Although some try, the game of soccer is too immediate and too fluid for coaches to micromanage.

So it is with this chapter. I will try to provide some suggestions on how to handle frequent transgender social situations. If you are transgender, it is up to you to use the suggestions you find valuable. I will not be there to coach you from the sidelines. You may be able to find better solutions than I have suggested. And that is how it should be. Figuring out how to get through adverse situations by yourself will make you a stronger person. If you are a transgender ally or just interested in being transgender, the suggestions will provide some insight into what it is like to be transgender. You might also use some of the suggestions in your own life to deal with stressful situations.

This chapter presents situations and solutions that are prioritized according to their importance for things like keeping transgender people alive and getting along with non-transgender people.

COPING STRATEGIES

Transgender people face many situations that are psychologically and physically stressful. The situations vary with regard to the potential for physical damage, but a transgender person needs to practice **active coping strategies** in order to protect themselves from psychological harm at the time and heal themselves thereafter.

Transgender people should learn to use active coping strategies to deal with stressful situations. Such coping strategies are taught to those in the military and others who have to deal with stress and trauma. These active coping strategies are not new, and they are certainly not just for the weak. For example, the ancient **Zen Warriors** and **Samurai** practiced relaxation techniques that allowed them to cope with the stress of battle in order to make good tactical decisions. Similarly, when I was a male athlete, my college football coach always told us to find a quiet place inside your head to keep poised during a game.

Studies showed that the most resilient U.S. Special Forces soldiers were found to naturally use some of these coping strategies without even being trained on them. The strenuous Special Forces selection and training process must have weeded those out who did not have coping strategies. People in civilian life have found that yoga and meditation classes help them relieve stress. It has only been in the past few years that the effects of psychological stress have been recognized and dealt with. Unfortunately, this recent improvement in stress resilience research was due to the increased frequency of psychological injuries of returning soldiers from recent wars. Many had been saved from physical harm by modern medical trauma treatment but later suffered from posttraumatic stress syndrome. This has recently also been recognized in civilians who suffer from psychological damage due to the stress of disasters or crimes. Such strategies have been found to provide the means for people to have power over their stressful experiences and feel less helpless.

Because they experience culturally sanctioned rejection, almost all transgender people experience stressful situations. The two primary techniques that transgender people can use to protect and heal themselves are (1) relaxation response and (2) positive interpretation of events. A lot is known about them, but we will only cover the basics in this book. You can learn about them in more detail from the Veterans Administration website[1] and there is even an app for learning and self-coaching at http://www.ptsd.va.gov/public/materials/apps/PTSDCoach.asp.

The **relaxation response** must be practiced so that a transgender person can voluntarily relax in the presence of stress. That does not mean that you will fall asleep when stressful events occur, but it does mean that you can relax your body to more effectively deal with the situation. Getting "uptight" interferes with performance. Relaxation practice can take many forms: yoga, meditation, biofeedback, and certain Lamaze techniques. A transgender person does not need to take classes or have a teacher, although it does not hurt to do so. Just try getting into a relaxed position and tensing one muscle after another and remember that relaxing feeling once the tension is removed. Do this all over your body to relax every muscle, and you will start to experience the relaxation response. A transgender person should practice until they can automatically relax in the face of stress. (Actually all people should do this.) Being relaxed does not mean that you ignore the situation or that you are not active. It simply means that you can more easily call on the right actions and thoughts when your mind is calm.

Positive interpretation of events is a little trickier than the relaxation response because it is not as visible and occurs in your thinking and verbalizations. But you will feel better if you practice it. The idea is that events only have the meaning that you give them. So why not give them a positive interpretation that will serve you and avoid stress? Many people, including transgender people, fall into the trap of negative interpretation. If they are confronted with a stressful event, they will assume the worst, known as "awfulizing." Just like Chicken Little, they assume that "the sky is falling" when they do not need to do so. That sets off an emotional reaction that may cause psychological harm and interfere with mental and physical performance.

Like relaxation, positive interpretation requires daily practice. Practice interpreting events in a positive way. If a tree falls, think to yourself that the tree cannot fall anymore, so no one will be hurt in the future by it. If a transgender person gets a catcall saying that they are beautiful, they do not need to interpret it as a microassault; they can interpret it as "maybe I am beautiful." This does not mean that a transgender person should not take action to remove themselves from the hostile situations or report a criminal offender. Positive interpretation is an attempt to reduce toxic negative emotions that can cause damage. Make jokes about stressful events, "Gee, that guy is really insecure in his gender." It also helps to share your positive interpretations with friends and counselors, because it gives a transgender person more practice in verbalizing positive reinterpretations.

I practice both relaxation and positive interpretation in the face of stressful events, but I probably need more relaxation practice than I get. I picked up these techniques and understood their importance in somewhat random professional and life events. I was surprised that my college football coach would talk about relaxing in order to maintain performance in a game. He talked about getting into a mindset that was calm while engaging in violent sport. And he actually used the word "poise," which until that time I had only associated with femininity. Another event was going through Lamaze class relaxation techniques, which husbands learn as well as the pregnant ladies. I have used these techniques particularly to relax on rough airplane trips. I get my focal point somewhere on the plane and go through relaxation processes. At one point in my career, I was studying methods of pain relief when I learned that relaxation actually raises the pain threshold and can be used therapeutically. It also helps whenever someone experiences pain from physical trauma. I learned positive interpretation from an Esalen-like course that I took, which was my one and only excursion into humanistic psychology. Awfulizing will actually make things worse. At another point in my career, I had the opportunity to study stress and posttraumatic stress for the U.S. Army. I developed a theory of stress and stress resilience that explains how memories of traumatic events can be reduced by relaxation during recall.

Since I am transgender, I have had to use my knowledge of these techniques to deal with rejection, either from catcalls or denial of using the ladies restroom or driving to support groups. Fortunately, I have not encountered extremely stressful situations like being physically attacked, but I attribute that to careful planning to avoid such situations. I will also share that knowledge later in this chapter in "Violence" section.

SUICIDE

The attempted suicide rate for transgender people is around 40%, whereas the population rate is about 1.3%. Suicide is a major problem among transgender people. It happens mostly in teenage and young adult years, when the suicide rate is the highest for non-transgender people as well. The actual rate may be higher because sometimes we do not always know the reason for attempted or actual suicides.

If you or someone you know think(s) about suicide, get help immediately. You can call 911 or various helplines such as:

- Transgender Lifeline in the United States: 877-565-8860
- Transgender Lifeline Canada: 877-330-6366

- The Trevor Project LGBTQ Hotline: 866-488-7386
- The National (U.S.) Suicide Prevention Hotline: 800-273-8255

Call 911. There are various suicide hotlines at the state and city level, but the 911 operators will know all about them.

The Trevor Project also supports text help: Text the word "Trevor" to 202-304-1200.

The National Suicide Prevention Hotline also supports chat at http://www.suicidepreventionlifeline.org/gethelp/lifelinechat.aspx.

In the United Kingdom, the emergency numbers are 999 and 112. The Samaritan helpline numbers are:

- +44 (0) 8457 90 90 90 (United Kingdom—local rate)
- +44 (0) 8457 90 91 92 (U.K. minicom)
- 1850 60 90 90 (Republic of Ireland (ROI)—local rate)
- 1850 60 90 91 (ROI minicom).

According to the Trevor Project, the telltale signs of potential suicide are:

Do you or someone you know . . .?

- Not care about their future: "It won't matter soon anyway."
- Put themselves down—and think they deserve it: "I don't deserve to live. I suck."
- Express hopelessness: "Things will never get better for me."
- Say goodbye to important people: "You're the best friend I've ever had. I'll miss you."
- Have a specific plan for suicide: "I've thought about how I'd do it."
- Talk about feeling suicidal: "Life is so hard. Lately I've felt like ending it all."

Have you or someone you know been . . .?

- Using drugs or alcohol more than usual
- Acting differently than usual
- Giving away their most valuable possessions
- Losing interest in their favorite things to do
- Admiring people who have died by suicide
- Planning for death by writing a will or letter
- Eating or sleeping more or less than usual
- Feeling more sick, tired or achy than usual

It goes without saying that transgender people should not attempt suicide. Transgender allies <u>should first try listening</u>. Listening is sometimes all it takes to get the person who is thinking about suicide to delay or not to do it. Causing delay may be enough until the professionals arrive or get on the phone line. If you need to talk, try to summarize what the potential suicide victim just said. That is a common trick among mental health professionals to keep a person talking. Do not attempt to contradict their expressions of how they feel but instead try to echo the person's thoughts.

Reasoning arguments may not always prevent transgender people from committing suicide, but here are some reasons that may have an impact:

- Help is available almost anywhere anytime and the people who answer the phone are understanding and will help you.
- A transgender person may think they are alone but they are not. Both transgender people and providers are there for them. Many transgender people have been there and know all about it.
- Getting through this time in your life, although stressful, will make you, a transgender person, stronger. If a transgender person can figure out how to avoid attempting suicide, they can get through almost anything. After this, nothing will seem as stressful or hard.
- Things are getting better. More people tolerate and accept transgender people than ever before. With the push to train providers, more people will understand being transgender. With transgender people becoming more visible, more people will find out that being transgender is nothing to be feared or hated. Soon everyone will know a transgender person and that is how things get better. And things will get better for transgender people as they mature.
- A transgender person who commits suicide deprives the remaining human beings of their presence and their talents. There are transgender people who have accomplished great feats in science and the humanities. Who knows what you will do?
- A transgender person who commits suicide injures those around them. A transgender person should not use suicide in retaliation for rejection by family or community. (When I thought about suicide, this was the argument I used to talk myself out of it.)
- A transgender person who commits suicide misses out on all the good things in their future. Sure, life is full of bad things but they can be overcome. Death cannot.
- Some transgender person might attempt to commit suicide as a means of getting attention. There are lots of better, less dangerous ways to get

attention. And there is always the possibility that you will succeed in maiming or killing yourself.

- Everyone does not experience what a transgender person does. A transgender person has unique insights into what gender is and can see what it is like to live in both genders. The Native American Two-Spirits were valued for just this insight, which allowed them to be tribal leaders.
- Most religions discourage suicide and if a transgender person believes in one of those religions, they are violating their own beliefs.

VIOLENCE

We defined various types of violence that transgender people experience in Chapter 4. In this section, I am going to provide some suggestions for dealing with these verbal and physical forms of physical rejection.

Microassaults involve small verbal and non-physical acts that injure transgender people because of the threat of physical violence and the negative information that they carry. Microassaults are not unique to transgender people, at least 57% of women and 25% of men report being verbally harassed on the street. Microassaults also occur in public places such as shopping centers and schools.

Although microassaults may seem petty, they actually cause physical and mental injury, particularly if they are frequent. They cause rises in blood pressure and release of adrenaline and stress hormones. They subject the body to mental stress, which can cause depression and anger. All these effects can lead to posttraumatic stress syndrome in which uncontrolled emotions can reoccur at a later time. Transgender people are subject to some of the same sorts of microaggressions as non-transgender people, but transgender people are also subject to the microaggression of misgendering.

The best way to deal with microassaults is to avoid them. Transgender people typically know who and where the likely microassaults will come from. Word gets around. If a person never experiences a particular microassault, then it cannot hurt them.

If avoidance is not possible, I suggest that a transgender person should try to ignore the microassault. They should not let on that they have heard the "catcall" or insult because it may encourage the perpetrator. Wearing earphones or looking like you are having a telephone sometimes helps "sell" the idea that you did not hear the insult. Hopefully the perpetrator will get tired of hurling "catcalls" or insults and stop.

However, there are times, particularly when the perpetrator is close by or follows a transgender person, when communication is necessary. This situation calls for direct communications like "Please stop that." However, transgender people should not allow themselves to get into an argument. Sometimes a disarming or humorous comment works to fend attackers off but those are gambles. Best suggestion is to move to get out of the situation with safety. This is where your relaxation response training is particularly important to help you make decisions about what to do. As for the application of positive interpretation, just feel good "that you are not the ignorant person who just catcalled you" or "they must lead a boring life if they have to do this" or "at least they noticed me and I do look good."

I was walking with a girlfriend in a public market. I had on a pretty red pair of capris and beautiful paisley blouse, which was purple and red. It looked like about 200 little peacock feather trains. Most of the people were friendly but there were some workmen taking a lunch break sitting along our way. One of them said to me, "Hey, baby. That's a pretty shirt." I said the first thing that came to mind which was "Yes, I think this blouse is pretty, I like it a lot." We moved on into the market and I did not realize it until my friend had said something but my pace had quickened in fear. You cannot totally control your feelings but after she told me, I managed to slow down, calm down, and enjoy the rest of the day.

Most of the catcalls and insults in public are aimed at women. Some people think that this is a result of the evolution of gender resulting from sex differences, but as we discussed in Chapter 4, this theory is flawed. It is more likely that these insults are attempts at domination and behavior control through verbal bullying. As a result of these microaggressions, women have developed a large repertoire of things to say in reply. But none of them seem to stop the abuse.

Now the test of whether you really can use the relaxation reflex during microaggressions is whether you can remember the details of what the person looked like, what they said, and for whom they were working. (I flunked this test in the previous example in the marketplace.) The reason you want to be able to do this is to report the perpetrator either to the police, to their employers, or to whoever owns the public space (e.g., shopping mall). Assault and sexual harassment are illegal in the United States. If workers engage in sexual harassment, their employers are legally responsible and can be penalized as well as the worker. It does not matter what organization a person works for or what your business relationship is with them if any, they are still subject to the law.

Bullying may involve both non-physical microassaults as well as microbatteries. Although people have known about bullying for a long time, scientific study of bullying did not begin until the 1980s in Europe. Workplace bullying was studied first, followed by school bullying around 2000. Bullying also takes place in cyberspace with direct as well as indirect microassaults. Direct assaults may involve personal attacks or transmitting messages designed to upset the recipient, known as "trolling." Indirect microassaults involve family and friends of a person. We now know that bullying contributes to transgender as well as non-transgender suicide attempts.

Workplace bullying, including the bullying of transgender people, is illegal according to U.S. law and legal opinions issued by the Department of Justice. Yet it still persists despite widespread workplace training. In most cases of workplace bullying, job discrimination is involved, which also violates civil rights in workplace laws.

So, what are some suggestions for the transgender worker or any worker to deal with workplace bullying?

First, a transgender person should document every incident they can as soon as possible after they are safe and totally calmed down. The who, what, when, where, and how list should work.

Second, a transgender person should go about their work as they would normally because they do not want to give management an excuse to fire them. The violated person may have to take a sick day off to collect their thoughts and chill out. Most bullied people do need some time away before reporting the bullying. You should use that day off to develop an argument in dollars and cents how much the bully will ultimately cost the company in dollars. Include the expenses of rehiring, retraining, and medical injury treatment. As a rule of thumb, it costs an employer at least 150% of an employee's annual salary if they have to get rid of an employee and rehire and retrain a new employee.

Third, a transgender person should never use physical violence against a bully at work. It may be grounds for disciplinary action or dismissal, and there is a tendency to blame the bullied victim.

Fourth, start looking for another job. Decide whether you intend to leave the business or not. After a person is targeted by a bully on the job, two-thirds of the time they will be laid off, fired, or leave, regardless of whether they report the bullying or not.

Fifth, a transgender person must report the bullying to the human resources or personnel office. Bullying can have some long-term medical effects, which will prevent a person from maintaining a job at all. A transgender person cannot risk that. If the human resources department will not take action, then report it to the highest ranking person you can, preferably, and officer of the corporation. They have a legal responsibility to act. Make the business argument that the bully is costing the business money. Tell them if you intend to leave or not. If you are leaving, tell them that you are reporting the bullying because other people may be bullied by the same person in the future.

Fifth, consider consulting an attorney who is expert in workplace and employment law and tolerates transgender people.

School bullying in the United States remains a tough problem in spite of large-scale anti-bullying programs. Such programs originally involved the training of teachers and administrators that increased awareness. However, bullying actually increased due to these programs as shown by studies in 2012 and 2013. It appeared that the anti-bullying training given to students and teachers actually resulted in better-trained bullies, not in elimination of bullying. The results of these studies indicated that some changes in strategy were needed. The results indicated that efforts should be redirected toward improving the school environment, rather than targeting bullying per se. The results also indicated expansion of training from students, teachers, and administrators to include school bus drivers, janitors, secretarial staff, and all professionals. We are still awaiting studies to see if this approach works. A transgender person should cooperate with anti-bullying campaigns but not depend on them. Sometimes these campaigns have an anonymous reporting mechanism that can be of value.

More recently in 2014, educators in Finland have had success with anti-bullying programs in which the emphasis was placed on training peer bystanders how to intervene in bullying situations. That is, training students how to talk to both the student bully and their victim before, during, and after an incident. They found a significant decrease in bullying. This result is consistent with numerous psychology studies of bystander behavior, indicating that bystanders will hesitate to intervene in emergencies unless they are trained. When I was in graduate school, the psychology professors were running bystander studies. Several of my fellow students spent their time simulating emergencies in the basement by blowing smoke into conference rooms full of study participants to fake a fire or by faking electrocutions over closed-circuit television. It was surprising but with groups of college students, usually no one would report such emergencies or attempt to aid the "victims." A room could be filled with smoke with zero visibility, but they did nothing. But when they started testing groups from the public at large, they found something interesting. They found that certain participants were "screwing up" the results by reporting emergencies when other bystanders would hesitate. It turned out that these participants were people like ship captains, firemen, and police who had been trained to act in times of emergencies.

So what are some suggestions for dealing with bullying? First is to avoid contact with bullies, if you can. Second, after you use your relaxation response to calm down from an episode, write down some notes. The who, what, when, where, and how should work. You will need them for reporting the bully. When you make the report, you will be stressed, so it is best to have a written record to help yourself.

Third, the old advice about assaulting a bully is bad advice because, among other things, it teaches the bully that you accept violence. Teachers and administrators who are not sympathetic to transgender people may very well punish a transgender student, rather than the bully if the transgender person gets into a fight. Victim blaming is often involved in bullying incidents, and commission of microbatteries or violence will reinforce this tendency. In short, beating up the bully will not solve anything.

Fourth, know that anti-bullying campaigns are still struggling to find the right strategies, and a transgender person cannot yet rely on them to be effective.

Fifth, bystander behavior is important. Transgender people should try to change bystander behavior through school organizations and building a social network. Many schools have gay-straight alliances, which are groups that include GLBT students to discuss such issues as bullying. Some students have also had success by networking and forming new friendships. The goal is to put social pressure on bullies through their friends who now know transgender students are nice people too.

There are severe acts of assault and battery that rise to the level of criminal activity, either misdemeanors or, if more severe, felonies. These assaults may cause trauma resulting in bloodshed, broken bones, concussion, rape, or loss of life. If a transgender person is afraid that they might be attacked, they may consider going to self-defense school. I do not want to discourage a transgender person or any person from doing that, but here are some fundamental suggestions that any good self-defense school will tell you, whether they teach martial arts, woman self-defense, karate, Krav Maga, judo, or some other discipline:

- Plan not to be in the environment where such violence is likely.
- Plan your movements to avoid unlit areas at night and isolated places.
- Be cautious about who you are with; many acts of violence are committed by dates, friends, or coworkers.
- Put your purse on your shoulder, not across your body.
- Take out your car keys well in advance before reaching your car.
- Be aware of your surroundings, particularly at night.

- If attacked, and you can get away safely, run.
- Do not threaten the attacker with pepper spray, gun, or other weapon.
- If the attacker wants to rob you, give them what they ask for.
- If the attacker tries to hit you or injure you, make plenty of noise and use the techniques that the self-defense school taught you. If you have not been to self-defense school, punch or kick anything you think is sensitive on the attacker's body.
- If the attacker leaves, make plenty of noise and call 911.

We will discuss each of these in turn.

Avoidance of dangerous areas and situations is the first priority, although a transgender person cannot always do this. Many transgender people often live in poorer neighborhoods in which crime is frequent. If you cannot avoid an area, make some plans regarding safe areas to park and locate escape routes. If you are going into a new area, use one of the online mapping tools to do what soldiers call a "map reconnaissance" to plan how to avoid dangerous situations. Be especially wary of unlit and isolated areas at night. Although I trust the organizers of my support groups and meet-ups, I always research the environment in advance. I will not go to a gathering if I am concerned about my safety. Although most of Atlanta is generally an island of tolerance and acceptance, one does not have to go far to find prejudice and violence.

Be careful of elevators and confined spaces. If you are uncomfortable with who is already in the elevator, get out and wait for the next one. I had a transwoman friend in Washington who by day presented as a woman at her business and at the university where she taught software development. By night she was a loving masculine father with a wife and two children. Her situation was a bit of a reversal from the usual transgender situation. One day she had some work at the Pentagon and boarded an elevator with a young officer who proceeded to try to embrace and kiss her. Boy did he have a surprise coming! But try not to get into such situations.

Be cautious about who you hang out with. It is best to be in a group, rather than with just one companion. Even if you think you know them well, many cases of assault, particularly sexual assault, are done by people you know, whether they are individual dates, friends, or coworkers.

Transwomen should put their shoulder bag over their shoulder as all women should, not across their bodies. In many cases, purse straps are surprisingly strong, and if someone attempts to snatch your purse, you will be dragged along with your purse and be hurt. Take as little of value with you in your purse, and do not fight if someone tries to take it. Transpeople should be careful about telling people they are transgender in public places like bars and clubs. Some people prey on transpeople, and there is no need to advertise.

It is important to take out your keys in advance of getting to your car for three reasons: (1) you do not want to be fumbling around at your car so that someone can launch a surprise attack; (2) keys can be good personal defense weapons; and (3) key rings make good locations for whistles and other noisemakers.

Be aware of your surroundings, people approaching, and the next escape route. The military calls this "situation awareness." I made the mistake one night of going to a meeting site in a dangerous area of Washington, DC. I was dressed *en femme* and was walking back to my car in my highest heels when I became aware that I was being shadowed. I crossed the street to avoid him; he crossed the street to my side. The maneuvers were repeated. The third time I crossed, I used my military command voice and yelled at him, "Leave me alone." He was so surprised that he turned around and fled in the opposite direction. Transwomen prefer to use their feminine voices, but there are times when a loud commanding voice is useful.

Although self-defense courses teach physical means of protection, most of them teach that the first line of defense is to get away from the scene. A fight that never happens is a fight won. As Mr. Han, a martial arts instructor in the *Karate Kid* movie, said, "The best fights are the ones we avoid."

When I go to night meetings, I usually take a tote bag for my shoes. Going to and coming from the meeting, I wear my unfashionable running shoes but while at the meeting there I put on my heels. It is more comfortable that way and safer too, in case I need to move quickly to avoid an attacker.

There are many weapons sold in the name of self-protection, but unless a transgender person is practiced in using them, they are more likely to be used on the transgender victim than on the attacker. It is one thing to shoot at a gun range, quite another to struggle with an attacker over a gun in your pocket or purse. Having a gun around also provides an easy method of suicide to which transgender people are especially susceptible. Remember that about 40% of transgender people attempt it and one of them may be a friend who can get momentary access to your gun.

If a potential attacker wants to rob you, give them what they ask for. Whatever you give them, it is not worth your health. Try to minimize what you take with you, if possible. I live in a relatively safe neighborhood in Midtown Atlanta, but even in broad daylight, there are robbers who specialize in muggings for things like smartphones. Although I usually carry a phone on my walks through the neighborhood, if they ask for my phone I will readily give it to them, rather than fight over it. Besides, I can always go to my computer and track or disable the phone through the Internet.

If you are physically attacked, make as much noise as you can. Use your whistle, noisemaker, and special app on your cell phone. Some of these noise-making devices can reach the level of painful noise, and you can leave them behind if you decide to flee. If you cannot get away and have to defend yourself, use the techniques you learned in self-defense school. If you did not go to self-defense school, just try to hit every sensitive area on the attacker's body. Use whatever is in the environment as a weapon: fire extinguishers, garden hoses, or trashcans. Try to get separation from your attacker as soon as possible and leave the scene. Remember your relaxation response; it will help you to decide what to do.

After you drive your attacker away, continue making noise and call the police or get someone else to do so. Do not pursue the attacker. Get medical help even if you do not think you need it. Many injuries show up later when you are not juiced up on adrenaline and stress hormones.

When the police come, know that most policemen are more professional now in their treatment of transgender people because it makes their job easier. Many are now trained to ask what pronouns to use and to tolerate transgender people in order to get the information they need to do their jobs. But many policemen only know about transgender people from the transgender prostitutes they encounter. Some are still suspicious of transgender people and assume that they are the instigators and not the victims. They may arrest the transgender person, rather than pursuing the attacker. Stories about improper arrests are true. Some really bad apples regard getting sexual favors from transgender prostitutes as a side benefit of their jobs and use coercion and force to get these "benefits." They may sexually attack transgender people even if they are not prostitutes. Although police training about being transgender is improving, it is still not uniform throughout the United States. It is best to have a witness when you talk to the police. The only real long-term defense from police harassment is community action and culture change.

In the outskirts of Atlanta is a small town where tales of police harassment and sexual assault began to be recognized. A community action group approached the mayor and city council and picketed city hall, until they did something about the police misconduct. The city now has official procedures for dealing with GLBT people and the police received training. The bad apples were fired. The mayor has apologized. Not to say that it would not happen in the future, but the community group remains vigilant. I last saw the group on television picketing the same city hall because a prosecutor had repeatedly misgendered and harassed a transgender defendant in traffic court. We will see how they do.

SECRECY

I was in the closet as a transwoman for over 40 years, so I have some suggestions on how to survive in secrecy, although I encourage transgender people to come out as much as possible for the sake of their own health and well-being. I had some unintentional help along the way, because I worked for various military and intelligence agencies for which secrecy was paramount. I learned some techniques from them that I ironically used against them in order to preserve my privacy as a transwoman. I was never a spy, but I did learn some spycraft.

The two principles of keeping secrets that I followed are <u>denial</u> and <u>deception</u>. Denial meant preventing others from knowing that I was transgender by crossdressing in private, by crossdressing anonymously in public, or by limiting the number of people who knew. Deception involved making people believe that I was a masculine, all-American boy, and therefore a man, so they would not even suspect that I was transgender.

For me, denial started after I told my mother that I was a girl at age 4 and she vigorously rejected it. Not wanting to be on the wrong side of my mother and an embarrassment to the family, I started crossdressing in private and did so for many years. Denial of the information from my family that I was doing this was difficult at first because I was using my mother's clothing and we lived in a small house. My parents trusted me to be alone, so they would go run errands without me. When I was alone in the house, the crossdressing started. First suggestion to transgender people when you are in this sort of situation is to complete the crossdressing and makeup session on time. I used to use an alarm clock to tell me when it was time to clean up and put things back. Second suggestion is to always put everything back in the same place before your parents get back home. This is a skill that Bruce Jenner, now Caitlyn Jenner, knew to master:

> I marked the closet so when I put it back (the dress); I could put it all back, everything back, so I wouldn't get caught.
> —*Bruce Jenner: The Interview*, ABC, 2015[2]

When I was old enough to buy or steal women's clothing, I had to hide it from my parents and later my wife. My wife was not my size, so I had to steal clothing from my mother when I visited her. She did not seem to miss it.

In this case, finding a hiding place for the clothes was important. At first, I would hide the clothes in a box of discarded clothes, but when I had acquired too many, I hid the clothing in a box that I put in the attic. (By the way, do not steal clothing from a store because of embarrassment; most stores do not care whether the clothes match your gender and are glad to get the sale.)

Taking makeup off used to be more of a problem than it is now. Back then, everything was sold with its distinctive smell but today most makeup is odorless, a tribute to FDA safety standards that got rid of some unsafe chemicals. It was also due to concern by users that all the smells would conflict with one another or cause allergies. I had to use cold cream and scrub to get it all off. The point of this is that a transgender person living in secret has to deny trances of being transgender to not only the visual sense but also all five senses.

Denial of information that I had a set of women's clothing became a problem when I was a working adult and had a family. I had a second bag that I took on business trips, which contained clothing, makeup, and a wig. A transgender person living in secrecy has to resolve to themselves that in case of imminent discovery, they must be prepared to throw everything away. They also need to throw away clothing that does not fit in the suitcase or storage container. Dumping clothing and makeup in this way is painful, but that is the price you pay for denial.

The principle of deception as applied to being a closeted transgender person is that one has to put on a convincing show that one is following the gender behavior category assigned at birth. In the intelligence and military world, this is known as creating a **"cover story."** In order to form a cover story, a transgender person has to learn the expectations for a gender behavior category. Although I abhorred masculine behavior, I studied it in great detail. To be effective, a cover story has to have a germ of truth in it. The germ of truth in my cover story was that I was pretty good in solving puzzles, which led to my involvement in military technology and to understanding the strategy and tactics of athletics and the military. I actually make a living developing military technology, although I would have rather done something else.

My cover story included playing football in junior high school, high school, and college and volunteering for the military once I got to college. Our college military unit practiced mountain and winter warfare, which made the story even better. I became a "student of the game" and learned all that I could about being masculine in warfare. I cultivated what is known as a "command" voice for drill and learned to shout orders. And my mother was so proud! No one seemed to notice that I was rotten at other masculine behaviors like fighting and dating women. I also went to two schools that were all-male. My first college, Dartmouth College, had a particularly macho reputation at the time. Pretending that I was masculine was uncomfortable and sometimes I made mistakes.

My cover story continued after school through my job that involved developing technologies for the military. I interacted with all kinds of macho warriors who needed the technology. I did not mind developing the technology for them at all because at the time we were on the brink of having the Cold War heating up. I did find some of the really macho ones to be comical, but the most competent were intelligent, considerate, and caring. I kept a continuing association with athletics. My cover story included being a football referee for 14 years as well as a soccer and basketball coach for 6 years. Who would have suspected I was transgender?

I do not recommend secrecy for transgender people. The secrecy that I used to protect my transgender behavior probably warped my life and probably warps other transgender lives. If I had not built my cover story the way I did, I might never have gone into military technology development. Being in the closet is painfully lonely, and guarding ones secret makes social interactions stressful and awkward. But sometimes, living in secret is the only way that some transgender people can survive, particularly transgender children. They have to silently wait until things get better as they age.

ETIQUETTE

The purpose of etiquette is to provide rules and guidelines for behavior, particularly verbal behavior. The objective of etiquette is to avoid offending people. Etiquette can be different from situation to situation. Transgender people are in the process of developing their own etiquette. No doubt some transgender people will take issue with some of my suggestions. Transgender people are all individuals and have strong feelings about how they expect to be treated, based on years of rejection. Transgender people do not agree on a lot of things, and etiquette is one of them. There is as yet no standardized Emily Post or Amy Vanderbilt book on transgender etiquette. Transgender etiquette is still evolving. Transgender etiquette should guide both interactions between and with transgender people. Transgender people of all types, whether they only cross-dress once a month or full time, deserve respect and not to be offended.

Following proper etiquette by non-transgender people by involves some relearning, which takes time and effort. Transgender people cannot expect immediate changes in people, because the wrong behaviors are too well practiced. These behaviors are ingrained and difficult to change like riding a bicycle or talking in a particular language. It is like demanding that people learn a new way of riding a bicycle without falling or learn a new language without making mistakes. Transgender people need to act as teachers and coach people toward the correct behavior. They need to again fall back on their relaxation response and their positive interpretation skills.

When I correct someone for the first time, I always say, "Some transgender people would be very offended by your behavior or speech," but I will teach you how not to offend them. I recently corrected my housekeeper, but it took several tries for her to learn to use feminine pronouns with me instead of masculine pronouns. And in the South, every adult is either a Sir or a Ma'am, so it took her a little time to learn that I was a Ma'am. All transgender people can expect is for others to make the effort to relearn. If I sense that a person is not making the effort or is deliberately offending a transgender person, that is a different situation and I do get upset. But I always come from a place where I believe that people do not want to offend transgender people or anyone for that matter. If they prove otherwise, they are my enemy.

So here are my suggestions:

- Know some basic definitions about being transgender.
- Always use transgender as an adjective, as in "a transgender person."
- Always ask a transgender person for their preferred pronouns and use them.
- Avoid taboo words like "transvestite" and "tranny."
- Do not ask a transgender person about surgeries, particularly GPS.
- Do not ask about sexual function, organ size, or whether they can have an orgasm.
- Do not ask a transgender person for their "real" or "previous" name.
- Do not refer to "becoming a woman" or "becoming a man."
- Do not say that you are sorry that a person is transgender.
- Do not refer to being transgender as a conscious lifestyle choice.
- Do not refer to being transgender as gender dysphoria (GD) disorder or gender identity disorder (GID).
- Do compliment transgender people about their appearance, for example, clothes, jewelry, bulging muscles, or leather jackets if you really like them.
- For print and media, follow the Associated Press (AP), GLAAD, or Trans Media Watch (United Kingdom) guidelines on writing about being transgender.

Each of these suggestions is discussed below.

After extensive media coverage of prominent transgender people, there is no excuse for not knowing the definitions surrounding being transgender.

There are not only definitions in Chapter 2 of this book but you can also find them on the Internet on Wiki and numerous advocacy sites. Everyone should know words like "transgender," "transsexual," "sex," and "gender." Transgender people may become somewhat annoyed if a whole conversation merely consists of defining these terms.

Always use transgender as an adjective as in "being transgender" or a "transgender person" or "transgender people." Transgender people will take offense if it is used in any other way. It is not a noun as in "a transgender" or "transgenders" as if transgender people belong to another species. It is also not proper to use the word "transgendered" because it implies that someone had to do something to make a person transgender.

A polite person will always ask for a transgender person's preferred pronouns at the beginning of their conversation. Many transgender people will prefer traditional pronouns (he/she; him/her) but selecting the ones associated with their congruent gender behavior category, not their birth sex.

Increasingly, the convention in many business and academic meetings, particularly those involving millennials, is to go around the room and ask each person to introduce themselves and identify their preferred pronouns. It is not just due to transgender participation. Some young people are genderqueer and some women see conventional pronouns as sexist and that they encourage or maintain male superiority. There are a dozen or so alternative gender-neutral pronoun systems like **ze/hir** instead of he/him or she/her, but none has reached general acceptance. People using alternative gender pronouns should expect to provide help to most people. Use of Sir, Mr., Mrs., Ms., and Madam should be consistent with preferred pronouns.

Deliberately using the wrong gender pronouns is a microassault, one of the microaggressions. This is termed **misgendering**. In addition to using the pronouns associated with the transgender person's gender behavior category assigned at birth, some people go farther and call transgender people "it" or "he-she" or "shim." Repeated misgendering can result in psychological as well as physical damage. It is regarded as contributing to a hostile school or workplace environment, which has legal implications for organizations. A recent opinion letter from the U.S. attorney general includes transgender people as a protected class, which means that they can more easily sue organizations for damages.

Transgender people have several taboo words that should not be used in conjunction with being transgender. These include "transvestite," "post-op/pre-op," "he-she," "shim," and "tranny." As we indicated in Chapter 2, "transvestite" has the meaning that being transgender is motivated by the sexual arousal that accompanies crossdressing. This claim has been refuted by scientific studies but is still widely believed, because people some-time get sexually aroused themselves when they see a transgender person. This is probably due to the novelty of seeing a different kind of person. "Shim" is a combination of she and him used for microassaults, like she-he. "Pre-op" and "post-op" refer to those who have or have not had transsexual GPS as part of transsexual transition. These words should not be used because there is stigma attached by some that GPS surgery is required to complete transition and become a "real" transsexual. This is erroneous because most transsexuals never have GPS before completing transition; only about 25% of MTF have it. GPS is not the ultimate goal of transsexual transi-tion. The goal is to feel like your body is aligned with your congruent gender behavior category.

Probably the most controversial taboo word for transgender people is the word "tranny." It started out being a term of endearment, then became a taboo word, was rehabilitated, and now is a taboo word again. My suggestion is not to use the word, unless you are sure that it does not offend those present.

Most transsexuals will no longer answer questions about transsexual GPS because the answers are often used in sensationalistic journalism. These include questions about the surgeries themselves as well as questions about resulting sexual function or whether the transsexual can achieve orgasm. My suggestion is that a transgender person should not engage in conversa-tions about such matters and only say that in general the results of GPS are generally good. As Joy Ladin, a transsexual poet and writer, said:

> Asking intimate questions about someone's body is the same whether that per-son is trans or not, so if you wouldn't walk up to someone at a party and say, "Do you have one testicle or two?" you probably shouldn't ask a trans person if they've had genital surgery.
>
> —Joy Ladin in "A Transgender Guide to
> Answering Intrusive Questions"[3]

Do not ask a transgender person about their "real" or "previous" name. Many transgender people are still in secrecy or in partial secrecy and do not want to reveal this information. Transsexuals do not want to be asked because their previous name may bring up bad memories, and a new name to some symbolizes progress in transition. Transsexuals sometimes refer to their previous name as their **dead name**, which gives you a sense of how they feel about it.

Do not ask about when a transgender person became a girl/woman or boy/man. Most transgender people know their congruent gender behavior category from early childhood. As they remember it, they have always been a man or a woman, depending on their congruent gender behavior category. They may have spent some time behaving in the other category because of secrecy, but they have always known what gender they belong to. Remember that some transgender people may still not be full-time in their congruent gender. One does not "become" a gender, they are and always have been their gender.

Do not say that you are sorry that a person is transgender. They may have had hard economic or social experiences due to cultural rejection, which may warrant an expression of sympathy. However, there is no reason to be sorry that a person is transgender; it is a biological predisposition that cannot be changed. In fact, many transgender people are proud because they get to have unique experiences that others do not. Most would not take the "cure" if there was one.

Do not refer to being transgender as a conscious lifestyle choice. Psychology research clearly shows that there is no such thing as a conscious choice because any choice is made well before conscious awareness. Our subconscious mechanisms do the deciding, including biological gender behavior predisposition. Consciousness is just along for the ride. Being transgender is no more conscious than the predisposition to be left-handed or to be good at math or music.

Gender identity disorder (GID) and gender dysphoria (GD) are controversial terms, because they imply that transgender people have a disease that makes them behave the way they do. Disorder is just another word for disease, usually one without a known cause. These terms both appear in catalogs of diseases for insurance claims. GID has been replaced with GD in one list. However, this is meaningless because the term is still in the list and the title of the list ends in the word "disorders." Hopefully, in the future, being transgender terms will disappear altogether and being transsexual will only appear in a list of normal medical concerns like normal pregnancy and not in a list of disorders. That being said, these terms are thrown around in the media and in public conversations by transgender people and others, because mental health professionals have passed these psychiatric terms on inappropriately to transgender patients and the public. Closer reading of the descriptions of both GID and GD reveals that these terms do not apply, unless a transgender person becomes disabled or is in severe distress because they are transgender and has seen a mental health professional to get help. That does not apply to most transgender people; in fact most transgender people never go to a mental health professional. Transsexuals have to see a mental health professional to be screened for transition, not for a disease.

As you would with other people, do compliment transgender people about their appearance, for example, clothes, jewelry, nice figure, or bulging muscles if you really like them. Such compliments are part of mainstream etiquette and if they are genuine, they are fine. They tell the transgender person that you appreciate all the trouble they have taken in order to look good.

Journalists and writers should use the AP, *Washington Post*, or Trans Media Watch (United Kingdom) style guides to determine how to write about transgender people, including which pronouns to use. The guides essentially say that a writer should use the pronoun associated with the person's declared gender behavior category and if no declaration is available, then use the gender category that they live in. Recently the use of the third person plural "they" in place of the third person singular he/she has become accepted in cases where gender behavior category cannot easily be determined or a gender-neutral pronoun is desired. The *Washington Post* has led the way in this. The guides are deliberately not followed by publications with anti-transgender political agendas. The result is that they do harm to the reputations of individual transgender people and opinions of being transgender. When you read such articles, just fall back on your relaxation reflex. Journalists should also refer to transgender people by their chosen name, even if they have not changed it yet and never put their name in quotes.

IDENTIFICATION

Having accurate identity documents is vital for transgender people to vote, drive a car, travel, use a credit card, and enter public buildings. Unfortunately, there are often barriers to obtain identification documents for those who present full time in their congruent gender behavior category. This includes both transsexual and non-transsexual transgender people. It is important to have identification documents with appropriate names, pictures, and sex markers. In the United States, the hodgepodge of state laws makes it difficult. It is even more difficult because state laws are constantly being changed. In this section, we will provide suggestions for the five major U.S. identity documents: court order for name change, birth certificate, passport, driver's license, and death certificate. (Yes, transgender people are culturally rejected even after death.)

The best way to start through this maze of laws and practices is to consult the NCTE[4] website, which summarizes all of the requirements for identification by states. A transgender person will need to consult the requirements for both the state they were born in and also the current state in which they reside. Birth certificates can only be changed or amended by the state of birth. For example, in my case, I have to consult the requirements for birth certificates by the state of New Jersey and name change and driver's license requirements for the state of Georgia where I live.

Usually, the first step in getting correct identification documents is to establish a transgender person's name. Name changes can usually be obtained pretty easily by filling out a form at a local court (e.g., superior court or family court) in the county where one resides. A person can usually change their name to whatever they want to within reason as long as they are not doing it to commit fraud or escape debts. It is up to the judgment of the court if the name is acceptable. For example, a judge will not let you change your name to something that is obscene. Requirements may vary from state to state. For example, in Georgia, a name change has to be advertised in a local legal publication for a period of time. Occasionally, a persnickety judge will reject an application because the person is transgender, but this is rare and is almost always overturned on appeal. (A judge in rural Georgia recently denied an FTM the right to the name Elijah. We are now awaiting the appeal.) However, appeals require a lawyer and increased expense. The regular procedure is usually quick and easy. The transgender person must remember to immediately change documentation on bank records, credit cards, Social Security records, and other legal documents. They should also have a copy of the court order with them at all times, until all of these things are changed. In some states, after a name change, people also have a limited time to get a new driver's license.

Some states will change birth certificates and some will only amend them, leaving a person's birth name and sex marker on the certificate. Requirements for changing birth certificates for transgender people usually include a name change and a letter from a doctor. In some states, the doctor has to state that the person has completed transsexual transition and transsexual GPS. In others, all they have to do is say that a person is transitioning and intends to live in their congruent gender. In some states, like California, a medical letter is unnecessary. The simple procedure is for a mental health professional to fill out a form. It is usually possible to change or amend both birth name and birth sex marker at the same time. However, one state, Tennessee, will not change sex markers at all.

The next identification document to discuss is the passport. Most people do not have them, but they can be handy for transgender people. They are valid for air travel identification and entry into Federal buildings. The sex marker on a passport can be changed with just a letter from a doctor saying that the transgender person has received some type of treatment for being transgender. The only inconvenience is that you have to apply in person at a local postal service location with a name change court order and identification document with a picture and a signature. No need to show a state ID, a previous passport will suffice. It is handy because a passport is often the only identification needed to issue new driver's licenses, particularly under the REAL ID Act (see later). A corrected passport also helps with changing Social Security and immigration records.

The most commonly used identification document in the United States is the driver's license. There are two issues with regard to these documents. First, there is the problem of getting sex markers and name change. The other issue involves getting a picture showing your normal presentation. The requirements for changing name and sex marker vary from state to state. For example, Georgia requires a name change court order, a doctor's letter that specifies that a person has had transsexual GPS, and a government-issued photo identification (a passport works) and notification of sex marker change with the Social Security Administration. Although renewal of driver's licenses can usually be accomplished by mail, the states are in the process of issuing new driver's licenses because of the Federal REAL ID law. This requires a personal appearance and documents that establish citizenship, which effectively makes driver's licenses into national identification documents. The result is that most clerks in Department of Motor Vehicles (DMV) are over-worked. If someone presents a passport that is the gold standard for citizenship, they may not ask for or examine any other documentation.

Getting a picture on one's license that reflects normal presentation is sometimes difficult, particularly for non-transsexual transgender people. There have been several court cases in which a division of motor vehicle official refused to grant a license, because they thought that the picture of the person did not match the sex marker on the license. In many states, the rule is that the picture should match the normal presentation of a person. However, some DMV officials take it upon themselves to make a transgender person take off makeup or a wig, even if that is the way they look all the time. This happens with non-transgender people too. Court cases usually are decided in favor of discriminated people, but some people cannot afford such lawsuits themselves.

I have some suggestions about this situation. If a clerk refuses to give a transgender person a license, they should immediately ask for the supervisor who may have a better understanding of the rules. If that does not work, most states allow people to go to any of several offices. If they are turned down, a transgender person should use their relaxation responses and walk out of the office without comment. Wait a day or so and go to a different office, which will have a different set of clerks and officials. This "doorknob rattling" approach is perfectly legal and actually works. If not, then contact one of several advocacy groups that will write a letter to the head of the DMV threatening a lawsuit. That usually brings a settlement.

Unfortunately, rejection of being transgender sometimes transcends death. A transgender person should make arrangements with the executor of their will for the executor to take control of the death certificate and interment process. An executor is the dead person's representative to pay debts and settle all unfinished business. Governments do not typically issue death certificates; they are issued by funeral homes. In some cases, family members have interposed themselves to force the funeral home to issue a death certificate or even bury the transgender person with the wrong legal name, birth date and sex. If the death certificate is incorrect, it creates all sorts of problems because the Social Security Administration keeps a "Death Index" database that is the legal authority for determining such things as survivor benefits and burial benefits. So a transgender person should provide instructions to the future executor of their estate as to the exact legal name and sex marker for the death certificate and how they should be buried.

TRANSPORTATION SECURITY ADMINISTRATION (TSA)

The TSA uses body scanners to prevent travelers from bringing weapons and explosives on airline flights. The TSA has just announced the expansion of their scanner program. Terrorists have gotten clever about hiding moldable "plastic" or other explosives in their shoes, underwear, or brassieres or strapping to their bodies. The body scanners create very detailed images of what is beneath clothing. Initially, they were deemed so good that they represented a potential invasion of privacy if the images were released.

The manufacturers developed a computer system to analyze the image data and meet TSA requirements for privacy, but its algorithms required that the machine know the sex of the traveler. The TSA did not object to this, even though it causes problems for transgender people. For males, the computer ignores patterns where male genitalia would normally be located and detects patterns in the chest area, which might be explosives. For females, the computer ignores normal breast tissue patterns and detects patterns in the genital area that are not characteristic of normal female genitalia. The idea is that TSA agents are responsible to determine the sex of a traveler from their outward appearance and push either a pink or blue button on the scanner that tells the computer what to look for and what to ignore.

The problem, of course, is that no one can reliably determine sex from outward appearance. Some people are transgender, some are intersex, some people are genderqueer, and some people dress androgynously like the Japanese Kei subculture. The scanner and computer may see and detect breast binders, breast forms, and genital simulation "packers" as potential explosives. The TSA rules are supposed to allow transgender people to wear these devices, but the scanner may declare them as "alerts."

If a person flunks the scanner test, they are subjected to a "pat-down" guided by the scanner as to where a same-sex agent should feel to identify the detected pattern, termed an "alert." Transgender people are supposed to be able to select the sex of the officer doing the pat-down, but my experience is that the TSA agents will begin the pat-down before a person even gets out of the scanner, so there is no time to express a choice. The TSA says that one can always avoid the scanner and get a pat-down, but both the pat-down and the TSA agent talk are humiliating in the public inspection area because lots of people can hear it. You can opt for a private pat-down with a witness but all of this takes time that many people do not have. All of this may cause transgender people to panic and get upset, which is an indicator TSA uses to single out people for more scrutiny.

I will tell you my suggestions about how to deal with the TSA by telling you how I do it. First, I try to get to the airport early, so if I do encounter a problem, I would not miss my flight. I am registered with the TSA Secure Flight Program as a frequent traveler, which allows me to go through a line that may not be scanned but merely inspected for metal weapons. I watch the lines carefully to get in one where the scanner is not the primary inspection device. I will have previously picked a gender to present in. For me, it is usually the masculine gender behavior category because I stand nearly six feet high and have a big broad shoulders and frame. I wear a nondescript black pantsuit that could serve as business clothing for masculine or feminine presentation, in case my luggage gets lost. I do not wear makeup. If I trigger an alert for having breasts, the pat-down usually goes quickly and easily. I have triggered alerts for having breasts, even though I have AA small cup size. Lots of older men have gynecomastia or enlarged breasts, which by now the TSA people know all too well.

I put my bra, makeup, panties, heels, and jewelry in my carry-on bag that goes separately through the X-ray carry-on inspection device. I put my purse in my computer bag, so it is not visible as a feminine gender indicator. I have been questioned by TSA a couple of times as to why I have a woman's purse but explained that lots of men have such purses these days "what with cell phones and iPads getting bigger and all." I have learned that it is better to get the purse out of sight. If asked why there is feminine clothing in my carry-ons, I am prepared to tell them that it belongs to my wife, and this has always worked. I make my body underneath my clothes as masculine as possible by lightly binding my breasts with a tight T-shirt and wear boxers, not briefs. The scanner detects papers and driver's licenses, so I always put my boarding pass and license in one of the little dishes that they give you to go through the carry-on X-ray. Otherwise, I might be rejected for carrying them in my pockets. I do not want to give them any scanner signature that would make them reject me, because they may want to look at other parts of my body. Once I get through security, I go immediately to the closest family restroom and put on my feminine clothes and makeup. I do not like using family restrooms as a rule because it signals that there is something different about me, but there is more room for changing there.

If I decide to go in a feminine gender, much of my behavior is the same, except that I wear a tight pair of athletic panties and an underwire bra. I put on no makeup in case they see my identification. A different set of TSA agents check identification than that does the carry-on and body inspection, so the latter do not usually see my identification. The underwire bra is a "convincing detail" that shrieks to the computer and the TSA agents that I am a female. They probably think that no one would wear such an uncomfortable garment unless they were a female and in that they are probably correct. I occasionally get clocked because of the underwire but again the pat-down goes quickly. I am sure TSA agents all know about underwires, and this gives them something to focus on rather than some of my other body characteristics. It provides a "shiny object" to distract them. If clocked in my feminine gender, I plead my case as being a transsexual with breasts and need a supporting bra. And that is close to the truth, except that I very seldom wear an underwire in other contexts because they are uncomfortable. I may whip out my "carry letter" from my psychologist that says I should be permitted to present as a woman because that is part of my "treatment." A glimpse of officialdom is usually enough to get me through.

Once a transgender person gets to the gate, they are not out of the woods. TSA sometimes does a second screening at the gate. The two times this has happened to me, I was crosspresenting and I immediately went to the family restroom and shed my lipstick and jewelry. I got all the metal off of my body because they do not have scanners at the gates, only metal detectors. They can look through my carry-ons all they want; there are no weapons or explosives in them and that is really all they care about at that point.

TSA policy is constantly changing. Best place to keep up with how TSA changes affect transgender people is at the National Center for Transgender Equality[5] web page.

RESTROOMS

Anti-transgender people are making it harder for transgender people to go to the restroom type that matches with their congruent gender behavior category. They apparently are doing this as useless retaliation for losing the same-sex marriage cases in the Supreme Court and because they believe from their religion that being transgender is somehow immoral. Since transgender people have aligned themselves with the GLBTQQIA community, these people are trying to make being transgender a wedge issue and discourage transgender people from being visible. While they may talk about "privacy," the real reason is resistance to cultural change.

Mental health professionals say that transgender people will experience psychological damage if they are not allowed to go to the restroom that matches their congruent gender behavior category. Damage is also done if they are forced to go to a family restroom instead of a gendered one. Family restrooms are okay for changing clothes because there is more room in them. Both transgender and non-transgender persons take advantage. But to a transgender person, being assigned to anything but their congruent restroom is humiliating and degrading. Use of a restroom that is not congruent may result in complaints about soliciting for prostitution or other complaints.

So what should a transgender person do? Here are my suggestions. First, find a safe bathroom that is controlled by an organization that tolerates being transgender. There are several websites that can help you find them whether in restaurants, highway stops, or other places of business. After the North Carolina bathroom law, a transgender person started a website to list businesses that were transgender friendly and allowed transgender people to use their congruent restroom. She started by going around to the businesses, telling them that she was transgender and asking if she were a customer, could she use the woman's restroom. Before long, businesses were calling her to get on the list. Large businesses, like Target, are also setting similar policies. Businesses are transgender friendly because they have transgender employees, and they do not want to discourage transgender customers, all of whom may have families and relatives. In addition, they have customers who are in favor of transgender nondiscrimination.

Second, spend as little time as possible in the restroom. You are there to relieve yourself, not to socialize or fix your makeup. You do not want to give anyone a reason to report you. Do not take a "selfie" and post it to your Facebook or other social media page. There may be other people in the rest-room and they would not appreciate a photo being published including them.

Third, if you get involved with some sort of law enforcement, politely plead ignorance and ask which restroom you should use. Enforcement of these laws is impractical and most police forces have better things to do. Colleges are pleading ignorance and waiting to be told how to enforce the new laws. Many local cities do not police restrooms even in the South, unless there is some sort of crime in progress. They do not care which restroom you use. This is the case in Atlanta. Police are not used to asking for birth certificates and most would not know what birth certificates from other states even look like. Birth certificates do not always include sex markers. My original certificate did not. Evidently, the governor of North Carolina cannot find police to enforce his own law. Recently, several transgender advocates used the congruent restrooms next to his office on their visit with him to talk about his law and there were no police about. Finally, your "carry letter" from a mental health professional should also specify that you should be able to go to the correct restroom. "Carry letters" have no legal standing, but a policeman may think twice about contravening a doctor's order. I always carry mine in my purse.

NOTES

1. Veterans Administration website on PTSD, http://www.ptsd.va.gov/public/materials/apps/PTSDCoach.asp (confirmed May 2, 2016).

2. Diane Sawyer, *Bruce Jenner: The Interview* (American Broadcasting Company, April 24, 2015).

3. L. Italie, "A Transgender Guide to Answering Intrusive Questions." Quoting Joy Ladin (Associated Press article, *Providence Journal*, 2011), http://www.providence journal.com/features/lifestyle/content/20140803-a-transgender-guide-to-answering-intrusive-questions.ece (confirmed May 2, 2016).

4. National Center for Transgender Equality web page. Identification documents. http://www.transequality.org/documents (confirmed May 2, 2016).

5. National Center for Transgender Equality web page. Travel. http://www.transequality.org/issues/travel (confirmed May 2, 2016).

CHAPTER 8

The Gift of Being Transgender

INTRODUCTION

It may sound strange to call being transgender a gift considering how much misery it causes for transgender people and others. Transgender people are rejected because they violate cultural norms by behaving in a gender behavior category to which they were not assigned according to birth sex. Transgender people are subject to violence, homelessness, discrimination, and even murder, all of which are, in part, sanctioned by culture. Transgender people also have families, friends, loved ones, and allies that suffer because of their association, friendship, and love.

But, as the saying goes, every cloud has a silver lining and so it is with being transgender. Around the edges of the dark clouds, there are silver rays shining through. People benefit from being transgender and all non-transgender people benefit as well. It may be hard to see the benefits because of the storm clouds but they are there. Some of these benefits may seem less tangible than the miseries of being transgender, but they have long-term importance for our species.

This chapter is organized in four parts:

- Personal enrichment
- Enlightenment of the human condition
- GLBT civil rights movement
- Contributions to science

PERSONAL ENRICHMENT

As was described in Chapter 3, Native Americans in previous times recognized the need to have gender behavior categories that were not exclusively assigned by birth sex. Some of these people belonged to two gender behavior categories—the Two-Spirits. They were selected based on their expressed childhood spiritual experiences, behaviors, and vocational talents. Because they moved back and forth between categories, their lives were enriched. People in the tribe recognized their knowledge and wisdom based on their enriched lives, so the Two-Spirits were often appointed as tribal leaders. Some became leaders of whole nations of Native American tribes.

Transgender people have experiences that most other people never have and in this respect they are enriched. They become keen observers of behavior to identify the rules, norms, and conventions of the two gender behavior categories. To function and behave in two very different gender behavior categories takes learning nearly twice as much about gender as other people. Sometimes transgender people do not learn about their congruent gender category until they come out at an older age. They miss out on learning experiences in teenage and young adult years. When they are behaving in their incongruent gender category, they learn how to be good actors without going to any acting school. They learn without any instruction from the military and intelligence organizations how to deceive other people by denial and deception. They carry the burden of these lies and deceits and realize that they cannot be authentic people without shedding them. They learn to detect the lies of politicians and hatemongers and for that reason make excellent advocates. Transgender people learn to see through and eventually question authority because of their behavioral insights; they make good citizens and voters.

Some negative experiences wear transgender people down, but some can toughen them and build resilience and practice coping strategies. These negative experiences are unnecessary and as artificial as the cultural gender system that sanctions them. While some are injured by trauma and suffer from "posttraumatic stress syndrome," the innately resilient and those who practice coping strategies come out of the trauma with "posttraumatic growth" of character and purpose. As Nietzsche wrote:

> From life's school of war, that which does not kill me makes me stronger.
> —Nietzsche, *Twilight of the Idols*, 1889[1]

Given what we now know today about coping strategies (see Chapter 7: "Coping with Transgender Issues"), Nietzsche might now amend his quote to be:

> From life's school of war, that which does not kill those who know how to cope, makes them stronger.

Most transgender people say that they would not take the "cure" for being transgender if there was one. Rather than referring to gender dysphoria, they refer to "gender euphoria." This is an indication that being transgender can be an uplifting and enriching experience. I felt and still feel like I am floating on air and totally relaxed when I dress and present as femininely as possible.

All people are enriched from knowing about being transgender because it forces people to think. We are in a period when the public is fascinated by transgender people and want to know more about being transgender, just as occurred in the 1950s with the emergence of Christine Jorgensen into American society. One of the hardest things to do is to get people out of their comfort zone and force them to think. Scientists see a definite increase in brain activity when something new is encountered and triggers thinking. Most cisgender people automatically assume that everyone is like them until they see and know a transgender person. They may not come to the right conclusions about transgender people at first, but at least they start to pay attention. Many people are ignorant of biology and conflicts with culture, but transgender people force other people to learn about these things.

ENLIGHTENMENT OF THE HUMAN CONDITION

Learning about being transgender leads to some profound insights into the human condition.

When people contend that they have never met a transgender person and then are confronted with the statistics that show that being transgender is not rare at all, they are forced to realize that their original contention is probably wrong. They <u>have</u> met transgender people; they just did not know it. If you are in a meeting room with 100 males all other things being equal, odds are that at least 1 or 2 are transgender. Some doctors say that they have never treated a transgender patient. Faced with the large number of patients most doctors see, they are almost certainly wrong. They just did not know what to look for or gain enough patient trust. So much for the claims of modern "patient-centered" treatment where mutual trust is touted.

Many people believe that transgender children and adults are on the street because they want to be there. But once people understand that they are there because they were rejected by their families as sanctioned by culture, <u>they may come to realize the damage that culture can do</u>. Of course, transgender people are not the only ones damaged by culture, but with the current focus on being transgender, they represent highly visible casualties. If people see the transgender casualties, they might begin to see some of the other damages that culture causes. By continuing to reject transgender and other minorities, societies pay a terrible price not only in economic loss but also in human loss.

Being transgender makes it clear that biology is diverse and cannot be easily categorized by culture. Diversity is a strength of biology that increases the odds of survival for species. Many cultures have recognized that they need more than two gender behavior categories because of the diversity of their offspring. Unlike these cultures, our current Western culture tries to force-fit all people into neat binary categories of sex, gender, and sexual orientation. When people do not fit into the arbitrary categories that culture has constructed, they are rejected. But these rejected people are human beings and can and do make positive contributions to society if given a chance. Because of the current interest in being transgender, people are starting to realize the past accomplishments of transgender people in engineering, science, and the arts.

We can learn another lesson from cultures with nonbinary gender systems, and it is that we should allow children to cross traditional gender lines to reach their potential. Remember that these cultures assigned children to one or more gender behavior categories based on their expressions of interest as well as their sex. There is no reason that a male child should be told that they cannot play with dolls, and there is a current study that shows male and female children actually prefer doll play until 3 or 4 years old. At that point or earlier, their families tell them that it is inappropriate on the basis of gender. Who knows, the male child that plays with dolls may grow up to be a pediatrician just as my stepson did. A male child may show interest in dance or music but those should not be considered as sissy pursuits. Children will learn what they like or do not like according to their own tastes and biological predispositions, given the freedom to experiment based on parental and community support.

There is a myth that humans are a clean slate or *tabula rasa* for education and experience to write on and that humans do not bring biological predispositions with them. Being transgender is just one in a long line of behaviors that clearly involves human biological predisposition. The one that is most familiar is handedness. While it is possible for a human who is less right-handed to learn how to write and do other things with their right hand, some of these tasks become extremely difficult and require much practice. It is curious that many transsexual people are less right-handed. There are other recognized predispositions like "talents" for musical and mathematics. In science, this nature-nurture controversy has been going on for decades, and being transgender makes us see that both nature and nurture are involved. Transgender people have a biological predisposition for one gender or the other, but they cannot express this predisposition until they learn about gender, which occurs by age 2–3.

From the science that we know about being transgender, our parents are probably off the hook in terms of being blamed for childrearing practices that cause being transgender. Child rearing, with all its critics, does not cause being transgender; child studies have ruled out every parental childrearing mistake suggested to date. There is a tendency among people to blame child rearing for all sorts of childhood misbehaviors when the kids may have a biological predisposition or may be negatively impacted by culture. Yet historically, parents have taken the wrap needlessly, particularly mothers.

From studying transgender children we do know that <u>there is something for which some parents should receive blame</u>. Many transgender children are abused physically and verbally by their parents, because the parents feel an obligation based on culture to reject transgender behavior. There is no evidence that the abuse causes being transgender, but it clearly puts many transgender kids out into the street. Parents are only partially to blame, because they feel social pressure from their communities, churches, and sometimes governments to uphold what they perceive as the accepted culture. The way to reduce transgender child abuse in the long term is to encourage community, church, and government leaders to advocate tolerance and acceptance and change the culture.

Many people automatically believe that sex, gender, sexual orientation, and sexual arousal are all aligned. The fact that transgender people exist means that sex and gender are independent of one another. Feminists ought to revel in that fact, but many seem not to be able to understand that transwomen and transmen are real women and real men and have probably been so since birth or shortly thereafter. Their contention that transgender people are not real is hurtful and forms a rationale for discrimination. The fact that transgender people can have several sexual orientations that can change through transsexual transition also means that sexual orientation is independent from sex and gender. People are attracted to particular people regardless of sex and gender. There are an increasing number of couples who manage to stay together despite one of their members being transgender.

> The heart wants what the heart wants—or else it does not care.
> —Emily Dickinson, *The Letters*, 1862[2]

As this quote indicates, emotions like love are not under conscious control. Scientific evidence suggests that sexual attraction and romance are mediated by brain systems and hormones that are subconscious and different from sex and gender. Some transitioning transsexual people change their sexual orientation. <u>It is the only established process that does change sexual</u>

orientation. Being transgender is the phenomenon that makes clear the independence of sex, gender, and sexual orientation.

The fact that transgender people lose their acquired sexual arousal responses with exposure to their gender presentations (e.g., MTF clothing and makeup) also means that sexual arousal is independent of sex, gender, and sexual orientation. Being transgender forces us to realize that sexual arousal is a learned response, because it is unlearned by transgender people as they crosspresent.

GLBT CIVIL RIGHTS MOVEMENT

It is probably not accurate to say that only transgender people started the GLBT civil rights movement, but they certainly were at the forefront. Transgender people played major roles in the confrontations with the police at Cooper's Donuts in Los Angeles (1959), Compton's Cafeteria in San Francisco (1966), and Stonewall Inn in New York (1969). In all these confrontations, one of inflammatory issues was police harassment of transgender individuals who refused to take it anymore. These confrontations developed into riots. The events mark the beginnings of the modern GLBT civil rights movement, a gift, in part, from transgender people.

During the early years of the movement, separate organization advocated for gay, lesbian, and transgender rights. They sometimes tried to cooperate, but transgender people were "thrown under the bus" when they attempted to speak or show their flag at rallies and were deliberately dropped from a Federal bill that would provide employment discrimination protections in 2007. Although some advocacy organizations claim that they represent all of GLBT Americans, transgender people still support separate advocacy organizations of their own.

Fractures in the movement notwithstanding, the GLBT movement continues and has many notable accomplishments, including repeal of Don't Ask, Don't Tell legislation and legalization of same-sex marriage.

CONTRIBUTIONS TO SCIENCE

Knowledge and awareness of transgender people have opened up areas of science that were obscure. The involvement of these scientific areas in transgender science has given them new meaning and urgency. These scientific areas can now be coordinated and focused on a research agenda. Resources for transgender research are meager by some standards, and close coordination by researchers could produce greater impact.

First and foremost, the existence of transgender people is an example of biological diversity. Diversity is a feature of nature on this planet that allows a species to continue as environments change. At the local level, diversity provides more flexibility for groups to organize to survive. The North American Native Americans could not afford to waste manpower, so their members would pitch in to do whatever was needed. There were few restrictions based on sex that is not the case in modern culture, although this is changing. They had gender behavior categories that allowed specialization of skills, but survival always came first.

The existence of transgender people brings biological diversity out of the forgotten academic darkness. Knowledge and teaching about gender and sexual diversity have been suppressed in academia by culture, as Joan Roughgarden, a transsexual scientist, detailed in her book, *Nature's Rainbow*:

> But as I reflected on my academic sojourn, I wondered why we did not already know about nature's diversity in gender and sexuality. I came to see the book's [her book, *Nature's Rainbow*] main message as an indictment of academia for suppressing and denying diversity.
>
> And in the social sciences, variation in gender and sexuality is considered irrational and personal agency is denied. Gender and sexuality variant people are thought to be motivated by mindless devotion to primitive gods, or compelled by farfetched psychological urges, or brainwashed by social conventions and so on: there is always some reason to avoid taking gender- and sexually-variant people seriously.
>
> The fundamental problem is that our academic disciplines are all rooted in Western culture, which discriminates against diversity.
>
> —Joan Roughgarden, *Nature's Rainbow*[3]

The existence of transgender people provides an opportunity to study the interplay between genetics, epigenetics, and learning on behavior, because being transgender allows us to isolate gender predisposition. We can also compare transgender with other people on these factors to determine how gender behavior predisposition is formed. In order to explore this area, we will need support for comparison research on the genome and epigenome of transgender versus non-transgender people.

It appears that both genetic and epigenetic factors are involved in gender predisposition. There is evidence that genes start by setting a predisposition, but epigenetics can interfere. Neither of these factors can have influence unless children learn about gender behavior categories, which most seem to easily do by ages 2–3. Since the 1800s, psychologists have debated whether nature or nurture was more important in forming behavior. Nature referred to biology, while nurture referred to environmental influences. We now see that there are several factors involved in formation of behavior and that they interact. Understanding of the factors underlying being transgender provides yet another example that contributes to the resolution of this artificial debate.

Being transgender helps to clarify that the traditional evolutionary theory of gender based on sex must give way to the kinship evolutionary theory which puts survival of the group first. As we discussed in Chapter 4, the traditional theory says that people evolve into particular roles and behaviors because of their sex. The kinship theory says that, independent of sex and gender, human survival depends on the survival of the group; a group with diverse talents and behaviors will have a better chance to survive. Many people, usually without knowing it, use the traditional theory to support discrimination of transgender people, women, and other minorities. Such people are enamored by the "rugged individualist" notion of the traditional sex-based theory, which is undercut by the "cooperate and graduate" approach of kinship theory. If a person does not behave as the traditional theory predicts, then they are rejected and believed to have some kind of disease. This has been reflected in our culture and unfortunately in our psychiatry.

Making decisions about being transgender provides support for the "naturalistic decision making" theory of how people actually make decisions as opposed to structured, complex, overly elaborate methods. Transgender decisions, like most all decisions under time pressure, are "come as you are" affairs in which available knowledge is used for the decision as opposed to extensive fact gathering and meticulous analysis. The naturalistic decision-making philosophy is "visualize the likely outcomes and choose."

Being transgender dramatizes how decisions are made in the human nervous system. Decisions are not made at the conscious level, if there is one. Decisions are made by subconscious processes long before any consciousness function is informed about them. Through some complicated voting scheme these subconscious processes make a decision. Transgender people decide to behave in their congruent gender behavior category because of a biological gender predisposition that is contained in one or more of these subconscious processes. Sometimes other processes get more votes and the congruent predisposition is overruled. But gender predisposition continues to vote throughout the lifetime of a transgender person. Lana and Lilly Wachowski, transwomen filmmakers, describe a similar subconscious process in *The Matrix*:

> I know *exactly* what you mean. Let me tell you why you're here. You're here because you know something. What you know you can't explain, but you feel it. You've felt it your entire life. That there is something wrong with the world.

You don't know what it is, but it's there, like a splinter in your mind, driving
you mad. It is this feeling that has brought you to me.
                              —Morpheus, The Wachowskis, *The Matrix*, 1999[4]

A transgender person may not crossdress or may remain in the closet for years but
in many cases, they will ultimately express their gender predisposition openly.

Transgender people have helped to continue the rollback of psychodynamic explanations of human behavior by insisting that being transgender is
not a disease. Those who believe in such psychodynamic explanations are
now being forced instead to base their treatment of patients based on scientific evidence. Chapter 3 summarized the scientific evidence for biological
involvement in being transgender. The downfall of psychodynamic explanations of gender and sexual diversity began with the recognition that homosexuality was a naturally occurring phenomena. We can now visualize
physiological correlates of diversity with the technologies for brain scanning.

The point at the end of the spear is the transgender depathology movement, which seeks to exorcise old refuted psychiatric notions and replace
them with evidence-based treatment. As Joan Roughgarden observed:

Yet the absence of a scientific definition of disease implies that the diagnosis of
disease is often a value-loaded exercise in prejudice.
                              —Joan Roughgarden, *Nature's Rainbow*, 2004[5]

Depathologization of transgender people helps everyone in the long run by
demonstrating that other behavioral phenomena can be conceptualized as
natural processes rather than diseases.

The recent awareness of transgender people has caused scientists and
others to go back and look at gender diversity in other cultures. Social
anthropology studies on gender diverse cultures started in the late 19th century. There are many lessons learned through past studies such as the recognized need for more than two gender behavior categories and the need to
allow movement between them. This is in direct contradiction to the current
Western binary, cisgender, and inflexible gender system. However, there are
still gender diverse cultures that exist today. There are still several cultures
around the world that deserve more study, notably the *Muxe* of our Mexico
neighbor, *Guevadoces* in the Dominican Republic and Turkey, and several
subcultures in Southeast Asia.

The **Guevadoces** appear to be female until puberty because of a genetic
block of forming an enzyme and change sex organs when puberty starts.
The phenomenon was described in the best-selling book *Middlesex*.[6] Hopefully, the recent awareness of transgender people will awaken the social

anthropology community to more extensively study such phenomena. The payoff will be in understanding how cultures deal with gender diversity and gender change. There may be other payoffs. For example, the last study of the *Guevadoces* resulted in the discovery of the drug Finasteride, which is useful for treating enlargement of the prostate gland and treating transsexual people as well. I take it every day.

BEING TRANSGENDER IS A GIFT OF ADVENTURE FROM NATURE

Being transgender is the gift of a human adventure from nature. Human diversity, including gender diversity, allows humans to adapt to new circumstances also gives transgender people a wild ride. Amusement park rides have nothing on being transgender. There are ups and downs, joys and despairs, but many transgender people manage to be resilient, carry on, and sometimes enjoy the ride.

Many would say that the ride was worth it.

NOTES

1. Friedrich Nietzsche, *Twilight of the Idols* (First Edition 1889, Penguin Classics, 1990), Chapter I, 133.

2. Emily Dickinson, *The Letters* (First Edition 1862, Everyman's Library, 2011) Letter 262, 1.

3. Joan Roughgarden, *Nature's Rainbow* (Berkeley, CA: University of California Press, 2004), 4.

4. The Wachowskis, *The Matrix* (Warner Brothers, 1999).

5. Roughgarden, *Nature's Rainbow*, 3.

6. Jeffrey Eugenides, *Middlesex* (New York: Picador, 2002).

CHAPTER 9

Future Hope

There's a simple way to look at gender. Once upon a time, someone drew a line in the sands of culture and proclaimed with great self-importance, "On this side you are a man; on the other side you are a woman." It's time for the winds of change to blow the line away.

—Kate Bornstein, *Gender Outlaw*[1]

INTRODUCTION

Transgender people have every reason to be hopeful about the future. We still have more tough work to do in certain areas, but our advocates know how to deal with the challenges of legal and cultural change. Although transgender people do not agree about a lot of things because of their diversity, there are some things on which we all do agree. We should focus on them. The push for improvement has to come from the ground up both with respect to laws and cultural change. But we will take top-down help too, including several recent legal precedents and rulings by the Department of Energy (DOE), Department of Labor (DOL), and Equal Employment Opportunity Commission (EEOC). The push for change sometimes triggers backlash, which we are experiencing right now in the form of discriminatory restroom, "religious freedom" and public accommodation laws. Our current gender system is changing and transgender people are in a good position to encourage favorable change. As with many movements, the change begins with young people.

In our lifetimes, many of us baby boomers experienced movements for change, starting with the successful civil rights movement, the successful antiwar movement, the failed Equal Rights Amendment, the AIDS awareness movement, the Don't Ask, Don't Tell repeal, the semi-successful Occupy Wall Street, and the successful same-sex marriage legalization movement. I was a baby when Gandhi's India independence movement succeeded;

so I do not remember that. I do remember seeing him and his followers block the railroad in old magazine pictures, but as a child, I did not really understand why he was doing it. His nonviolent methods were used in many of the other movements in my lifetime. Through lessons learned in all these movements, advocacy has come of age in terms of its methods and effectiveness.

LEGAL ADVOCACY

Legal advocacy includes passing beneficial laws, fighting discriminatory laws, and monitoring their implementation. Our arsenal to do this includes:

- Finding partners
- Educating lawmakers and the public
- Lawsuits
- Amicus briefs
- Lobbying for laws
- Lobbying for executive orders
- Demonstrations and rallies
- Non-violent protests

Finding partners is an important first step in advocacy. Transgender people cannot do it alone. Partnering goes both ways, because injustice for one group means potential injustice for everyone. There is a hodgepodge of organizations that advocate for transgender people. Because of history and demographics, some of these organizations do not like one another and some are controversial with transgender people. Transgender people have been slighted in the past because some LGBT groups did not want us to be seen, or to talk at rallies, or even for our pride flag to be seen. (Yes, we actually do have a flag.) The most visible example was the failed enactment of the Federal Employment Non-Discrimination Act (ENDA) in 2007 when a partnership of advocacy organizations was formed to lobby for it. However, some organizations allowed transgender protections in a bill to be deleted in order to try to get protection for their own groups. As the saying goes, transgender people were "thrown under the bus." It is easy for people in some of these organizations to melt back into the population for work or recreation activities, but transgender people cannot easily do that without giving up their congruent gender presentation.

Partnering goes both ways. For example, many transgender advocacy organizations supported same-sex marriage and repeal of the Don't Ask, Don't Tell law. Besides, there were many cases of transgender people whose marriages were in legal jeopardy. And there were some transgender people who could not legally marry, unless the laws were changed and sex no longer became an obstacle.

We still have to partner with other advocates to fight injustice or the opposition will drive a wedge between us like they did with ENDA. I am reminded of a poem by Martin Niemoller who was a pastor during the Holocaust:

> First they came for the Socialists, and I did not speak out—
> Because I was not a Socialist.
> Then they came for the Trade Unionists, and I did not speak out—
> Because I was not a Trade Unionist.
> Then they came for the Jews, and I did not speak out—
> Because I was not a Jew.
> Then they came for me—and there was no one left to speak for me.
>   —Martin Niemoller, 1946[2]

Because of all the current pending and passed legislation targeting transgender people, I feel like we are the ones being targeted at this time but some other group who we are allied with may be next, say the intersex people, or the genderqueer/gender fluid people.

More recently, transgender organizations have partnered with businesses that find it in their economic interest to support transgender legal causes. Fights in many states to avoid or overturn discriminatory laws against being transgender were won because businesses, large and small, vocally objected and voted with their money. Businesses realize that transgender people make both good employees and customers, so it is in their interest to support them.

Transgender advocates know how to educate legislators, courts, and the public on being transgender. Sometimes this is a problem because journalists are often out for sensationalist stories and have difficulty with understanding the details about being transgender. Much to my chagrin, however, almost no transgender science is presented and much of what is presented is incorrect. That is one of the reasons for writing this book.

There are several organizations that partner with transgender organizations to file lawsuits on behalf of transgender people. These include the American Civil Liberties Union (ACLU), Lambda Legal, and Transgender Legal Defense And Education Fund (TLDEF). For example, the ACLU just filed suit to have the recently passed discrimination law affecting transgender people in North Carolina. There are organizations that file *amicus* briefs with courts in such cases. *Amicus* is the Latin word for friend and the organizations that file these briefs are known as "friends of the court." Various organizations file *amicus* briefs, including the American Psychological Association (APA), businesses, and even the Federal government. I am currently working on a committee for the APA to develop *amicus* briefs for transgender cases.

Transgender people have obtained legal precedents through lawsuits. The precedents serve to protect other transgender people who have similar cases. In fact, transgender people may have more precedent protection than GLB people. The courts have interpreted discrimination against transgender people in hiring and in the workplace as sex discrimination. Sex discrimination is protected under civil rights statutes and the Equal Protection Clause of the U.S. Constitution. Legal precedents help transgender people, but they often have to file lawsuits to take advantage of these precedents. Such lawsuits take time and money. There were so many successful cases that the Federal Equal Opportunity Commission took, what is called, legal notice and now provides policy and legal protection. However, obtaining protection often requires filing formal complaints with the Commission.

Transgender advocates have experience in lobbying for laws. Lobbying involves contacting government officials, including legislative and executive groups in support of legislation. There is nothing unseemly about lobbying *per se*, and transgender people have a perfect right to talk to their elected representatives. Advocates sometimes encourage transgender people to attend "lobbying days." There is nothing more formidable than a group of transgender people and advocates going to talk or give presentations to legislators. The typical strategy is similar to the one used in advocating for same-sex marriage, involving passage of supporting legislation starting at the city level. The laws at this level may not have much effect, but they build pressure for state laws. In the case of same-sex marriage laws, a law was passed in the city of San Francisco and the mayor, Gavin Newsom, actually started issuing marriage licenses until the state stepped in. However, this built momentum to ultimately win the fight in California. The U.S. Supreme Court finally decided the issue, because allowing some states to have same-sex marriage and some not would have led to chaos of marriages not being recognized by individual states.

Lobbying for executive orders is an important precursor to getting laws passed supporting transgender rights. One recent executive order that affected my company was one issued by President Obama, prohibiting transgender discrimination in contracting by the Department of Defense. Even if an executive order is rescinded, it gets businesses and people behaving that way and they come to realize the benefits. In this case, it is unlikely that businesses working for the Department of Defense will go back to discrimination because it would affect their public image and they benefit from having a wider group of contractors to select from.

Advocacy typically involves demonstrations and rallies in support of transgender legal issues, starting at the local and state levels and moving up to the Federal level. For example, there have been several large LGBT marches in Washington, mostly to get the Federal government to deal with the AIDS epidemic and other issues.

Changing the law may require nonviolent protests if governing authorities do not take prompt action. Arrests of protestors usually occur. This is one way to show that transgender people are serious about obtaining their rights and the rights of their partners. As an example, one of the protestors who was arrested for chaining herself to the White House fence to urge repeal of the Don't Ask, Don't Tell law was a transwoman who had served in the U.S. Navy.

CULTURAL CHANGE

Cultural change is harder than changing laws because people tend to learn deeply held cultural norms and habits. Cultural change involves trying to change the behavior of people, which can create uncertainty and anxiety. Being exposed to the idea of being transgender causes some to experience fear, hatred, or even unwanted sexual arousal, because being transgender is novel and a violation of existing cultural gender behavior categories. Transgender people are sometimes wrongly stereotyped as criminals by law enforcement and those who see transgender people engaging in street crime. However, most transgender people are not criminals and are upstanding citizens. In turn, transgender people may not trust police and others because of their stereotyping and emotional reactions.

There are many in our society who know how to accomplish cultural change in businesses and communities. Some have changed corporate culture in various ways, including accepting transgender people. It is little different for changing an entire culture about being transgender but some of the same processes are involved. Cultural change for being transgender involves deliberate action to:

- Increase transgender visibility
- Increase personal relationships with transgender people
- Depathologize being transgender

- Educate
- Find allies and champions in organizations
- Develop a vision of the new culture
- Commit to small, measureable behavioral changes
- Encourage champions and allies model behavior
- Celebrate success and models of success
- Continue measureable behavior changes
- Nonviolent protest

Transgender people should increase their visibility whenever possible. This should take place as often as possible but should be done safely. There are even specially designated days and opportunities to increase visibility. As I write this chapter in the spring, this year's Transgender Awareness Day will be occurring soon and then there is the Transgender Day of Remembrance in the fall. But transgender people should also be visible on a daily basis. Every day that I go out to the supermarket or shopping, I make sure that I am as feminine as possible, even though I am 6 feet tall and weigh as much as a football tackle. There is no way that I can pass, but people are getting used to seeing me. Sometimes I even get nice comments on my dress or my courage. We know being visible works to change culture because the gay and lesbian communities made it a priority as a foundation for their efforts to obtain protections and same-sex marriage rights. For LGB groups, a key was the pride parades that now take place all over the world. People saw that LGB people could celebrate and be happy, and later transgender people joined in. It took courage for the LGB community to do this, but it takes even more courage for transgender people to do it.

The next activity in cultural change is to make personal relationships with as many people as possible and let them know that you are transgender. That was the second priority for the LGB community in the same-sex marriage fight. People changed their attitudes toward LGB because they found a family member or a friend who was LGB. Even Dick Cheney changed when he realized that he had an out lesbian daughter. Lesbian couples even invited skeptical Congressmen to dinner.

The percentage of people who know a transgender person is now almost up to 20%, but a few years ago, it was less than 5%. The LGB groups saw similar increases during their campaigns. Transgender people have a ways to go to be more visible and make friends who will become allies. It is hard for people to reject transgender folks that they know, even if the culture says they should. As President Obama said:

I think what you're seeing is a profound recognition on the part of the American people that gays and lesbians and transgender persons are our brothers, our sisters, our children, our cousins, our friends, our co-workers, and that they've got to be treated like every other American. And I think that principle will win out.

—Barack Obama, June 18, 2011[3]

People now want to meet transgender people because some have become celebrities. There are many more high-profile transgender people and transsexuals in public life than ever before. People are curious and want to ask questions. We need to take advantage of this by telling our stories. This is yet another reason for transgender people to be informed and an important part of that is being informed about science. Many of the questions that cisgender people ask concern science. We need to up our science game. I have seen too many transgender people, including advocates, saying that they do not know what science says about being transgender. Those critical of being transgender make up their own pseudoscience and we need to be science literate to answer their challenges.

Transgender people and their mental health advocates have succeeded in reducing transgender pathologization but it is not entirely gone. Pathologization means that people demean and humiliate transgender people by saying that they are disordered or diseased. Until recently, the psychiatric community supported pathologization by listing being transgender as a disorder in insurance claims' directories. The often ignored fine print was that the transgender person had to be debilitated or distressed by being transgender to be considered "disordered." But due to the work of many people, including transgender mental health professionals, pathologization by psychiatry seems to be fading. This gives critics and hatemongers less authority to say that transgender people are diseased or disordered and therefore should not be respected and have the rights they deserve.

Transgender people have been educating cisgender people for years on aspects of being transgender. There is survey evidence that about 65% of transgender people have to educate their own doctors about it. Transgender people have always been willing to provide educational talks to schools, churches, the public, the media, as well as various groups, but the demand is greatly increasing. Too often, people are only interested in intimate details, but when transgender people do these talks, they carry the unspoken message that there is nothing to fear or hate about a transgender person. They become ambassadors for other transgender people. If you are going to give talks, better get prepared with the message and oh, yes, with transgender science.

There are lots of ways to educate people besides giving talks. Social media is now popular in all its forms. I sometimes wonder whether I spend too much time blogging or telling about science online, but social media is an important way to get the message out. If transgender people were not on social media, they would not know one another as much as they do or be able help educate people. Social media is also where young people hang out and many are sympathetic to needed cultural change. Transgender people write books about their experience. TV, movies, and plays educate about transgender people, although they are often too interested in ratings and profits to provide a coherent message. A relatively untapped vehicle for education is books of fiction. No one has yet written a popular great American novel involving transgender people that can change attitudes on a large scale. But the race to write such a novel is on. In the past, novels have helped change culture by allowing large audiences to know about how it felt to be in particular situations or be a certain type of person. Novels create emotional learning.

> Up until the last few years, all we'd get to publish were our autobiographies, tales of women trapped in the bodies of men or men pining away in the bodies of women.
>
> —Kate Bornstein, *Gender Outlaw*[4]

The organization Out and Equal has considerable experience in changing culture within corporations with regard to GLBTQ issues. They often work with internal corporate groups to effect change. I am a certified Out and Equal instructor, so I have been to their course that teaches corporate people about making things better for GLBTQ people through cultural change. Change in addressing schools and nonbusiness organizations is a little trickier. The best example in that area is the organization True Child that provides education, tools, and consulting help to reduce the adverse impacts of rigid gender behavior categories for students. In particular they have targeted reproductive health; bullying and harassment; science technology engineering and mathematics (STEM), and academic underachieving. They discourage rigid gender roles that can discourage girls from pursuing careers in STEM. It is up to the organizations concerned to actually use True Child tools and procedures. An example of a recent initiative is Transform California that involves over 30 organizations seeking to increase transgender acceptance in the state through education.

Inside corporations there are usually GLBTQ employee groups that seek to make things better. One of the first things that they should do is to find allies, whether in the human resources department or elsewhere. The other thing they should do is to look for champions in management that will stand up for their needs. The same goes for other organizations except that it is not so common to find employee groups and allies and champions in non-business organizations. But schools may have GLBTQ student groups or gay-straight alliance groups. School groups may find champions on the school board or a city mayor. If the goal is to change community culture, then allies and champions need to be found in religious, fraternal, and even professional groups. In some situations, there is social risk associated with aligning with the GLBTQ groups, but this makes good allies even more valuable.

In the past year, I went to a GLAAD meeting that had a panel of religious leaders who spoke about their communities and GLBTQ issues. During the question and answer period that followed, the question was asked, "Why don't you preach more about GLBTQ tolerance?" The reply by one outspoken clergyman was simply "Money." She explained that clergymen resist talking about tolerance because they are afraid that they will lose their congregations and therefore their monetary support. A man with a gay child got up right in front of me and said that this had happened in his congregation. They had lost half their members overnight because of sermons advocating tolerance. This is also an example of how behavioral change, in this case, sermons on tolerance, may have to proceed in small steps.

There are various ways to identify the vision of the organization or community after the desired changes have occurred. In corporations, this is sometimes set by upper management, but it is important that interpretation and implementation take place at the lowest level possible. Edicts from upper management may be resisted or ignored. Buy-in by employees or community residents requires participation at the lowest level.

Edwards Deming was one of the best managers in the car industry. His thing was improving quality. He helped resurrect the Japanese auto industry after World War II and later helped Ford Motor Company when it was nearly bankrupt. Both times it was through improvements in car quality. He found that people would buy and pay more for quality cars. Rather than issuing a lot of orders to improve quality from upper management downward, he started quality circles of employees who worked in the parts department or on the assembly line. He reasoned that the lower level employees had the best experience and knowledge about how to improve quality. He then measured improvements in quality to give the groups feedback. Although Deming was not interested in GLBTQ issues, he is a model for changing corporate and community culture. <u>Changes have to start from smaller groups inside organizations and societies</u>.

Champions and leaders need to visibly model new behaviors by participating in cultural change activities and giving credit to people and internal groups at the lowest levels. They need to provide good examples by making it point to use correct names and pronouns for transgender people. They need to be scrupulous not to commit microassaults even in jest because they might be misconstrued. In short, they need to set a good example of the desired behavior.

The essence of cultural change is behavioral change, so the objective of groups, allies, and champions is to change behavior. In order to avoid resistance to change, they should start out with very small changes, which can be measured. In the case of True Child, improvements in school grades and numbers of females going into STEM might serve as things to measure.

The next thing to do in cultural change is to celebrate success by participants and champions. This is more than giving out trophies and sharing social events; it is recognition that the culture has changed, if only a little. The process of incremental improvements and celebrations should be continued even after the original vision is realized, because new visions can be developed that build on previous successes. In the case of GLBTQ issues, an original vision to improve tolerance may turn into a new vision that involves using diversity to attract new employees and customers.

Changing the culture may require nonviolent protests to dramatize the harm that culture does to transgender people. This is one way to show that transgender people are serious about changing culture.

So in our culture we have the know-how to change laws and culture. We just need transgender people, allies, and champions to make it happen. The next section suggests how to apply our know-how to an important problem for transgender people to solve.

TRANSGENDER PEOPLE ON THE STREET

The most glaring problem in the transgender community is the tragic homelessness of many transgender people. Homelessness leads to living on the street and participation in illegal street crime such as prostitution and drug dealing. Transgender people on the street are <u>not</u> there because they want to be. For a time Janet Mock, a transgender journalist, was a sex worker:

> Many people believe trans women choose to engage in the sex trade rather than get a real job. That belief is misguided because sex work is work, and it's often the only work available to marginalized women. Systemic oppression creates

circumstances that push many women to choose sex work as a means of survival, and I was one of those women, choosing survival.

—Janet Mock, *Redefining Realness*[5]

Illegal activities lead to permanent inability to hold jobs due to criminal records and being put on sex-crimes registries. The results are devastating for the transgender people involved, and it is no wonder that the attempted suicide rate of transgender people is so high. For society, homelessness and street crimes result in a high rate of poverty and a reservoir of HIV and sexually transmitted diseases (STDs). Transgender criminals on the street give the transgender community a bad reputation. For some people, the only time they see transgender people is when they drive by a line of transgender prostitutes on the street. The media makes it worse by showing videos of these transgender criminals on the street to sensationalize stories. Finally, transgender people in the street divide the transgender community on the basis of genetic heritage and socioeconomic status.

I do not claim to have all the answers to this problem, but in this section, we will use the problem to illustrate how cultural change and legal change processes might be used to reduce it.

The root cause of transgender people being homeless is family rejection, sanctioned by culture. Children are either thrown out of their homes by their families or they leave because of microaggressions or violence directed at them. To attack this root cause, culture needs to be changed in many communities and in the broader public. Surveys indicate that family acceptance of transgender youth protects against depression, substance abuse, and suicide. Family acceptance also results in higher self-esteem among transgender youth. Unfortunately, surveys also show that high religious involvement in families is associated with low levels of acceptance of transgender youth. Community leaders advocate rejection of transgender people from the pulpit or political campaigns. The current spate of anti-transgender "bathroom bills" is an example of how politicians can use being transgender as a "wedge" issue to run on. Victimizing minority groups is standard political practice. In many cases, the communities are so negative toward transgender people that it is difficult to change the culture. Janet Mock laments this situation:

... I think of the hundreds of thousands of LGBTQ (lesbian, gay, bisexual, transgender, queer or questioning) youth who are flung from intolerant homes, from families who reject them when they reveal themselves. Of the estimated 1.6 million homeless and runaway American youth, as many as 40% are LGBTQ ... .

—Janet Mock, *Redefining Realness*[6]

Using the Deming model, initially focus on cultural change and the very local level, which means starting with church groups, community centers, and businesses. If one organization will not immediately talk about transgender tolerance and acceptance, find one that will. The idea is to demonstrate positive results that will be contagious. Clergymen do get together and compare notes, so the word spreads. All one needs is for one clergyman or lay minister to start preaching tolerance and more may follow. Holding families together should be rewarded, and talking about successes is usually more pleasant than fire and brimstone. Building from the bottom up also applies to political districts. Start with a city or county that can be convinced to change and build up to the state and national levels.

So what needs to be done? First of all, transgender people need to be visible in the community. A transperson should attend each one of the churches and community centers in the target area periodically. I have never heard of a transgender person being thrown out of a church service, but I suppose it may have happened. If they are thrown out, the community organizations can be shamed on social media. Talk to people and make friends if possible. Next, if you are able to do public speaking, go out to all the community organizations you can talk to and answer questions. With the current interest in being transgender, that should not be a problem. And make some more friends. If you are not a churchgoer or a talker, there are still lots of things a transgender person can do to change community culture. Who is going to coordinate all those visits? There are roles for people to coordinate if they do not do the talking. If you have the fire in your belly, run for public office, starting at the school board level and working up. Even if you lose, you will have spread the message.

Another cultural change strategy is to tackle the problem of housing. Many transgender people are not admitted to homeless shelters because of religious or other objections. There are volunteer transgender organizations that are trying to provide shelters where needed and the Federal government has a policy that a shelter cannot collect Federal money if it discriminates. Long-term housing is also needed. Some cities, like Chicago, have taken the bull by the horns and provide housing for transgender people. This direct approach provides a residence so that transgender people can get off the street, get counseling, get jobs, and be reunited with their families in some cases. There are also volunteer organizations trying to provide long-term housing. For the transgender person fortunate to have a place to live, they can either support laws that encourage transgender housing or they can help a volunteer organization.

As to changes in the laws to deal with the problem of transgender people in the street, here are some suggestions. The most obvious suggestion is to set up arrest diversion programs. These allow transgender people accused of street crimes to go into counseling and vocational programs, rather than being convicted. Conviction brings with it a criminal record, and in some cases getting put on a sex-crimes registry. Both of these prohibit future employment. The goal is for the arrested transgender person to get a job. This may require vocational training or completion of a high school degree. Such programs require legislation and funding by local cities and counties, which transgender people should initiate and/or support. And transgender people can act as volunteers in the effort.

Public health initiatives are needed to get transgender people off the street or at least stay healthy. Free or government clinics provide such treatment including counseling, HIV/STD testing, and access to hormones for transsexuals. Such clinics usually provide biweekly injections and tests for transsexual people on the street. Some of these injections are for transsexual transition, but others are to stop the spread of STDs. Of course, such public health initiatives also benefit society as a whole by limiting the HIV/STD reservoir that transgender people on the street provide. Free clinics often need volunteers to help with setup, administration, fund raising and other tasks, so there are ways for transgender people and their allies to participate. Planned Parenthood also recently started providing access to hormones for transsexual HT treatment.

Who is going to do all this? Transgender people and their allies. If transgender people want a better world, they need to create it. The good news is that people in the transgender community know how to do this, and there has been no better time than today. It is time for transgender people to come out into the light and change the world or at least one aspect of it.

THE FUTURE OF GENDER

Gender behavior has declined in its importance over the past 40 years. The breadwinner family model with a male earning all the income necessary for the family and a female taking care of the house and children has all but vanished. The male breadwinner model is akin to the traditional sex-based evolutionary theory (see Biological Theories of Gender Development in Chapter 4. in which tasks, genetics and gender are closely linked with sex and pregnancy. The breadwinner model was touted during World War II and for the first 30 years afterward, when the United States enjoyed economic preeminence in the world. However, since that time U.S. incomes have not increased as quickly as before. Multiple breadwinners are now needed to maintain families. The nature of work in the United States has changed with manufacturing disappearing and with service and information jobs on the increase. The U.S. military now needs people who can operate increasingly complex weaponry, and even combat roles are now open up to women. Female warriors can become stronger now, because bodybuilding and fitness training are no longer a male dominated mystery. Just about every gym in the country can provide weight and fitness training.

For those who grew up in the male breadwinner model, many found it distasteful:

> I have come to see that gender system created by this culture as a particularly malevolent and divisive construct, made all the more dangerous by the seeming inability of the culture to question gender, its own creation.
> —Kate Bornstein, *Gender Outlaw*[7]

Truth be told, the post–World War II breadwinner model was a wartime and postwar dream and an illusion. All family members in the United States, had contributed to family incomes since the country's inception, sometimes unfortunately, including the children. Family farming required participation by all in the family, usually without compensation. In urban areas, females took in laundry and cleaned houses to make money. After females demonstrated that they could contribute to the war effort through manufacturing *ala* Rosie the Riveter, females never left the workforce. (Rosie the Riveter is an icon used to symbolize those women who contributed to the World War II effort by doing jobs like shipbuilding, airplane and munitions manufacturing, previously assigned to males. During the war, there was a big expansion of such jobs with no males to fill them.) While politicians and others were spouting the breadwinner model, the real model was Rosie the Riveter, and her predecessors and successors. Statistics show that even before the war, 25% of females were engaged in work in industry, outside the home. Before 1941, 30% of females participating in the workforce had been there for 10 years, and 50% of them had been there for over 5 years. Today, females constitute about 56% of the workforce. Females started out by earning less than half of wages as males for the same jobs. Now that number is 89% and, with continuing advocacy, promises to go up.

The breadwinner model never did apply to my family. If I look back at my family during the period when I was growing up in post–World War II America, all but one of my aunts had jobs outside the home. The only one not to have an outside job took care of the schedule of her husband, who was a doctor. The same is true with all of my female cousins who all currently work outside the home. My mother, but not my father, had a college degree. She was the first college graduate in my family. More of my aunts than my uncles actually had college degrees. Even today, although both of my female children have outside jobs, one of their male spouses stays home to take care of the kids.

With the slowing of the U.S. economy through war and several recessions since the 1980s, many females became the breadwinners of the home because they were in the workforce and they had talents that were in demand. Females realized that they could gain skills and earn more money by going to college, so now more females than males are going to college. Today 25% of females make more than their male spouses.

Under these economic conditions, the kinship theory of gender evolution would predict that the importance of gender should decline. The Native Americans crossed gender lines to perform tasks for the survival of their families and their tribes. Just as these Native American cultures did, people today are ignoring traditional gender behavior categories to work where they are most productive and earn the most to take care of their families. Most employers are now more prone to hire on the basis of education, skills, and other talents, rather than the sex or gender of a person, although there is still residual resistance.. Dressing up for work is no longer a priority in some jobs, and both males and females wear jeans and casual clothing in many service and knowledge jobs. Gender based dressing up for travel has all but vanished due to increased security measures and the need to adapt to uncomfortable airplanes.

The future will be created by the young. Young people aged 14–34 have taken note of economic conditions and worldwide commerce trends and now say in a survey by the Intelligence Group, a consumer research organization as quoted in *USA Today*, that gender is unimportant to them. The survey found in general that:

> ... gender is less a definer of identity today than it was for prior generations. Rather than adhering to traditional gender roles, young people are interpreting what gender means to them personally.
> —Sharon Jayson, *USA Today*, July 2, 2014[8]

In the survey, more than two-thirds said that gender does not define who they are and more than 60% said that gender lines have been blurred.

Many young single females see work as a means of security and independence in an uncertain world. About 6% females report that they are unhappy with their assigned gender behavior category. Females report that they are unhappy with restrictive gender rules, including culturally required appearance and presentation.

The future of gender is with the young. Where young people are accepting of being transgender, cultural change has already occurred. Where older people are not accepting in the subcultures of the geographic South and

Midwest, we can anticipate that the traditional binary, cisgender, and inflexible gender culture will resist change. Will the young in these latter subcultures follow their traditional sex-based gender culture of their parents, or will they follow along with their peers who accept transgender people?

I believe that given current conditions, young people in nonaccepting subcultures will generally follow their accepting peers for three reasons:

1. The Internet
2. Cultural change efforts
3. Economics

The Internet provides information and social contacts based on interests, not on geography. It is used extensively by both accepting and nonaccepting subcultures. Young people use it extensively. The Internet is a communication capability that was not existent in previous historical times. In the past, the U.S. subcultures that were not accepting of minorities, such as the South, were geographically isolated. Information exchange is important and so is social networking. People in these nonaccepting subcultures, especially the young, can get information to see that transgender people are real people. They can see that transgender people are humans deserving civil and legal rights like everyone else.

Cultural change efforts are underway in the nonaccepting subcultures to improve transgender tolerance and acceptance. There are transgender advocacy organizations that are building acceptance in local areas, working toward acceptance at the county and state levels. Last summer, the organization GLAAD toured the South and collected video stories of GLBT people, which have been widely distributed to encourage acceptance.

Judging by the restroom law controversies, economics will play a big role in gaining acceptance for transgender people. The fundamental economic fact is that many of these nonaccepting subcultures, particularly in the South, are also areas of poverty and low economic activity. Skilled workers in these areas tend to leave because they can find better jobs elsewhere. These subcultures receive far more in aid from the Federal government than they contribute to the Federal budget in taxes and fees. The recent growth in these areas is not due to organic economic activities of local economies. It comes largely from encouraging businesses to move there, using tax abatements and other incentives. In these abatement deals, assessment of taxes is often delayed for several years, with the agreement by businesses to provide jobs for the local economy. Paradoxically, economic growth through tax abatements has two effects that support cultural change. Because so many workers have left the areas, new workers will need to move from other areas of the United States, bringing their accepting culture with them. The second effect is that some migrating transgender-accepting businesses will insist that workers and customers be protected from discrimination, because it is good for their business. This is already happening in states with discriminatory laws such as North Carolina. Rejecting transgender people is bad for business in terms of attracting both workers and customers. Enlightened business leaders will continue to insist in tolerance and acceptance of transgender people

Businesses that move to nonaccepting geographic areas are not anchored to those areas by the availability of raw materials or local economic features. So if the subcultures will not change, they can easily pick up and move when the tax abatements expire or if businesses start to lose employees or customers because of discrimination. Tolerant skilled workers who migrate to these tax-abated jobs will leave when the businesses leave. This will also subject these areas to increased risk of economic collapse. It is noteworthy that the state of New York is already engaged in a campaign to encourage big businesses to move to their state from states with discriminatory laws. Their current targets are Texas, Mississippi, and North Carolina.

If cultural change about GLBT people does not come to young people in these nonaccepting subcultures, the United States runs the risk of experiencing a geographical, economic, and cultural schism, which will be hard to heal. The last time such schisms existed, the United States was afflicted with a civil war and its negative aftereffects. It is up to young transgender people to play their part in cultural change. They should concentrate on their peers who live in non-accepting geographic areas.

NOTES

1. Kate Bornstein, *Gender Outlaw: On Men, Women, and the Rest of Us* (New York: Routledge, 1994), 22.

2. Martin Niemoller, quoted in Harold Marcuse, "The Origin and Reception of Martin Niemoller's Quotation" (University of California, Santa Barbara Version, July 31, 2014).

3. Sheryl Gay Stolberg, "Obama's Gay Views Evolving" (*New York Times*, June 18, 2011), http://www.nytimes.com/2011/06/19/us/politics/19marriage.html?_r=0 (confirmed July 10, 2016).

4. Bornstein, *Gender Outlaw*, 12.

5. Janet Mock, *Redefining Realness: My Path to Womanhood, Identity, Love and So Much More* (New York: Atria Books, 2014), 199–200.

6. Ibid., 109.

7. Bornstein, *Gender Outlaw*, 12.

8. Sharon Jayson, "Gender Loses Its Impact with the Young" (*USA Today*, July 2, 2014), http://www.usatoday.com/story/news/nation/2014/06/21/gender-millennials-dormitories-sex/10573099/ (confirmed July 10, 2016).

CHAPTER 10

FAQ

J ust about every morning, I flip on my laptop and wade through the overnight search engine "hits" on being transgender. Scientific articles I find are read and put into my database. References to scientific articles go into the queue for library research. The vast majority of the "hits" are trash but some are either pro- or anti-transgender articles that suggest questions that science should address. The most frequently asked questions are included in this chapter under categories from "A to Z" with current answers based on science and my experience.

ATHLETICS

Are Transgender People Allowed to Participate in the Olympics and International Competition?

At the international athletic and Olympic level both FTM and MTF can compete, according to recent policy decisions. No transsexual GPS is required, but the athlete has to declare their sex that they cannot change for four years. FTM can compete without restriction on male teams. MTF have to be on HT and below a particular blood testosterone level for at least a year. It is not clear whether this blood testosterone requirement will continue because of court cases. The National Collegiate Athletic Association (NCAA) has a similar policy as the Olympics and international organization, except there is no blood testosterone restriction for MTF. The NCAA also has rules for transgender people taking hormones. FTM can compete on either male or female teams. In order to encourage participation, the NCAA has new rules for mixed male/female teams. Athletics below the NCAA level are governed by state athletic associations whose policies on transgender athletes vary.

Are Transgender People Allowed to Participate
in High School Competition?

High school athletics is governed by state athletic associations. Policies for participation by transgender people vary from state to state.

How Do the Olympics and International Athletics
Determine the Sex of a Potential Competitor?

Right now it is unclear how Olympics and international athletics will determine the sex for assignment in male or female competition categories. The usual problem is a competitor who seeks to compete with females, not with males. The experts on the Olympic medical panels have eliminated chromosomes, DNA genes, and external genitalia examinations as being unreliable. Last year an international court for athletics struck down the use of blood testosterone levels to determine sex.

BIOLOGY

What Is the Evidence for a Biological Basis
for Being Transgender?

There are several sources of evidence that support the idea that being transgender involves both DNA genetic and epigenetic factors. DNA genetics appear to be the primary factor from twin and family studies, transgender DNA markers, and various biomarkers such as handedness and brain/body structure. But not every identical twin has an identical twin transsexual or transgender person, which means that epigenetic mechanisms can block being transgender. This is known as the **Two-Factor Theory** of Being Transgender. This theory is detailed in Chapter 3.

Why Are There Transgender People?

No one knows for sure but here is a reasonable explanation based on the kinship theory of human behavior evolution (see Chapter 4 in the "Biological Theories of Gender Development" Section). Transgender people are part of the biodiversity of nature involved in human evolution. The kinship theory of human evolution holds that it is the survival of the family, clan, tribe, or group that is important to continuing the species. With this perspective, it may be that the gender behavior predisposition traits have provided needed flexibility in performing survival tasks. For this reason, gender behavior predispositions that are independent of sex genetics continue in our genetic makeup. This is contrasted with the traditional theory of human evolution that holds that survival tasks are allocated on the basis of sex alone, with no male performing feminine tasks and no female performing masculine tasks. This theory is often cited to validate the current Western gender system, although many using the theory do not realize it. There is ample social anthropology evidence to refute the traditional theory, including gender diverse cultures, changes in occupations of gender behavior categories in the 20th century, which is too short a time for DNA evolution to take place, and studies of contemporary hunter-gatherer societies, which show that females perform many tasks previously thought to be male-only.

Are Transgender Brains Different from Cisgender Brains?

Yes, there are differences in several places, as described in Chapter 3: There Are Biological Differences in Structure and Function between the Brains of Transgender People and Non-Transgender People. During MTF transsexual hormone therapy, the volume of places in the hypothalamus decreases by about 30 cc in adults, perhaps reflecting that some parts of the male nervous sexual system are no longer important. Unfortunately, these differences could not be fully characterized in the study because the MRI machine being used did not have adequate resolution.

Are Transgender People Intersex?

They are not usually considered as intersex. Being intersex has to do with sex organ formation, whereas being transgender has to do with biological gender predisposition and behavior. Being transgender and being intersex involve different DNA genes as far as we know from the existing studies. Intersex has to do with differences in development of the sex organs and there are a large number of difference patterns, so the number of intersex people can vary from 0.3% to 1% to 3% of live births, depending on which patterns you include in the total. Most of these intersex differences are due to DNA genetics. The DNA formation responsible for being intersex can be in any of the chromosomes. Although a special gene in the sex chromosome Y can kick off the formation of male sex organs, the recipe for forming these organs actually resides in the genes in the non-sex chromosomes. Some of the intersex conditions are so severe that the sex of a newborn baby cannot be determined with accuracy. Some of the milder conditions, like undescended testicles in males, are very common and can be easily fixed by surgery.

Are Transgender People as Intelligent as Non-Transgender People?

There is a wide variation in intelligence and knowledge among transgender people, just like non-transgender people. We know that most transgender people are intelligent enough to learn how to behave in both gender behavior categories, which requires intelligence. Successful transgender people can be found in jobs requiring higher learning in medicine, science, mathematics, engineering, and technology. We also know that about 65% of transgender people teach their medical providers how to treat them. Transgender people make very complicated decisions about their lives than non-transgender people do and for the most part are pretty good at them. All that said there are no direct scientific comparison studies between transgender and non-transgender people on intelligence or knowledge. Defining how to measure intelligence is difficult because there are many different kinds of intelligence. Judging by the raging controversy over whether there are differences in intelligence in non-transgender people between males and females, any such studies are likely to be difficult to interpret.

If One Identical Twin of a Twin Pair Is Transgender/ Transsexual, Why Is Not the Other Twin Always Transgender/Transsexual?

Identical twins start out at conception with identical DNA genes, but during pregnancy, there are epigenetic mechanisms and during the lifespan that alter the DNA or alter its expression. By the time that identical twins are born, there are already considerable differences between identical twins, which continue to develop throughout life.

Do Not All the Cells in the Body Contain Identical DNA and Chromosomes That Can Be Used to Determine Sex?

No. There are several reasons that this is not true. First, some people do not have XX or XY sex chromosomes, but instead they have all sorts of combinations, like XXY, XXX, XYY, and XYYY. Some of the combinations result in miscarriages but many do not. Even though one may have XY sex chromosomes, it does not necessarily mean that one will have male genitalia, as the intersex condition of androgen insensitivity syndrome (AIS) demonstrates. People with AIS usually have XY chromosomes but all have a defect in their androgen receptor gene that prevents testosterone from acting to form male genitalia.

Second, each person shares cells with their mother *in utero* during pregnancy. Both chromosomes and DNA are transferred. The cell transfer goes both ways, so later children are likely to pick up some of the cells from their older brothers and sisters as well as from their mother and maybe even from her mother and siblings.

Third, many people have blood transfusions and transplants, which involve tissues that do not have the same DNA and chromosomes. In fact, cells containing DNA from male bone marrow donors have been found in the brains of female recipients. It appears that the brain is a safe haven for cells that are not those of a person's original DNA at conception. They otherwise might be destroyed by the immune system.

Fourth, many people are **mosaics**, meaning that they have more than one type of DNA. One of the most obvious differences occurs in people when one eye has a different color from the other, because it has a different configuration of the 15 or so genes that determine eye color. All females are mosaics because they have two X chromosomes. They have duplicate genes in each position on the X chromosome, but only one can be expressed in each cell. The result is that each cell in a female has a different combination of DNA gene expressions from the two X chromosomes.

Fifth, genes do not always stay still; they hop from one position to another and from one chromosome to another on the DNA molecule on a cell-by-cell basis. The gene that kicks off male body development (SRY) is usually on the Y chromosome, but it has been found missing on the Y chromosome and present on other chromosomes. These hopping genes are called **transposons.** So the DNA of one cell in the body may look considerably different from another. The SRY gene can even appear in the DNA of people with XX chromosomes and male organs are formed. When scientists go to look for genes in identified positions on DNA molecule, they only appear where they are supposed to about 65% of the time.

Sixth, some people are called **tetragametic chimeras** because they developed from two cells that merged immediately after conception. These people have different types of DNA in different parts of their bodies. If one of the two cells carried the genetic recipe for male body development and the other for female body development, such people may have a mixture of male and female organs. We did not know about people with this genetic situation until genetic testing started for legal and medical purposes, but such testing is rapidly expanding.

Seventh, the DNA of every neural cells in the brain is unique with over 1,000 different places where they are different from the surrounding neural cells. We are just beginning to understand the involvement of DNA changes, but some of them appear to be involved in learning mechanisms. This is consistent with the brain being a "safe haven" for cells with different DNA.

Because of these reasons, the use of chromosomes or DNA to determine sex is not reliable. Medical experts working for the Olympics and international athletics organizations currently agree.

Why Are Transsexual People Used in Biological Studies Instead of Both Transsexual and Non-Transsexual Transgender People?

There are two reasons, one theoretical and one practical. Because transsexual people take the radical step of physically changing their bodies, some researchers believe that they have a stronger transgender motivation. They reason that if they are looking for an experimental effect comparing transgender to non-transgender people on some measurement, then it will take fewer transsexual study participants to show the effect. This difference in transgender motivation comes from clinical impressions and is scientifically unproven. The practical reason is that transsexuals are more readily available for research because in many countries, transsexuals must report to government or private gender clinics in order to go through transition. At these clinics, they are more accessible for research. Most non-transsexual transgender people never report to a gender clinic, so they are hard to identify and less available for research.

Is There a Relationship between Being Transgender and Handedness?

Yes. Several studies have found that both MTF and FTM transsexuals are less right-handed than non-transsexual controls. Handedness does not mean that one is totally right-handed or left-handed. It means that given a set of common tasks, transgender people are more likely to use their left hand than their right. Unfortunately, there are no large-scale studies on non-transsexual transgender people. Understanding this relationship may help explain genetic or epigenetic factors in being transgender, because studies show that handedness can be inherited through DNA.

Is There a Relationship between Being on the Autism Spectrum and Being Transgender?

Several studies indicate that there is an overlap of people who are both on the **autism spectrum (AS)** as well as being transgender. Being on the

AS means that a person is different in terms of social interaction and verbal communication from others. The overlap figures range between 6% and 20%. These studies are suspect because they use relatively small clinical populations and invalidated scales. Because people on the AS are less sensitive to others' feelings, they may more readily admit being transgender because they cannot sense or expect a negative reaction. It would be good to have more information on this possible overlap because we know that some people on the AS are there because they have a genetic predisposition, inherited from their parents. It is suspected that AS may also triggered by environmental epigenetics.

CHILDREN

Are Children Mature Enough to Know That They Are Transgender?

Children have mastered the basics of gender by the age of 2–3, and most transgender children come to the realization that they are transgender by age 4–5. Today, more transgender children are going through social transition in time to take puberty blocking hormones by age 8. Mental health and medical professionals supervise decisions about transgender children. One of their primary concerns is to be sure that transgender children have enough knowledge and are mature enough to proceed. Providers are looking for signs that a child is insistent, persistent, and consistent about their transgender behavior.

Should Children Play with Toys according to Their Sex?

Playing with toys is one way children learn about the world and themselves. Children should play with whatever toys interest them as long as they are safe toys. A recent study indicates that both sex children prefer enjoy playing with dolls up until age 2 ½. They are probably attracted to dolls because babies are drawn to human facial features as soon as they are born and their eyes are open. Parents and family teach children about gender and one of the early lessons they teach is what are the appropriate toys for each gender. However, some children have toy preferences that do not agree with what their parents think they ought to be but that does not make them transgender. Male artists have to start playing with art supplies, which their parents might think is too girly. Future male chefs may want to play in the kitchen. Future male musicians may prefer musical devices, rather than playing with trucks. Future female engineers need access to trucks and building materials.

Playing with toys is self-regulating. Children will play with toys that inter-est them and grow tired of toys that no longer hold their attention if parental interference is not a factor. Give them both "masculine" and "feminine" toys and see what they do. Later, they will tell you what they want. Trying to change their gender preferences is fruitless, as the ineffectiveness of reparative therapy and psychotherapy has demonstrated.

I have never found a large-scale scientific study that compared the toys that transgender and non-transgender children actually play with. I do not remember playing much with dolls as a child, although they were available. I was more interested in electricity, electronics, and radio. As my mother put it, "all you want to do is play with things with a wire on one end and a noise on the other."

I remember being able to play at cooking because my mother said that someday I might need to cook for my family or myself. She was right about that. She said that there was nothing sissy about cooking because all of the great chefs were male. (This may seem sexist but at the time it was probably true. This was before Julia Child became famous.) I remember that both my parents allowed me to play with and learn about their professional equip-ment. They taught me their particular skills whether they were considered masculine or feminine. When I was old enough, my father taught me to fire and clean pistols and rifles (he was a wildlife manager and used them for defense when necessary against hunters that were already armed), how to play sports, and surveying. It was the result of his teaching me about surveying, using aerial photography, that set me on a career involving remote sensing from airplanes and space. My mother taught me "domestic" basic skills of cleaning and sewing. Although today, I have forgotten most of it; I can barely sew on a button. Her major contribution to me was to teach me to read at an early age because she was an elementary schoolteacher.

Is Being Transgender Caused by Child Abuse, Child Trauma, Family Loss, or Disruption?

There is no evidence that being transgender is caused by negative child-hood experiences. All of the empirical studies of transgender children indi-cate that parental relationships are not responsible for being transgender. However, there is abundant evidence that many transgender children are ver-bally and physically abused by their families, because their transgender behav-ior is a violation of the cultural gender system. None of these studies indicates that abuse is the cause of being transgender.

Do Medical Providers Encourage Children to Be Transgender?

No. Guidelines from the World Professional Association for Transgender Health have been set up to insure that any treatment for being transgender is undertaken with caution. Decisions about children require a team of parents, mental health professionals, medical doctors, and endocrinologists to agree. Reversible treatments are undertaken before irreversible treatments. Decisions on treatments are based on success with previous treatments. For example, social transition must be complete before puberty blocking hormone treatment can begin. There is plenty of opportunity for a child to change their behavior or for parents to change their minds.

What Happens to Transgender Children When They Grow Up? Do They Become Transsexuals or Homosexuals or What?

There has been a notion abroad among psychiatric circles that transgender children will grow up to be homosexual or transsexual. (There is nothing wrong with being homosexual or transsexual, of course.) However, the idea has been used to scare parents into unproven treatments for transgender children. There are no effective treatments to "cure" transgender children or transgender adults for that matter.

This idea comes from a few studies of a few transgender children in clinics. Findings from clinics are always biased because the numbers of children under study are small and because children with multiple problems tend to be referred there. Many times they have multiple problems in addition to the problems that go with being transgender. The gender clinic at Harvard reports a 41% co-occurrence of being transgender with other problems. So the children are very few in number, and they are the worst off in terms of problems. The other difficulty with these studies is that they do have adequate data on a longitudinal basis, over decades, in order to characterize outcomes. They have high dropout rates and there are increasing incentives for teens and young adults not to admit in later life that they are still transgender. So these studies are useless for answering the question at hand.

We know that some transgender children grow up to be transgender adults. Some transgender adults may not have revealed themselves as transgender children. Many, like me, were in the closet starting almost as soon as they knew they were transgender. If I had been asked whether I performed transgender behavior on surveys or studies, I certainly would have lied.

We know that some transgender adults are also gay or lesbian or asexual, but there is no way of knowing for sure whether they were gay or lesbian or asexual as children, because sexual orientations do not usually solidify in childhood. Some transsexuals know they are transsexual as children, but some only come to that realization in later life. The "late bloomers" typically have been transgender for long periods of time until something triggers them to change.

The bottom line is that transgender children and their parents should have counseling help available, but there is no cure for being transgender and therefore no reason to seek one.

Why Does There Seem to Be a Large Increase in Transgender Children?

Many doctors believe that the underlying population frequency of being a transgender child has not changed, but previously it was a hidden issue. Rather than ignoring the issue, parents are now seeking help for these children. Counseling, supervised social transition and puberty blocking treatments have increased in frequency.

Are Transgender Children Just Confused about Gender?

No. Studies show that transgender children are as consistent in their knowledge of gender as non-transgender children, which means that they are not confused.

CULTURE

Why Do People Hate/Fear Transgender People?

Many people have strong emotions about transgender people. These emotions are alternatively labeled as hate, sexual arousal, or fear. What determines the reaction and label depends on previous experiences and the person's curiosity. Many humans have emotional reactions to someone or something that is unknown or unusual, although others are drawn to novel people and situations. Transgender people often do not appear or sound like other people, so they may be perceived as unusual. Humans have acute sensory capabilities to discriminate things like facial features, gait, and dress, so they can detect minor flaws in transgender presentation. People learn what is familiar from their experience with other people as well as from their parents, their communities, and their schooling. They may have heard mistaken ideas about transgender people, or they may have been exposed to transgender criminals who are not representative of the transgender community. Personal knowledge of transgender people will decrease the emotional reaction.

DEFINITIONS

Why Do You Call It Transsexual Genital Plastic Surgery (GPS) in This Book?

I call it that because all of the other terms used are inaccurate and because genital plastic surgery is the correct medical term used for similar procedures in non-transgender people, though the operations are normally less extensive than transsexual GPS. The changes made in transsexual GPS are only part of those used to change sex organs during transsexual transition. The alternatives are all misnomers. "Sex reassignment surgery" is incorrect because reassignment has to do with labeling and naming, not with surgery. Gender reassignment surgery and gender confirmation surgery are incorrect because the whole idea is that transsexuals already know their gender, so it does not have to be reassigned or confirmed. Most know from early childhood what their gender is. The purpose of transsexual GPS is to change their bodies so that they are more in anatomical and functional alignment with cultural expectations of their congruent gender. "Genital reconstructive surgery" is incorrect because the genitals are not being rebuilt after injury. "Sex realignment surgery" is incorrect because the body was not previously in or out of alignment. GPS is the term used to describe a surgery that improves the form, function, and appearance of the genitalia. Transsexual GPS improves the body to better meet cultural expectations of appearance and function for a person, with their congruent gender behavior category.

Why Do You Deemphasize the Use of Term "Gender Identity"?

There are two reasons. First, "gender identity" started out as a pathological term in the psychiatric community and still is used in the ICD listing of mental disorders. In psychiatric terms, one can claim to have the identity of Napoleon or Neil Armstrong, but those are delusions. Being transgender is not a delusion or a mental illness. Second, the word "identity" (and identify) is used in sociology to refer to membership in a group such as identifying as an American or an Atlantan or a writer or a soccer fan. It does not reflect anything objective like transgender behavior or how transgender people present themselves in a particular gender behavior category.

I interpret reports of gender identity to mean that a transgender person is giving a verbal report of their gender behavior as transwoman or transman. As scientific evidence, reports of gender identity are weaker than direct observation by a trained observer, but they cannot be dismissed altogether.

EDUCATION

What Restrooms Must a Transgender Student Use in Schools?

Title IX of Education Act bans discrimination on the basis of sex. This has been interpreted in Federal policy that a transgender student should go to the restroom and locker room, which is aligned with their congruent gender behavior category. Schools that do not follow this policy are subject to loss of Federal funds for education. There are severe health implications if transgender people are forced to use their noncongruent restroom or locker room. If they refrain from using a restroom because of potential humiliation and embarrassment, it may also cause urinary tract infections, dehydration, or bowel problems. Pediatricians who treat intersex children have expressed concern about the discriminatory restroom law in North Carolina. They are concerned about children who cannot be assigned sex at birth and whose birth certificates do not match their current sex. It may be traumatic for them to use a restroom based on the sex of their birth certificates.

The Federal government recently sent out guidelines for restroom and locker room use by transgender people in schools that supports the idea that transgender people should use the rooms in accordance with their congruent gender behavior category. This puts millions of dollars in jeopardy for Federal aid to education for noncompliance.

ELDERLY

What Happens to Transgender People When They Get Old?

The number of senior transgender people is growing along with the "baby boomer" bulge of senior non-transgender people. Transgender people face some unique challenges. Most elder care (80%) is provided by families, but transgender people are often estranged from their families because of transgender rejection. Transgender people experience discrimination in applying for assisted living and nursing home facilities, despite the fact that there is a Federal housing and urban development policy that interprets the Fair

Housing Act to protect transgender people. To meet the demand, assisted living facilities that specialize in accommodating GLBT people have been started. Transgender people can cope with aging by making sure that they develop a social network of family and friends. The Veterans Administration can provide financial help with assisted living if the transgender person served in the military.

EMPLOYMENT AND ECONOMICS

What Is Known about the Demographics of Transgender People? What Is Their Lifestyle Like?

Transgender people come from all walks of life and all socioeconomic strata. There are multibillionaire transgender people, like Jennifer Pritzker, and there are the abject poor. At least 25% of transgender people make less than $10,000 a year. There are many notable successful transgender people and some are listed on Lynn Conway's web page http://ai.eecs.umich.edu/people/conway/TSsuccesses/TSgallery1.html.

Transgender lives are generally not very exotic. Most transgender people manage to reproduce and have families. They take care of their families and homes. They are not confused or mentally ill. They generally love their mother and father, siblings, wives, and families. Most kept being transgender a secret for some period of time. Some are recreational transgender people and only crosspresent monthly or less often, but some go full time.

Most transgender people have relatively normal jobs and are not prostitutes or drug pushers. All they want to do when they go to the bathroom of their congruent gender is to pee or move their bowels. (There are absolutely no reports of transgender committing acts of violence in restrooms.) Many have seen a mental health professional only if they want to start transsexual transition or have marital or social problems. About 10% have started transsexual transition. Transgender people join the military at a rate 20 times that of other people and approximately 20,000 are currently in the U.S. military. There are many transgender veterans who fought for the United States or other countries.

Are Transgender People Protected from Employment Discrimination?

Transgender people are protected by some local and state laws. Some states, notably North Carolina, in 2016, have passed laws that nullify local city ordinances, which would have provided protection in Charlotte and other cities. Local ordinance protection can also be struck down by state courts if it conflicts with state constitutions.

There is no legislation at the Federal level that protects transgender people in employment. Transgender people have some protection based on legal precedents, which have ruled that protection is provided under sex discrimination provisions of the Federal Civil Rights Act. Because of these precedents, a Federal Equal Opportunity Commission policy now protects transgender people. But employment disputes are still likely to end up in expensive lawsuits or EEOC complaints which is a form of rights denial.

ETIQUETTE

What Pronouns Should One Use with Transgender People?

Transgender people usually prefer the pronouns associated with their congruent gender behavior category and presentation, but some prefer gender-neutral pronouns. Gender-neutral pronouns include using the third person plural "they" in place of the third person singular "she" and "he." There are also about a dozen invented pronoun systems like using **"ze"** for the third person plural but none have gained widespread use. It is polite for a person talking to a transgender person to ask for their pronoun preferences at the beginning of the conversation. In print, journalists should also use preferred pronouns, or if preferred pronouns are unknown, should use pronouns consistent with the way they live or lived. Both the AP wire service and GLAAD provide guidelines in the United States.

Is It All Right to Compliment a Transgender Person on Their Presentation?

Yes, it is fine to compliment a transgender person on aspects of their presentation, if you really mean it. However, it is rude to say things like "you almost could pass" or "you look just like a woman/man."

Should a Person Ask about the Genitals of a Transgender or Transsexual Person?

No. Transgender and transsexual people believe that this is their business and not anyone else's business. If they want to volunteer the information, that is their choice.

Should Transsexuals Be Asked Whether They Are Preop or Postop?

No. It is nobody's business but the transsexual. As Julia Serano, transgender author, explains:

> It is offensive that so many people feel it is okay to publicly refer to transsexuals as being "pre-op" or "post-op" when it would so clearly be degrading and demeaning to regularly describe all boys and men as either "circumcised" or "uncircumcised."
>
> —Julia Serano, *Whipping Girl*[1]

INCARCERATION

How Should Transgender People Be Treated in Incarceration Facilities?

Transgender people should be housed according to their congruent gender behavior category, not their birth sex. Searches should be done according to a person's congruent gender behavior category. If jailers are unsure, they should ask. They should not be normally housed in solitary confinement, because it constitutes cruel and unusual punishment. They should be protected from sexual assault. The rate of sexual assault among transgender inmates is 13 times higher than among cisgender inmates. The Federal Prison Rape Elimination Act requires that transgender people (1) should not be strip-searched to determine the status of their genitalia, (2) should not be housed according to birth sex, and (3) should be able to change and shower in private. However, even though states receive Federal money, some ignore these requirements, and private prisons are exempt from penalties due to a loophole in Federal law. Incarcerated transgender people should receive transgender healthcare, including GPS, because such treatments are medically necessary. The government is responsible for their health and welfare because of their incarceration.

LAW ENFORCEMENT

Why Does the TSA Give Transgender People a Hard Time?

There are four reasons why the TSA hassles transgender people. The first is that the Taliban and other terrorists have previously dressed in traditional feminine clothing, the burka, which covers their entire bodies. They have done this to smuggle suicide vests, explosives, and arms. This somehow got translated to the TSA agents that they should be wary of those pretending to be the opposite sex. Second, terrorists began to use their underwear and vests to transport explosives. So this got translated into the need to see under people's clothing and the development of radar scanners. Although assurances were given that transgender people could still wear bras, breast binders, and packers, TSA agents have not been adequately trained to deal with transgender people. Third, the TSA scanners have a flaw in that they need a human TSA agent to tell them the sex of each person being inspected. Otherwise the scanner manufacturers could not meet their contracted performance requirements and still maintain some semblance of privacy. The success of TSA agents in determining sex from external appearance has never been measured, but this task is obviously not easy. And fourth, the TSA heard that other countries like the United Kingdom and Israel were using behavioral interviews and checklists to spot terrorists, so they had to invent their own. Many of the criteria falsely cast suspicion on transgender people. The TSA quietly abandoned their checklist program without knowing why it did not work. I can tell you that the other countries use trained, experienced military and intelligence interrogators in order to have successful programs, which is not a requirement for TSA agents.

MEDICAL

Does Not the Affordable Care Act Provide Insurance Coverage for Transgender Medical Treatment?

Yes, but insurance companies do not offer it in most states. States set the policies for insurance carriers and many do not require coverage or continue to ban coverage for no good reason. Only eight states require GPS coverage in medical insurance policies. Medicare parts A and B require insurers to provide coverage for transgender people, but GPS is decided on an individual basis using medical need and applicable standards of care. Submission of claims for Medicare Parts A and B requires a "condition code 45" to allow computer processing, because computers are set up to compare sex markers with treatments to detect fraud. This code tells the computer that the claim is not fraudulent, even though there is a mismatch between sex marker and the list of authorized treatments. Medicare Advantage and Medicare Part D will not respond to a "condition code 45." Instead coverage requires a letter from a doctor stating that the patient has a "medical necessity" for the treatment.

MENTAL HEALTH

Are Transgender People More at Risk for Mental Health Disorders?

Probably not. There have been studies of clinical populations of transgender people who seem to be more likely to have mental health disorders as well as being transgender. But remember that these are clinical populations and not representative of all transgender people. Many of the ones with the multiple problems end up in clinics. About 40% of transgender people who go to clinics have other problems; some of them have organic mental disorders unrelated to being transgender. Transgender people are subject to "reactive depression" which can be treated with antidepressant drugs, but this type of depression is due to cultural rejection and stress, not to the depression caused by brain disorder. Most transgender people never go into a clinic or see a mental health provider for being transgender. Transgender people do need counseling help sometimes to deal with personal problems, just like everyone else. They also go to mental health providers to get permission letters for transsexual transition and GPS.

Do Transgender People Have "Split Personalities"?

No. The key feature of dissociative identity disorder or "split personalities" is that people cannot remember important information about what they did in one personality when they are in another personality. Part-time transgender people do assume two alternative behavior "roles" when crosspresenting and not crosspresenting. However, most people assume different behavioral roles. For example, at one time, I alternately assumed the roles of father, work supervisor, scientist, soccer coach, transgender person, and football official. Transgender people seem to be able to recall what happens in both their crosspresenting and not crosspresenting roles.

Can Being Transgender Be "Cured"?

No. Being transgender is not a disease or disorder but a naturally occurring phenomenon. There have been several attempts to try to change the gender behavior of transgender people so that they will behave in the gender behavior category that is culturally expected by their birth sex. Some people are still practicing methods of "conversion therapy" or "reparative therapy," but there is no evidence that these methods work. However, there is evidence that similar methods cause long-term harm when applied to homosexuality.

Conversion therapy has been rejected by many professional organizations, which consider it unethical. Laws in various states, provinces, and countries have been passed to outlaw conversion therapy. These laws primarily outlaw conversion therapy for homosexuality, but some also outlaw it for being transgender. Many legal precedents have found that such treatments constitute fraud.

Although psychotherapy is not a "cure," mental health professionals can provide counseling and patient management services. Psychotherapy, as opposed to counseling, may be needed for non-transgender-related problems. Patient management for transgender people means providing them with information on support groups and transgender-friendly businesses and organizations.

Do Transgender People Engage in Odd Forms of Sexual Behavior?

No. The sexual behavior of transgender people is the same as non-transgender people. Being transgender does not mean that one is a pedophile as some hatemongers have suggested.

MILITARY

Do Transgender People Serve in the U.S. Military?

Yes. Approximately 20,000 transgender people are in the military right now. Transgender people join the military at a rate 20 times that of non-transgender people. Transgender and transsexual people serve in the military of many of our NATO allies.

POPULATION FREQUENCIES

Transgender People Do Not Matter Because There Are So Few of Them?

This statement is wrong on two accounts. There are several million transgender people living in the United States. Approximately 1–2% are transwomen and 0.5% are transmen. These percentages are conservative. This is equivalent to the population of several states or large cities. In any room of 100 males, there is likely to be one or more a transgender person. My estimates are that the U.S. population contains approximately 0.35% MTF transsexuals and 0.15% FTM transsexuals. It appears that the number of

transgender people reporting for transition treatment in the United Kingdom is increasing at about 3–4% rate per year. . Estimates before 2000 were
based on those who entered transgender clinics, but most transgender people
never go to a clinic or see a mental health professional. The United States has
a tradition of respecting individual rights, and there are international agreements safeguarding transgender people, so even if being transgender were
rare, transgender people would still matter.

Are There More Transwomen than Transmen?

Yes. It is not clear why this is so. Some people attribute this to cultural
acceptance of females who are allowed by culture to dress in a masculine gender behavior category on a limited basis (tomboys) or permanent basis. Current estimate of the ratio based on population statistics is 5:1, but this ratio
has been steadily closing in recent years. The genetic mechanisms for each
appear to be different.

PUBLIC ACCOMMODATIONS

What Restroom Should a Transgender Person Use?

A transgender person should use the restroom that matches their congruent gender behavior category. Mental health professionals agree that anything else injures transgender people through humiliation, embarrassment,
and loss of authenticity. This includes being forced to use family restrooms
that are supposed "separate but equal." Use of restrooms on the job is governed by U.S. Department of Labor rules that require transgender people
have reasonable access to restrooms according to their congruent gender
behavior category. There are no reported cases of transgender people attacking other people in restrooms. However, 70% of transgender people report
harassment, being attacked, or being denied access to restrooms

SEXUAL ORIENTATION

Are Being Gay and Being Transgender the Same?

No. Being gay or lesbian means that one is attracted romantically to people of the same sex, called one's sexual orientation. Being transgender has
to do with gender behavior. Being transgender means that one behaves in
their congruent gender behavior category that was not the one assigned at
birth according to sex. Some transgender people are gay or lesbian but most

are not. Some transgender people change their sexual orientation to be attracted to the opposite sex as a result of transsexual transition (25% MTF become attracted to males and 40% FTM become attracted to females). Some transsexuals, approximately 15%, change their sex to asexual, which means that they are not attracted to either sex. Sexual orientation changes for MTF when they have GPS, while sexual orientation changes for FTM when they start HT.

SPIRITUALITY

Is Spirituality Sometimes Involved in Being Transgender?

Yes. Some people report that spiritual experiences guided them toward expressing transgender behavior. The Native Americans believed that spiritual experiences reported by a child in dreams were important criteria for assigning a child to one or more gender behavior categories. Those with spiritual experiences of two genders were Two-Spirits who were permitted to move at will between gender behavior categories. Even today there are transgender people who report that they were inspired to be transgender by spiritual experiences. Spirituality is not in conflict with science, because it does not require ethereal spirits or beings. One can have a spiritual experience by looking at the Milky Way or the moon or the planets or a flower or other aspects of nature. Unless we find an interface between ethereal spirits and our bodies, science has to conclude that mechanisms in the brain produce the experience of spirituality. Science has been unsuccessfully looking for such an interface for several centuries. But that does not mean that spirituality is unimportant. It is one of the most profound experiences of human beings.

Did God Make a Mistake by Creating Transgender People?

Being transgender is part of the biological natural diversity of the human species that has helped us to survive and prosper. Natural diversity has allowed at least some humans to pass on their genes to the next generation under adversity. If God created nature, then being transgender is a biological outcome of natural gender behavior diversity. If one does not believe that God created nature, then one has to observe that diversity is an integral feature of nature. Without it, life would have died out long ago because species could not adapt. If one does not believe in God, nature, or evolution, then one might fall back on the argument that God created man in his own image and therefore some part of God is transgender. Many religions teach that

God is infallible and that God does not make mistakes. So why would being transgender be an exception? If you do not believe in any of this, then take solace in the fact that the best international ethicists, regardless of their religious preferences, support the rights of transgender people.

SUICIDE

Does the High Rate of Attempted Suicide among Transgender People Indicate That They Are Mentally Ill?

No. Transgender people are typically under stress because of secrecy and cultural rejection. Depression and attempted suicide are natural reactions to these stresses and do not constitute mental illness. Most transgender people are not depressed because they have an organic mental illness caused by biological mechanisms. They have what is known as "situational" or "reactive depression" in response to cultural rejection. Many transgender people who attempt suicide are typically teenagers and young adults. The attempted suicide rates for this age group are higher than all age groups of all people, not just transgender people. Transgender people in this age group have the normal stress of puberty and growing up plus the stress of living in secrecy or openly and being rejected. It is no wonder that the rate of contemplated suicide is 80% and that the rate of attempted suicide among transgender people is at least 40%. The high rate of attempted suicide does not indicate mental illness but reflects natural reactions to adverse situations.

Do Some Transsexual People Attempt Suicide Because They Cannot Obtain GPS?

Yes. Some otherwise eligible transsexual people attempt suicide because they cannot afford or are prohibited by law or policy from obtaining GPS. These transsexual people are blocked from fulfilling relationships and having appropriate sex because GPS has not been performed. Obtaining GPS reduces this attempted suicide rate by approximately 75% for this group.

TRANSSEXUAL TRANSITION

Do All Transgender People Want to Undergo Transsexual Transition?

No. Some transgender people are happy with presenting in their congruent gender behavior category on a full-time or part-time basis without transsexual transition. They are not interested in modifying their bodies to support their transgender presentation. Transsexuals modify their bodies to make them more similar to what people in this binary, cisgender culture expect from their gender presentation.

Do Some Transgender People Take Unprescribed Sex Hormones?

Unfortunately, yes. In some countries, hormones can be legally obtained without a doctor's prescription and can be imported into the United States or other countries where prescriptions are required. Taking hormones obtained from these sources is dangerous because of offshore drug counterfeiting and lack of medical supervision. Counterfeit drugs may not contain their labeled medications or doses. Some contain ethinyl estradiol that can result in blood clots, which are life-threatening. (Estradiol valerate is much safer but it can also be counterfeited.) It is also dangerous because anyone taking such hormones should be monitored by a medical professional to look for side effects. Recent reports at the Charing Cross clinic in London indicate that 20% of those MTF seeking transsexual transition are already taking do-it-yourself hormones before their first appointment.

Does Transsexual Transition Really Change Sex?

Sex is defined by sex organs of reproduction, most all of which can undergo anatomical change during transsexual transition. Using chromosomes or DNA as a sex indicator is unreliable due to natural diversity. Both the Olympics and international athletics organizations have rejected these indicators. Transsexual transition changes sex organs. Transition can change breasts, internal genitalia, external genitalia, nervous system and brain, as well as the skin, hair, and other organs, all of which are involved in sex and/or sexual reproduction. Transsexual transition can change nearly all of the sex organs and the functionality of most, so it represents a change in sex.

Should Medical Treatment of Transgender People Be Covered by Insurance?

Yes. Several studies have been done which show that the medical expenses of transgender treatment, including transsexual GPS, are more than offset by expenses from treatment for depression and attempted suicide. Plus it reduces the human suffering of patients and family. Many companies provide such coverage in order to keep valuable transgender employees and reduce sick leave taken. The ACA does not yet force insurers to cover transgender health expenses but this is under consideration. Medicare will cover transgender healthcare, but each individual state determines what risks insurers must cover. In many cases, transgender healthcare expenses are reimbursed by insurers, with letters supporting medical need, but the patient must outlay the money up front. The Internal Revenue Service recognizes GPS as a deductible medical expense but not breast implant surgery.

Is GPS Necessary? Does It Improve Life?

All studies that I have seen indicate that it is medically necessary and improves life. It clearly reduces the frequency of suicide among eligible transsexuals. But transsexual GPS does not solve all of the social and cultural rejection problems that transsexual people face, nor should it be expected to. So it is recommended that transsexuals still have access to counseling even after transsexual GPS.

Do Transsexuals Regret Having GPS?

Very few. Most report improvements in their life. Best estimate is that less than 0.3% regret having GPS, but this number is steadily decreasing, thanks to preop precautions followed in the WPATH Standards of Care. Some studies that have been recently cited by anti-transgender pundits were not originally designed to assess regret. Their authors dispute interpretations that transsexual GPS regret is common. But GPS does not solve all of the social and cultural rejection problems that transsexual people face. So it is recommended that transsexuals still have access to counseling.

Why Do Transsexuals Go Overseas for Transsexual GPS?

Transsexuals may go to another country to get their GPS surgeries for three reasons.

One of the reasons is that costs of performing surgery plus travel often are less than getting the surgery in their home country. A second reason is that the demand in a particular country may be greater than the capability. In the United States, there are only a few surgeons and in Canada only two that do these operations. In many cases countries with national health services have not anticipated the demand, so people must go abroad or tolerate long waits for treatment and surgery. And in some countries, there are no transsexual GPS surgeons at all. For example, New Zealand is currently without a native transsexual GPS surgeon. The third reason is expertise. Serbia appears to be slightly ahead of other countries for FTM techniques, although

U.S. surgeons have cross-trained with the Serbian doctors and these techniques are now becoming available in the United States. The two leading countries for medical tourism to obtain transsexual GPS are currently Thailand for MTF and Serbia for FTM.

What Is on the Horizon for Transsexual Body Change?

Improvements in surgical and medical technique continue, especially for FTM transsexual GPS. Uterine transplants have been successful in non-transgender females, resulting in two births last year. Artificial vaginas and artificial penises have been grown in the laboratory but are not yet in use. Penile transplants have been demonstrated successful in non-transgender males. The U.S. Department of Defense is working to perfect its procedures for penile transplants, because it plans at least 60 transplants for those injured in war. Penile transplants continue to be conducted in other countries, notably South Africa.

NOTE

1. Julia Serano, *Whipping Girl: A Transsexual Woman on Sexism and the Scapegoating of Femininity* (New York: Seal Press, May 14, 2007), 32.

Bibliography

Addams, Calpernia. *Mark 947: A Life Shaped by God, Gender, and Force of Will.* Bloomington, IN: Writers Club Press, 2002.

Alden, J.P. *A Season for April, Part 1: Summer Storms.* Seattle, WA: Amazon Digital Services, 2013. Kindle edition. https://www.amazon.com/Season-April-Part-Summer-Storms-ebook/dp/B00DT4LHL0#navbar (confirmed July 5, 2016).

Amato, R. Madison. *I'm Your Daughter Too.* Seattle, WA: CreateSpace Independent Publishing Platform, 2014. https://www.amazon.com/Im-Your-Daughter-Too-transsexual/dp/1470097656/ref=sr_1_1?s=books&ie=UTF8&qid=1467731388&sr=1-1&keywords=I'm+Your+Daughter+Too (confirmed July 5, 2016).

Bevan, Thomas (Dana). *The Psychobiology of Transsexualism and Transgenderism.* Santa Barbara, CA: Praeger, 2014.

Bono, Chaz. *Transition: The Story of How I Became a Man* (with Billie Fitzpatrick). New York: Dutton, 2011.

Bornstein, Kate. *Gender Outlaw: On Men, Women, and the Rest of Us.* New York: Routledge, 1994.

Boylan, Jennifer Finney. *She's Not Here: A Life in Two Genders.* New York: Broadway Books, 2013.

Brown, Lester. *Two Spirit People: American Indian Lesbian Women and Gay Men.* New York: Harrington Park, 1997.

Colapinto, John. *As Nature Made Him.* New York: Harper Collins, 2000.

Cossey, Caroline. *My Story.* Boston, MA: Faber and Faber, 1991.

Costa, LeeRay, and Andrew Matzner. *Male Bodies, Women's Souls: Personal Narratives of Thailand's Transgendered Youth.* New York: Routledge, 2007.

Erhardt, Virginia. *Head over Heels: Wives Who Stay with Cross-Dressers and Transsexuals.* New York: Routledge, 2006.

Eugenides, Jeffrey. *Middlesex.* New York: Picador, 2002.

Grant, J., L. Mottet, J.E. Tanis, J. Herman, and M. Keisling. "Injustice at Every Turn." National Center for Transgender Equality and National Gay and Lesbian

Task Force, 2011. http://www.thetaskforce.org/static_html/downloads/reports/reports/ntds_full.pdf (confirmed May 1, 2016).

Gregorio, I.W. *None of the Above*. New York: Balzer and Bray, 2015.

Holland, A. *A Girl like Me: The Gwen Araujo Story*. Lifetime Made for TV Movie, 2006.

Hurst, Michael, and Robert Swope, R. *Casa Susanna*. New York: Powerhouse Books, 2014.

Italie, L. "A Transgender Guide to Answering Intrusive Questions." *Providence Journal* (August 3, 2011). http://www.providencejournal.com/features/lifestyle/content/20140803-a-transgender-guide-to-answering-intrusive-questions.ece (confirmed May 2, 2016).

Jacobs, Sue, Wesley Thomas, and Sabine Lang. *Two-Spirit People*: Native American Gender Identity, Sexuality and Spirituality. Urbana, IL: University of Illinois Press, 1997.

Kelly, Anita. *The Psychology of Secrets*. New York: Plenum, 2002.

Krieger, I. *Helping Your Transgender Teen: A Guide for Parents*. Seattle, WA: Amazon Digital Services, 2011. Kindle edition. https://www.amazon.com/dp/B004R1QBIS/ref=dp-kindle-redirect?_encoding=UTF8&btkr=1#nav-subnav (confirmed July 14, 2016).

Kuklin, Susan, and Tanya Eby. *Beyond Magenta: Transgender Teens Speak Out*. Seattle, WA: Amazon Digital Services, 2014. Kindle edition. https://www.amazon.com/Beyond-Magenta-Transgender-Teens-Speak/dp/0763656119 (confirmed July 5, 2016).

Lev, Arlene. *Transgender Emergence*. New York: Haworth Press, 2004.

Mock, Janet. *Redefining Realness: My Path to Womanhood, Identity, Love & So Much More*. New York: Atria Books, 2014.

Morris, Jan. *Conundrum*. New York: Harcourt, 1974.

Nanda, Serena. *Gender Diversity: Crosscultural Variations*. Prospect Heights, IL: Waveland. 2000.

National Center for Transgender Equality. *A Blueprint for Equality: A Federal Agenda for Transgender People*. National Center for Transgender Equality, 2012. http://www.transequality.org/issues/resources/a-blueprint-for-equality-a-federal-agenda-for-transgender-people-2015 (confirmed May 20, 2016).

National Center for Transgender Equality Webpage. Identification documents. http://www.transequality.org/documents (confirmed May 2, 2016).

Peters, Julie. *Luna: A Novel*. New York: Megan Tingley Books, 2002.

Prince, Virginia. *Understanding Cross-Dressing*. Capistrano Beach, CA: Sandy Thomas Publications, 1976. https://www.amazon.com/s/ref=nb_sb_noss?url=search-alias%3Ddigital-text&field-keywords=Understanding+Cross-Dressing (confirmed July 5, 2016).

Roscoe, Will. *Changing Ones: Third and Fourth Genders in Native North America*. New York: St. Martin's Griffin, 1998.

Roughgarden, Joan. *Nature's Rainbow*. Berkeley, CA: University of California Press, 2004.

Rudd, Peggy. *Crossdressing with Dignity*. Katy, TX: PM Publishers, 2011.

Trevor Project Website. http://www.thetrevorproject.org (confirmed May 2, 2016).

Veterans Administration Website on PTSD. http://www.ptsd.va.gov/public/materials/apps/PTSDCoach.asp (confirmed May 2, 2016).

Index

About the Author

THOMAS E. BEVAN, PhD, is president and owner of a company that conducts research on biopsychology applications, including capturing the science and experience of being transgender. Bevan is both an experienced biopsychologist and a transgender person, herself. Bevan is known in the transgender and academic communities as Dana Jennett Bevan. She has been a transgender person for over 50 years and a transsexual for 9 years, completing transition in 2014. She still publishes under her legal name (Thomas). She has published two previous books on transgender science. Her most recent one was Praeger's *The Psychobiology of Transsexualism and Transgenderism*. Bevan received her doctorate from Princeton University in physiological psychology and her bachelor's degree from Dartmouth College with Distinction in Psychology. Her previous book was entitled *The Transsexual Scientist*, which was self-published under the name Dana Bevan. She was full professor on the general faculty of the Georgia Institute of Technology and taught psychobiology there. Bevan has presented scientific papers at prominent transgender meetings, including WPATH, IFGE, First Event, and Southern Comfort. She developed several physiological psychology applications for the Department of Defense, receiving the Army Innovation Award for medical training technology. Bevan also developed the Integrated Theory of Stress Resilience for the military, which provides understanding of posttraumatic stress disorder. Bevan is a member of WPATH, the American Psychological Association, Human Factors Society (emerita), National Gay and Lesbian Chamber of Commerce, and Lesbians Who Tech. She blogs on biopsychology topics under the name of Dana Jennett Bevan at tgforum.com on a monthly basis.